Historical Biographies of Presidents

Books 1 and 2

Historical Biographies of Presidents

Books 1 and 2

Abraham Lincoln – Freedom Fighter and Teddy Roosevelt – The Soul of Progressive America

J.R. MacGregor

Historical Biographies of Presidents

Books 1 and 2

Copyright © 2021 JR MacGregor

All rights reserved. No portion of this book may be reproduced, stored in a retrieval system, or transmitted in any form or by any means – electronic, mechanical, photocopy, recording, scanning, or other – except for brief quotations in critical reviews or articles, without prior written permission of the publisher.

Published by CAC Publishing LLC

ISBN 978-1-950010-51-6 paperback

ISBN 978-1-950010-50-9 eBook

Table of Contents

Lincoln 8

Introduction 12

Chapter 1 - Foundations in American History 17

Chapter 2 - E Pluribus Unum 42

Chapter 3 - Phases of Life 47

Chapter 4 - Thomas Lincoln 57

Chapter 5 - Development 69

Chapter 6 - Young Adulthood 80

Chapter 7 - Spreading His Wings 88

Chapter 8 - First True Love 106

Chapter 9 - State Legislator 116

Chapter 10 - Marriage and Life After 129

Chapter 11 - Lincoln's Angels & Demons 163

Chapter 12 - Spiritual Center 181

Chapter 13 - National Politics 202

Chapter 14 - Politician 218

Chapter 15 - Electoral Math 233

Chapter 16 - The Presidency 241

Chapter 17 - Lincoln's War 265

Chapter 18 - Second Term 268

Chapter 19 - John Wilkes Booth 277

Chapter 20 - Last Act 283

Conclusion 286

Teddy Roosevelt 295

Introduction 299

Chapter 1 - Family 303

Chapter 2 - Life 318

Chapter 3 - Mind 327

Chapter 4 - Law 338

Chapter 5 - Politics 348

Chapter 6 - Cowboys 404

Chapter 7 - Presidency 415

Chapter 8 - Nationalism 430

Conclusion 561

Lincoln

Freedom Fighter

Lincoln

Freedom Fighter

A Biography of Abraham Lincoln

J.R. MacGregor

Lincoln - Freedom Fighter

Copyright © 2021 JR MacGregor

All rights reserved. No portion of this book may be reproduced, stored in a retrieval system, or transmitted in any form or by any means – electronic, mechanical, photocopy, recording, scanning, or other – except for brief quotations in critical reviews or articles, without prior written permission of the publisher.

Published by CAC Publishing LLC

ISBN 978-1-950010-48-6 paperback

ISBN 978-1-950010-47-9 eBook

Introduction

"I believe this Government cannot endure, permanently half slave and half free. I do not expect the Union to be dissolved--I do not expect the house to fall--but I do expect it will cease to be divided."

Abraham Lincoln, June 16, 1858

The presidency is more than just an office created by the force of the Articles of the U.S. Constitution. It is the hill upon which men of charisma ascend to lead a nation of diversity and to inspire an entire generation. Not all who aspire to the office, though, have the God-given resources to be successful. Even fewer stand the time in accomplishing a positive change so profound that he leaves the annals of history and enters the pantheon of legends. Abraham Lincoln was such a legend but not because he freed the slaves or fought the only civil war to unfold within these shores.

Lincoln is a legend because he made manifest the motto of the United States—*E Pluribus Unum*, from many, one. The joining of people and states was the goal of the unification that took years to articulate in a document, debate at conventions, and argue about at homes.

Before Lincoln, the country was splintered. It may have been under one national flag, but it was a collection of different cultures. It was still referred to as "these united states" instead of "this United States."

A president is not limited to the office that is given power by the Constitution. He is also the man who brings the country together by virtue of how he gets into office. The president is the only officeholder that every citizen has a hand in electing. Each citizen lends him an ear when he speaks, each citizen resonates when he tolls, and ignites when he lights the flames. Only the president can bring a country together and make the words *"that all men are created equal, that they are endowed by their Creator with certain unalienable rights, that among these are life, liberty and the pursuit of happiness"* manifest.

Lincoln embodied the presidency unlike many of the officeholders who had been elected to that office before him or since. Each man can only be fairly judged by how he handles the events that are presented to him during his presidency. So, while it is unfair to force another president into the same criteria one would judge someone like George Washington or FDR, Abraham Lincoln stood solitary in his accomplishments and lasting. You can't expect every president to win a war while in office or oversee the reunification of a country. Instead, you have to observe the factors he brought to the table and extrapolate his contributions from the good that came from his time.

In doing that, encapsulating Lincoln needs to be a lifetime endeavor that is spread across numerous books. To do it in just one requires just the salient points and for those points to be placed in context. That context comes in the form of a rags-to-riches story except it does not refer to wealth but to opportunity and accomplishment. Moving slowly but resolutely the way he did, from the backwater of zero opportunity to the capital of a vibrant democracy, is nothing short of inspired. Add to that, observing and empathizing with the challenges he faced inside elevated his accomplishments that were already stratospheric in its continuation to the way we live our lives today.

It turns out that it was his inner rotten demons that made his outer better angles take flight. There was a darkness within Lincoln that would have crushed most men. It is not the demons that deserve attention; it is the angels he summoned to lift him out of the depths and raise him to the heavens.

Depression colored him inside but never stained his soul. He used the power and stamina of his mind to beat back the negative thoughts that filled his head. The story of the life that was handed to him was the typical frontier story. It was filled with anecdotes of hard work, fears of uncertain days ahead, visions of self-sufficient acts, tears from the loss of loved ones, and heroic battles with the elements.

Depression was not a unique issue among frontiersmen back then. It was also a prevalent condition that afflicted immigrants who had fled their country in fear of hardship and landed in a country that was nothing but wilderness and uncertainty. Depression had even touched Lincoln's father, which caused him to act and perform differently from most other men. It was a cause of heartache for young Lincoln, who eventually thought it better to leave his father's side and make it on his own.

All this—the life that he lived as a child, a son, a brother, and a frontiersman—happened on the backdrop of a new nation that was a nation in name only until he came along and made it a nation in spirit as well.

Chapter 1 - Foundations in American History

"The best way to predict your future is to create it."

Abraham Lincoln, Sixteenth President of the United States

On February 12, 1809, the day President Lincoln was born, the United States of America numbered only seventeen states: Rhode Island, Vermont, Connecticut, New York, Pennsylvania, Delaware, Maryland, Virginia, Ohio, Kentucky, Tennessee, New Jersey, North Carolina, South Carolina, and Georgia.

All were located east of the Mississippi River.

Indiana Territory, Louisiana Territory, and Orleans Territory were located west of the Mississippi River and would not become states until later. This state of things made for a very different country during a very different period of time.

The banding together of a coalition of colonies to fend off King George and his taxation without representation had only happened a mere three decades before. The U.S. Constitution had only been in effect for twenty-two years, superseding the law of individual states and giving rise to the Office of the President, Congress, and the Supreme Court, which was the arbiter of conflict in laws between the states and the federal Constitution, and now they felt more that they were begrudgingly stuck with each other—instead of being stronger—united.

The states were delineated by more than just lines drawn on a map. They were divided by geography in many places, by self-interest everywhere, and all were injected with the self-interest of politicians, who found strength in division rather that unification. One of the side effects democracies have to endure is the fear-mongering of us versus them by shortsighted politicians.

The Founding Fathers of the United States understood that local politics between competing localities would take on an us-versus-them shade and needed a mechanism to balance that. At the same time, they understood that no man can make the decision his neighbor would because each man occupies the well in his own shoes and can't possibly understand the predicament of his neighbor who made a decision differently from him.

The day Lincoln was born Thomas Jefferson was serving out the last few weeks of his term as president. The election of 1808, a few weeks earlier, had yielded president-elect James Madison, who would be sworn in a few weeks later on March 4 and see Jefferson return to Monticello.

The Honorable John Marshall was Chief Justice of the Supreme Court, which that same year as Lincoln's humble birth in the backwoods of Kentucky, had been part of a majority decision to enforce the supremacy of the court in matters of deciding the extent of states' rights versus federal power and jurisdiction. Half a century later it would become the one of the central thrusts that powered Lincoln's political ascendancy.

At a granular level, the issue of states' rights versus federal supremacy had been stewing. Each man's loyalty was resoundingly to his state and his community. This was significantly more so than it was to the new republic. Loyalty to something larger than what he could traverse easily was beyond the imagination of the average man, who would typically live out his entire life without leaving his county or his state.

Reasons for loyalty also went beyond this issue of affinity. They even included and probably more so the issue of self-preservation and self-importance. These issues were the main drivers of the democracy practiced in the states and the well from which politicians sent to the capital drank. These politicians and their politics were critical elements of stoking the discord of difference.

To the farmers and settlers, neighboring states may have been easier to fathom, but distant reaches were illusory and unworthy of the extra thought. Sitting on a farm in Hodgenville, Kentucky, in 1800 and thinking about Cambridge, Massachusetts, was like sitting in Wichita, Kansas, today and thinking about somewhere far away, such as Somalia. They certainly didn't feel like countrymen, and the locals from each jurisdiction had differing issues to focus on. America today with all the technology and communication still bears this out.

Asking someone to pledge his loyalty to something so illusory was a stretch, especially when it came at the cost of his livelihood or in opposition to his own needs, principles, and beliefs. This was magnified when self-serving politicians expounded issues of division when it suited them and their aspirations.

What is commonplace to us today—visiting distant reaches of the country—was alien then to those who lived their entire lives within a few square miles of where they were born and where they would eventually die. This caused a wildly different mind-set of what one could be loyal to or call his home. It took men with imagination, like that of Jefferson and Lincoln, to see that the individual states, united, would evolve and develop into something much greater than just the sum of its parts. Jefferson was fighting for it in his lifetime, and Lincoln achieved it in his.

Each man is made up of more than a solitary experience or a singular ideal. We are all a compendium of impressions and a conglomerate of desires. So, too, was Lincoln. His ideals and vision of the nation stretched beyond the borders of a state. Perhaps it was because he had traveled from one backwoods town to the the next, spent time on one farm, then the next, sailed on rivers, journeyed across plains, and saw the expanse of the country from the lakes in the North to the Gulf in the South and from the shores in the East to the plains in the West. He understood the scope of the country as something beyond just a few counties.

Being a collection of states instead of being one country meant having soft borders. These borders between states complicated matters. They weren't just random lines drawn on a map. They represented the extent to which laws of different states would have effect.

Being a country of laws meant that no one man had power over the land, and it meant that equity and equanimity were guaranteed by the laws that defined the lines of demarcation between the states. It was these laws that gave rise and imbued life into the land. For every grain of tangible sand that made up the land, there was an intangible dome of protection that was created by the laws men agreed upon and instituted.

America was, is, and always will be a land of laws, but these laws, while on one hand were designed to protect those in its jurisdiction, could sometimes prove to be in opposition to laws that were designed to protect those in neighboring jurisdictions.

That disparity did not do anything to draw the people in different states together; instead, it seemed there was a state-sponsored effort to divide the people. But there wasn't. There just wasn't enough understanding of the mechanisms of the new republic.

It was important, though, that each state legislated the necessary framework to be able to provide for that particular state's unique conditions. That had positive and negative consequences. Because people, their movement, and their activity patterns are fluid, they naturally oscillate back and forth across these intangible borders. They create relationships, cement transactions, and advance through life impervious to the waning of one set of laws and the waxing of another across state lines.

In theory, it may not have been that important, but in practice it was a major hindrance and a source of widespread frustration. The differing state laws would often work in concert and worked well to facilitate interaction, but one state's laws would often inconvenience the citizens of a neighboring state. Such places as neighboring New Jersey and New York that shared the waters in New York Harbor found this to be a difficult issue and gave rise to mischief.

In areas where these differing laws came into contention, the Constitution had foreseen some areas this could happen and relegated these areas to the federal government's jurisdiction. That was, in part, the idea of the Union. It was not only convenient to bring about economies of scale, but it was also practical to have an impartial foundation of legal structures to cover matters that may involve cross-border issues.

Only the Supreme Court was empowered to adjudicate whether a state's law was its own business or ceded to the federal government by virtue of the U.S. Constitution. Criminal behavior in one state or conducted across state lines, for instance, would be problematic without federal law and the Constitution. The construction of the Constitution was supposed to be the buffer that managed the competing laws across borders and contradictory laws that were legislated down the road.

One issue that grew precarious because of this structure in law and order was the regulation and institution of slavery. Some states allowed it;

some states did not. To the states that allowed slavery, they were the engine of growth, the root of wealth, and the bane of humanity. To the states that didn't, the question was split. Should they mind their own business or should they enforce their morals on the states that allowed slavery? The issues of states' rights and slavery were on a collision course. The issue of morality and wealth was also on a collision course. The issue of racism and religion was also at odds with each other and so were so many other matters that rose with the sun at the dawn of the American story.

The question had even been put to the framers of the Constitution during the Constitutional Convention more than thirty years before Lincoln was even born. The South knew very well that there was disagreement with the immoral acts of slavery and that they needed some kind of protection to be able to preserve their institution. Even Thomas Jefferson was pushed back when his original draft of the Declaration of Independence was first presented. Parts of it were rejected because of its antislavery tone, and the delegates were afraid that if they took those back to their respective colonies the support for it would evaporate, and the Second Continental Congress would not be able to pass the Declaration. Slavery has had a significant clout in the history of the United States.

In the South, where slavery was a major part of life, they had already tried to use the neighboring states in the North as a slave net. They wanted the Constitution to enforce their (the South's) laws in the North so that the slaves who did run north would be caught and sent back. The argument that they wanted a federal system to act as a policeman or a bounty hunter is more accurate than the South wanting to promote a centralized government over states' rights.

Lincoln could see through the South's facade. He understood that the issues they were talking about undoubtedly led back to the issue of slavery. The politicians of the South had a vested interest in the fraught state of affairs and the systemic racism that had become the vessel in which it not only affected the soul of the individual but also the godliness of a nation.

Racism in the South was not sparked by the racism of hatred. It was fueled by the racism of economics. To the target of racism, that distinction was lost. Dehumanizing abuse by any other name is still as painful, but the distinction serves to understand that the moral vacuum that existed back then was so overwhelming that it managed to blind Christian eyes into reading the Bible to mean that racism, slavery, and abuse were God's will. Lincoln rejected this interpretation to the fullest and initially rejected the Bible because of it as well.

To racists, what they knew to be right was traded for dollars and cents and then masked in arcane passages from the Bible. The wealth and livelihood of the South was predicated on the suppression of an entire race of people but was masked in and sanctioned by the righteousness of religion.

Lincoln would have none of it. He rejected the South's fake interpretation of the Constitution and their understanding of the intent of the framers and the Founding Fathers. He was intimately familiar with the writings of his favorite president, Jefferson, and the books that Jefferson himself had relied on to shape his own mind and thoughts on the matter. While Lincoln did not need to study Greek and Latin to drink from the same intellectual trough as Jefferson, he merely had to study Jefferson's words.

Looking within, Lincoln could no longer sit still and take what was happening in the political realm of his country and the moral well of the nation. Both were fraying at the seams and destroying the intent of the Founding Fathers from within. It has always been said that America cannot be destroyed but from within. In the twenty-first century, the world is witnessing such an attempt, but in the mid-nineteenth century, the self-serving nature of the Southern politicians who fed the flames of fear on behalf of the influential owner class in society was the catalyst of chaos.

To understand Lincoln, it is important to understand the South and the politics of deception that was practiced by the politicians.

Because of their actions, the issues of states' rights and slavery become intertwined, making the latter the proxy for the former.

It wasn't about slavery alone, and it was not about power in the South in isolation. Over the last two hundred years, the two had become two sides of the same issue. Slavery had become a billion-dollar industry, and scrapping that stain off the fabric of society boiled to such stratospheric contention that they melded into one and the same.

At the start, in the first fifty years, the conveniences of unity were outweighed by the differences in opinion and practice. England presented a greater threat to their freedom and to their wealth. The magnates of the South saw independence as the lesser of two evils and one they could wield to their will.

For the first hundred years, the slave-owning class had their way, but it seemed that the differences were growing more stark. Around the time Lincoln began voicing his concerns against slavery and a certain part of the Whigs had started to champion the abolition movement, the South had begun to ramp up their slave dependencies.

To understand the reason behind the upswing in slave ownership and dependency, it is necessary to think about the world holistically. The Industrial Revolution, especially the part of it that had to do with the mechanization of the textile mills in Lancashire, England, and Scotland, not to mention the ones in France and Germany, were starting to shift their dependence on the cotton coming from America's South. This move created significant competitive forces and enormous wealth in the Deep South. There was also competition from South India and other parts of Asia, but the American South had the benefits of lower cost, which contributed to the slave labor. Without slave labor, it would have been likely that they would have lost their cost-competitive position.

To keep slaves in the South, they also needed states in the North to help capture them when they managed to flee. Under the auspices of this ability to enact law and have it enforced beyond their own borders, the South initially tried to use the Constitution to its benefit at the cost of the slaves and the North.

To think that it was only slavery that sparked the highlight of Lincoln's career would be simplifying a critical juncture in American history and diminishing the toil and effort that went into addressing it. To say that it was the problem of balancing states' rights with central governing would be insufficient in capturing the full reason. Together, they come closer to the truth but still do not encapsulate the full extent of the stakes Lincoln had to contend with.

Slavery, as contentious and fraught as it was on its own, was also the vessel that held a compendium of other frustrations and aspirations of the South under one umbrella. Those differences included ideological chasms, cultural asymmetries, moral divergence, and even religious interpretations.

The issue of states' rights had evolved into a matter of sovereignty. The South took on an air of its own distinct from the "Yankees" in an effort to draw the lines of culture, heritage, and governance. There was a concerted effort to distinguish the "Southern way" from the North, and it was part of the push toward secession.

The groundswell in the Southern states had already been agitated by the powers that were more interested in industry than integrity. Slavery, while painful, heartbreaking, and monstrous, was not the core matter of the secession effort. It is a common fallacy, one of many, among historians who romanticize the roots of the Civil War, the evil of the South, and the empathy shown by Lincoln. In reality, it was about keeping the Union intact for Lincoln, and it was about leaving the Union for the South so that they could have control of the vast riches of the South that was built on the backs of slaves. Any excuse would do.

The Civil War purged the toxic buildup of those differences for the country and became the yardstick to measure the resolve of one man while blood was spilled in the mud along the battle lines.

The moment Lincoln won the election, which no one thought he would, the South capitalized on the deep-seated hatred they had for him. Some historians even go so far as to say that there was a wish on the part of the financiers in the background who wanted Lincoln to win so that they could use it as an excuse to secede. If they framed it in such a way that Lincoln would end slavery, then the South would mobilize against him and be up for splitting the country. Remember that the South had already made strong international ties and had become an advanced agricultural center. They did not need the North any longer.

Much of the wealth they gained came from exports to Europe, which included, but was not limited to, textiles and agriculture. They did not need the demand from the market created by their Northern neighbors. To be able to keep their margins and be cost-competitive, they needed their slaves, and they did not want anyone, including the federal government, continuously harping on the matter. They were under the impression that at some point it would become a problem, and they wanted to get out before it did.

As for Lincoln, there are a number of documents that give evidence to the fact that while slavery was a matter of concern because it tore at the fabric of morality, his main concern was to preserve the Union. In his letter to Horace Greeley, publisher of the *New York Tribune*, he made his deepest intentions clear that his priority was for the cohesion of the Union.

Lincoln was a long shot as a candidate who went on to win. Unlike today's typical presidential elections, it was not a two-way battle between one party and the other. There were numerous parties and factions at that time, and four of them had fielded a candidate in 1860. Lincoln represented the new Republican Party. Stephen Douglas, Lincoln's political nemesis, represented the Northern Democrats, John Bell represented the Constitutional Union Party, and John

Breckenridge represented the Southern Democrats.

If the battle was directly between Douglas and Lincoln, then the outcome would have been very different. Out of the four men, only Lincoln's policy stood out in stark contrast to the policies of the other three. Lincoln's position was so different from that in the South that he knew he would not be able to garner many votes there. His job was to appeal to the North.

On the election issues that mattered in the South, the other three men had similar positions and cannibalized each other at the ballot box. Their positions also alienated them in the North in favor of Lincoln.

The Democratic Party of the mid-nineteenth century was not the same as today's Democratic Party. In 1850, a major problem arose with respect to slavery that split the Democratic Party into two groups—the Northern Democratic Party and the Southern Democratic Party.

There were three aspects to slavery that you have to understand to have a better appreciation of the events of the time and to better understand Lincoln's point of view. The first school of thought was that slavery was unacceptable. The second was that slavery was necessary, and the third was that each person should have the right to decide on slavery within their own state. This was the foundation of the problem.

Then came the second layer to complicate matters. Lincoln didn't like slavery, but he merely wanted to hold the Missouri Compromise to its word and let the states that already had slavery on the books continue in the same way but disallow new territories to legalize slavery when they joined the Union.

This meant that the new territories that came after he was in office would not allow slavery. He was not looking to abolish slavery in the South; he was just trying to make sure that slavery didn't spread across to the new land and the states that came later. Lincoln was clear about this. He did not think that it would be fair to subject the industries of the South to a set of laws that put them at a disadvantage. He also believed that what had already been settled upon should not be reversed.

Those in the North were not interested in slavery and were morally aghast at the continued expansion of it and supported the idea of limiting slavery to some states that were already in the union. But those in the South wanted to expand it to the new territories as well. This was the contention. It was not about removing slavery in the South. It was about not allowing the new states to allow it.

The South was afraid of tipping the scales in Congress. If the new states were against slavery, then legislation that came up in Congress would be in favor of abolitionist ideology. The South read the tea leaves on this matter. As the West was unfolding, people there were not inclined to be slave states.

By the time of the election of 1860, the country was hotly debating the issue, and the South had already threatened once again to secede if slavery were on the table. The Democratic Party split to assuage its members on both sides of the debate, which proved to be a costly mistake.

The two sides of the party then fielded their own candidates for the general election—Breckenridge in the South and Douglas in the North. This, by itself, split the vote. If this had not happened, Lincoln would not have won the majority of the votes, and the Union would have taken a very different direction.

Every crisis is an opportunity, and to Lincoln the secession of the South, which happened on April 12, 1861, was the opportunity that allowed him to cease slavery across the board even in the states that were already in the Union during the Declaration of Independence.

Electoral math was not a major discipline in those days, and neither was scientific polling. The two halves of the Democratic Party were not sure what such a split would mean. It was the same way that Hitler rose to power in Germany—a split in the voting block delivers the power to the third party—a house divided. Ironically, the man who delivered his speech about "a house divided" became president himself because of a divided house. During his entire presidency, from before his inauguration to when he died, Lincoln presided over a divided house.

As we have now seen in the election of 2016, America is not straightforward when it comes to the presidential election. The Founding Fathers instituted something called the Electoral College, and that had the direct impact of tempering the power and vagrancy of the popular vote. The idea, as we learn from our civic textbooks, is to avoid the election of a popular president or something of a fad. That's a topic for another day. However, it was not just the 2016 election that resulted in an unexpected result. It also yielded an unexpected result in the 1860 presidential election.

The North had a larger share of the Electoral College and a larger share of the total population. It was more than double, with about twenty-three million in the North and nine million in the South. The South was divided in their choice, splitting the vote between its three candidates—

Bell, Breckenridge, and with a little left over for Douglas. Lincoln was pretty much shut out in the South. Each of the three candidates split the vote, which was small to begin with.

In the North, Breckenridge and Bell didn't gain any traction, and they were not looking to follow the policy that Douglas had laid out. They wanted the new territories to be free from slavery. That tipped the North in Lincoln's favor, but Douglas did manage to come close. If the vote in the South had not been split, it is almost a certainty that Douglas would have repeated his victory over Lincoln as he had done in the Senate race a few years earlier.

Nonetheless, Lincoln did win with the help of Republican grassroots in the North, with Hannibal Hamlin's faction of the pro-abolition fervor, and the word of print from Horace Greeley, among many others.

Chapter 2 - E Pluribus Unum

It certainly was a long road from Hodgenville, Kentucky, to Ford's Theatre. As perilous, tortuous, and bloody as it had been, it was the most righteous of journeys that was taken by any occupant of the president of the United States bar none. It was not a life that enhanced the status quo. It was a life that altered the course of American history.

As we advance over the course of the book, it is to be understood that Lincoln's life and history-altering influence was not limited to his life in the White House. It went far beyond that. What influenced him is altogether another matter and predates his own birth. It was molded by Puritanical views, lack of formal education, frontier antics, and backwoods mannerisms.

A look at the history of the man must also be mingled with the history of the environment and circumstances that surrounded him. At the broad view, the country we know today did not exist in form or culture as it did at the time Lincoln came into adulthood, and it certainly did not exist while he was at the height of his presidency or the Civil War.

For the first point, there were three Americas. The first America was not only geographically in the North but was also psychologically Northerners, or Yankees as Southerners referred to them. Being a Northerner was as much a state of mind as it was to be a Southerner.

Then there were those in the geographically southern areas of the country, which we think of as the South. Their mind-set was distinct and their lifestyles totally different from those in the North. As pilgrims arrived, the landscape changed rapidly, and as each year passed, not only was the country expanding westward, but each frontier town, each port city, and also towns expanded rapidly with new immigrants in search of a new life. Growth fueled evolution, and evolution created culture. Southern culture evolved until it was occupied by a certain aristocracy—what we think of as the Southern Lady and the Southern Gentlemen. It's not difficult to imagine.

Finally, there were those areas that were neither Northern states nor Southern states. These folks were part of the territory that was expanding westward but had not yet been included in the Union. Volumes have been written about these histories of the United States, but it would be too lengthy to list them here, so we shall look at them so that we have enough context to place the man who stood at the crossroads of all three mindsets—the Northerner, the Southerner, and the frontiersman.

The Union was young at the time, with three forces tugging on it in different directions. There was the commercial force in terms of the resources that this new land possessed. From steel, oil, and gold in the ground to timber and agriculture above it, commerce was a major part of the American story and the primary force by the time Lincoln came to power. The world didn't stop just because the South seceded or because

Lincoln had become president. Commerce still proceeded, trade was still conducted, and fortunes were still being made—just think of Carnegie, Morgan, and Vanderbilt.

Then there were the alliances that created a delicate balance between the colonies and the Old World. It was, in part, driven by commerce, but it was also strategic in nature. The states that seceded from the Union were also the states that were the largest producers of cotton in the world, and Britain was a trading counterpart by far. Although Queen Victoria had initially proclaimed neutrality in the Civil War, as did all the other European countries, the British were gradually finding that it was better to be aligned with the South for commercial reasons.

This was also a major concern to Lincoln, who saw the dangers of the commercial ties the South had and the motivation to keep the status quo. The South definitely had the upper hand in negotiating the issue.

The merits of either side of the slavery debate are best left to another book for another time. For now, they are just there to place in context the resolve that Lincoln brought to the discussion and the steel he exemplified throughout the four years of his presidency.

There were two planks inherent in Lincoln's presidency: (1) his stated and vehement adherence to the constitution and (2) his love of the Union. The Civil War brought both to a head. Much of how he saw the Union was in part because of the role models that he adopted over the course of his readings.

Until Lincoln the United States of America was just a united federation of individual states. After Lincoln we became one nation, changing these united states to this United States. That was the true blessing of his presidency, and while he didn't see those actions and decisions in quite that romantic a light, the decisions he did make set the path to that conclusion, and for that we are eternally grateful because America is better when identified as one unit rather than an x number of parts. E Pluribus Unum was a motto that Lincoln adhered to and saw the wisdom of.

Chapter 3 - Phases of Life

"May the Almighty grant that the cause of truth, justice, and humanity, shall in no wise suffer at my hands."

Abraham Lincoln, May 21, 1860

For anyone who wants to truly appreciate the life of Abraham Lincoln, it can be best defined in four phases. His heritage and his youth are best placed in the first phase. It gives us the canvas on which to paint the accomplishments of the man against a backdrop of personal, societal, and systemic challenges.

The second covered his years as an adult that dovetailed into his time practicing law and his early political career. It was his time in law practice that raised his awareness of the nature of the country, what it meant, and the force to which it owed its existence. America is unique. It is not a country that was built the same way that others had been built. America was an experiment in self-governance.

His third phase was the period of time between his legislative career and the time he became president. It was during this time that he developed the manner of his thinking and the maturity of his planning. As the book will progressively reveal, Lincoln's ascendancy to the presidency and his reasons for doing so are not what they are always thought to be. It was not accidental. It was intentional. It was not altruistic. It was calculated. And, it was not enlightened. It was manipulative. In other words, he developed the skill necessary to be the consummate politician.

Then, finally, is the phase of his life that tested his mettle and changed the American promise from what it would have become to what it is today. This was the period that began the day he was elected and before he even took the oath of office. It was a combination of the issue of slavery, which was by all analytical accounts a convenient matter to discuss with the electorate but nonetheless a proxy of the real cause of battle. The South may have been at war because of slavery, but Lincoln was at war to hold the Union together. The issue of slavery, as important as it was back then, was second only to a subject that is largely misunderstood today and mostly forgotten.

By the time Lincoln had risen to prominence in Illinois, the South—those states that made up what was known to be the South—had already attempted to secede from the Union a number of times. The time just before the Civil War was by no means the first and only time.

As far back as the dawn of the age of Lincoln, Southern conservatism was a very different brand of thinking from what we think of conservatism to mean today.

Lincoln's studies had given him insight into the ideals of the men who were responsible for the founding of the country, and he began to see the wisdom of their perspective. Such men as Jefferson and Madison, who were initially opposed to certain common ideas, eventually started to see the benefit of one country comprised of numerous states. It was like a timber raft. The individual timbers would give it the stability it needed to carry more than just the same number of individual trunks would.

Lincoln, being a boat man, saw this clearly as well. Together, if they could work out their differences, they would be stronger against almost anything imaginable. Lincoln felt that the constant bickering of the states and the threats of secession had to stop. He also understood that such a goal could not be harnessed by just legislation. Something more needed to happen.

Lincoln was a well-read man. He had understood the playing field and how the dynamics had played out. In his writings, Lincoln had come to realize that the country was diverse because of three core factors. First was the geography and the climate. The American geography that he had personally experienced from his time in Kentucky and traveling up to Illinois allowed him to realize that the land was capable of different things in different places, causing people in those areas to ultimately behave differently. People are, after all, products of their environment.

For instance, it is not surprising that slavery flourished in the South because the plantations that were worked (before mechanization) were labor intensive and active almost throughout the year. In the North, different industries were prevalent and ones that did not necessarily lend themselves to intense slave labor.

The second reason the country was diverse in politics was that it was populated differently. The Southern states had low-density population centers, and most of the people were flung out and spread across a vast area. In was different in the North. The urban areas and countryside were more densely populated, which created a political landscape different from that of the South. In Congress, there were more representatives from the North than from the South. That meant that Southern interests, when they diverged from Northern interests, would be almost inconsequential in Congress. The North would automatically always have the power of the federal government behind them.

The South found this to be unacceptable and influenced their impression of the Northern states. It also resulted in the South choosing to deal directly in commerce outside the country. In time, they gradually did not see any advantages of remaining with the Union. It was not just in 1860 when the first seven states decided to leave the Union. Different combinations of Southern states had tried to do it in one form or another for the previous forty years since the Revolutionary War.

Lincoln had been studying the intricacies of the political landscape and the history of the United States. He was a student of history, law, and the actions of such men as Madison, Jefferson, and Washington. His candidacy, if he chose to run for president, would be a long shot. His aspirations to high office were motivated by a number of factors. He had been in Congress for years, and he had a solid grounding in the issues and understanding how the nuts and bolts of lawmaking and horse-trading were carried out.

He was trying to thread the political needle to be able to win the election. There were so many issues that he could run on, but every issue that he analyzed left him feeling that the issues that others saw to be what they championed were more popular in debate than his. The issues championed by his party were no longer sufficient to carry Lincoln to the destination of his dreams.

Lincoln was of the Whigs, the party founded by Henry Clay, one his childhood heroes. But within that party, Lincoln had done well as a four-term congressman and then descended into obscurity after retirement. He was nobody once he left congressional politics. To be able to aspire for higher office, he needed a grassroots movement that took interest in areas that were more widespread than just state issues, which were highly localized and did not offer any inspiration for a candidate with aspirations for national office.

When the Republican Party was founded some years later before the 1860 election, he realized that it could be his vehicle, if he chose, to ascend to the executive branch. In the first presidential election year since the forming of the Republican Party, Abraham Lincoln had been nominated as the vice-presidential candidate for the Republicans. The Republicans, however, lost the election that year at the presidential level but did surprisingly well at the congressional level. That year Democratic candidate James Buchanan was elected president.

Lincoln had no control over the manner in which the campaign was run. He was merely the VP candidate, and it was up to the man at the top of the ticket to determine the path and the crux of the campaign. It was also a new party at the time and was ultimately unproductive in its bid. The Republican Party was the second party that Lincoln had joined after being a Whig for the initial part of his political career.

The Whigs were popular between the 1830s and the 1850s, which was just before Lincoln had become active in congressional politics, and stayed relevant until he left. When he left Washington, D.C., he had every intention to return to the practice of law and do more for the country.

There are a number of reasons why Lincoln returned to the political stage after leaving Congress. Just as with all of us, our decisions are never based on just one reason. For Lincoln, too, there were many reasons, some consequential, some just a matter of convenience and preference. One of the reasons why he wanted to get back into the game was so that he could leave the house and put some distance between him and his wife. On the other end of the spectrum was a deeply personal reason—one that was rooted in his self-perception and self-esteem. Lincoln was a man who saw himself through the eyes of others. The years that he was away from the glare of the constituents he represented were some of the most difficult for him. He lived off the energy of public life, but he also hated the idea of losing. He had lost the race for the Senate to Stephen Douglas. There were two sides to his loss. The first was the low self-esteem that he suffered from. The second was his lack of a platform that would make sense. He needed to be able to reach across the landscape and sell himself. He knew that was not plausible.

The opportunity presented itself when the Kansas-Nebraska Bill passed Congress and was signed into law. The Kansas-Nebraska Act was a lightning rod that seemingly rolled back the Missouri Compromise and put slavery back in the center of the sphere of interest.

He knew that if he could meet every constituent, then he would not have a problem winning the contest. But there was no way to do that. He had to devise a different strategy, and he did.

Chapter 4 - Thomas Lincoln

One of the facets of any man is the childhood injections of morals, outlook, and motivations. Since children learn by mimicking, a boy, who soon sees the differences between his mother and his father, realizes that he should observe his father and be loved by his mother. When he observes his father, he finds a source to mimic and does the best he can to emulate. That is his psychological base. It is the way our species transmits continuity from one generation to the next while still maintaining the flexibility to adapt to changing conditions. From that paternal platform, his environment takes over, and he applies it, right or wrong, and faces the consequences, acceptable or otherwise, to gradually evolve and prompts a man to fill his own shoes.

Abraham Lincoln was the same. He was born into a family of love and hard work. His first glimpse of life came from seeing his father, while his first love was his mother. Much of Lincoln's character was set by the actions of his father and tempered by his mother's love. Getting to know his father then will go a long way in setting a sound foundation in understanding the sixteenth president.

Thomas Lincoln was the youngest son of Abraham Lincoln (the president's grandfather) and Bathsheba Lincoln. Mordecai and Josiah were older than Thomas and more successful later in life compared with young Thomas.

Thomas was the baby of the family both in terms of his age and that his two older brothers would take care of him. The family was well to do. They had been frontiersmen and built the homestead to be a profitable enterprise. Abraham Senior was a shrewd businessman and farmer, grounded in a strong work ethic, religion, and family. This was the fabric on which the Lincoln clan had been built on. When one is marinated in those qualities, it is hard to not become successful in life. This was born out by the president's two uncles, Mordecai and Josiah, who went on to become successful landowners and farmers.

For the first five years of his life, Thomas lived a fairly privileged childhood, being the center of everyone's attention. This had created a close bond with everyone in the family, but he primarily became close to his father.

By the time he was five years of age, little Thomas would wrap up his study and minimal chores and then follow his father in his daily work on the farm or when he had to go into town. He was by his father's side watching his brothers and just absorbing all it meant to be a Lincoln.

Part of their time together, Abraham Senior would relate the rich stories of the Lincoln family and how they came to Kentucky. Abraham's cousin, Daniel Boone the explorer, had made his way south from Virginia. They were among the first people to come to this part of the country. They went on to make connections and relationships with the Native Americans in the area.

Boone and Lincoln had done their best to expand the fur trade with local Indians in that part of the unexplored lands. Boone and Lincoln were enterprising young men who were looking to tap as much potential as they could on virgin soil. They traded for some time and became prosperous at it. It was said that Abraham Senior, who was a captain in the Revolutionary War and came from Amity, Pennsylvania, amassed more than $17,000 (equivalent to more than half a million dollars today) from this endeavor.

With part of that money, they set up a ranch and moved the whole family down to Kentucky. The business grew as the state did as well. The Lincoln family was well respected and well known across the district, then state of Kentucky.

When Thomas Lincoln (the president's father) was just eight years old, in May 1786, they were out in the field tending to the chores they typically did in the day. Mordecai was within shouting distance and closer to the barn, while Josiah was on another part of the property but also within earshot.

There was a contentious relationship between the settlers and the native tribes in the area, who would frequently lead raiding parties on the property of residents in the area. On a warm Kentucky summer day, they mounted an attack on the Lincoln farm. There hadn't been many attacks on the farm simply because Lincoln and Boone had always had a good relationship with the natives, and that made them stay clear of the Lincolns. But it was different that particular day.

As Thomas was crouching next to his father, the war party rode up the knoll and attacked both Lincolns. Abraham was struck and died instantly. The screaming commotion caught the attention of everyone within sight of the scene. Mordecai, the oldest of the Lincoln boys, had the presence of mind to run toward the barn, which was a short distance away, to retrieve a weapon.

In the meantime, the assassin had turned his sights on little Thomas, who was distraught. Fear aside, he was unable to process the killing of his father in such a bloody manner in front of him. He was too young and too scared to do anything.

Mordecai had also dispatched Josiah to the military stockade, Floyd's Station, located nearby on Beargrass Creek to get help. Mordecai was able to find his father's rifle and from a distance took aim at the man who was preparing to murder Thomas. From the barn, Mordecai killed him with one shot and saved his little brother.

At that moment, two things happened simultaneously. It changed the trajectory of Thomas, who became more withdrawn, while it emboldened Mordecai. The divergence of the two brothers forever altered their lives.

Not long thereafter Josiah arrived with the cavalry, and the war party rode away. This incident left a deep scar on young Thomas, who had the misfortune to have his father die in his arms and the fear of almost being killed himself.

That became the defining event in Thomas Lincoln's life, and subsequently the shadow of the father was cast on his son. Thomas could never seem to make the fortune that his brothers went on to make, and while Thomas was steadfast in his honesty and integrity, he never really could provide a comfortable life for his wife and children.

It was a key moment in the Lincoln family legacy. While the Lincolns that stemmed from Mordecai and Josiah did well, most of the others who descended from Thomas faded into the shadows of history. The other Lincolns had worked hard and provided for their family, and the typical American dream unfolded in front of them. Thomas, on the other hand, was the exact opposite.

After that incident, Thomas retreated into a shell, which was to be expected considering what he had just witnessed. His family gave him some time to recover, but even after two years he was still less engaged in life than everyone else in the household.

His academics suffered and so did his time with chores. He did, however, enjoy being alone and working with wood. He had some understanding of agriculture and farming but not to the degree any of his siblings did, and so he seemed to not be as successful as his father and brothers. Thomas was also prone to melancholy and fear. He was not able to muster any sort of risk tolerance or put aside any of his fear of doing almost anything that normal people would. Even his moods were not stable. The grew more despondent as he grew older and began spending hours in silence or talking about the old days when he would help his father and the time his father was murdered.

He drifted from one property to the next, earning a meager living with his woodworking skills. He had poor business acumen and little farming instinct. He even purchased land to farm that was filled with rocks and boulders, and he was unable to make anything of it. This inability to make a life like the one his brothers had frustrated him to a high degree. But whatever share of intelligence that had been taken away from him on that summer morning in Kentucky, it hadn't touched a sliver of his honesty, which he was liberally endowed with.

The one thing that determined his actions and fueled his thoughts was the nature of honesty that he eventually passed down to his son, who became president. He did not live long enough to see his son try for the vice presidency or eventually be elected president.

Within a decade of Thomas losing his father, he had moved to neighboring Washington County and away from the rest of his family. He continued with his carpentry work to provide for himself. His desire to move away from his family was not unlike what would eventually be the same trajectory that his son, Abraham, would do many years later.

He was not the kind of person who would settle down for long in one place. After spending a few years in Washington County, Thomas decided that he would find his calling by purchasing a farm, which he did with some of his inheritance and money that he had saved.

The 238-acre farm was located in Kentucky's Hardin County, just about fifty miles south-southwest of Louisville, Kentucky. He moved there in 1802 and started to work the farm and make a living. It was a time that he seemed to be coming out of his darkness. He was about 5' 10" tall, much shorter than his son would be later in life, and he weighed 190 lbs. Thomas was not the quickest on his feet, choosing to do work that didn't require a lot of movement.

The one strong feature that seemed to be a major part of his character was his frugality. When one is frugal, there are numerous benefits that arise, not least of which is the ability to save money. Frugality also allows the person to not be swayed and predisposed to lavish distractions. Thomas was certainly that way. He was not a person who was lavish or predisposed to a lifestyle of his standard, much less one that was above it. That kept him out of trouble. Lincoln, the president, observed this while he was growing up. There was not one pretentious bone in his body just as there were none in his father's.

In 1806, four years after settling in Washington County, and reducing his time on the farm in exchange for working as a carpenter in Elizabethtown, Thomas met a young seamstress who used to work in the Washington-Hardin area. Her job would take her from one county to the next, spending time in the homes where she worked. Nancy Hanks and Thomas Lincoln courted that same year and then married on June 12. After the wedding, they moved into a cabin close to where he worked with plans to start a family. As a family, they joined the congregation of the Little Mount Separate Baptist Church.

This church was in contention and had split from the South Fork Baptist Church in Hardin over the issue of slavery in 1807. The Lincolns were resolutely antislavery even back then, as they felt that it was not consistent with Bible teaching. Their first child, Sarah, was born in 1807.

After a short time in Elizabethtown, they moved to another cabin in Sinking Spring Farm in Nolan Creek just a few miles from the church and just outside Hodgenville. Here on a cold Sunday morning before daybreak, after a long night in labor, Nancy Lincoln, with the help of a young midwife, gave birth to a baby boy they named after his grandfather. It was April 12, 1809.

The delivery had weakened Nancy to the point that she lost a lot of weight after the birth. The couple tried for a third child not long after that and was blessed for a short while with another little boy. They named him Thomas, but he died shortly afterward much to the deep sorrow of his mother. The darkness rushed back into Thomas' life at that point, and the time for dark clouds and gloom returned after a long absence.

Chapter 5 - Development

Abraham Lincoln, son to Thomas Lincoln and grandson to his namesake, was born in the barest of log cabins in the backwoods of Hodgenville, Kentucky. Today, the town is populated with just over a thousand people, a stark contrast to the days when the Lincolns first arrived in the area. Back then it didn't even have so much as a High Street, and one's closest neighbor would have been a half a day's walk away.

Forget for a moment the weight of Lincoln's actions and how history has placed him on the pedestal that few occupy, and look at him as just any man. That would be the best way to start simply because before the choices and trials came to pass, he was nothing more and nothing less. At a young age, young Lincoln was of a happy disposition and good manners.

Lincoln had just about twelve months of schooling, cumulatively, across his entire life. He never saw the inside of a classroom at a young age as children do today, and when he did, he was already much older and only did so infrequently. This upbringing and lack of any significant schooling resulted in a naturally unpolished demeanor, although that was not the measure of his kindness. His rough edges were more so in contrast with the refined ways of the upper class but not subpar to it. He may not have known how to say something harsh in gentle terms, but he knew how to be gentle in harsh terms. It was his mark of sincerity and sensitivity.

Unlike men of success in that period of time, Lincoln had not entered the fray with a strong educational background and one that was polished in a way that Dickens referred to as gentlemen of sorts. In fact, Lincoln's mannerisms were gruff, even if they were on the right side of righteousness. It would be easy to mistake Lincoln for a loser if you were to see him in his element as a youth. Between the lack of formal education, his backwoods mannerisms, and his unusual appearance in stature and countenance, not many people would peg him for someone who had a resolve of steel and the ability to teach himself what he didn't know.

After teaching himself how to read, he realized there were two kinds of language that were spoken. The first was the kind that he and his fellow backwoodsmen engaged in, and the other was the language that the educated spoke.

Lincoln quickly realized that his peaceful demeanor and Puritan values were better represented by the version of communication that one would classify as being educated. The problem was that this occurred around the time when he was nearly in his late teens, and going to school was no longer a viable option. He also didn't have the opportunity to come into contact with men of eloquent demeanor and a polished veneer.

What he lacked in eloquence, however, he made up for in heart and intelligence. By heart, of course, we mean that he had the tenacity and stamina to do what needed to be done. Don't confuse heart with the romanticism of pity, empathy, or sympathy. Once he realized that what he had to do was improve the way he spoke, he looked around for books that would give him a better grasp of the language. What he found was a book on grammar. He found that *A New Guide to the English Tongue* by Thomas Dilworth was something that would be of great help, and he set about to get a copy.

The closest one that he could borrow was a few miles outside town, and so he walked to ask its owner if he could borrow the book. He was successful and studied it repeatedly from cover to cover and altered the way he spoke and the eloquence in the way he wrote. It allowed him to bridge the gap between the fate of his fortunes to pulling himself up by the scruff of his collar to a point that he could eloquently participate later in life in the Lincoln-Douglas debates, which set the trajectory for him to be elected president.

By the time Lincoln was seven years old, his family had moved to Indiana. It was 1816, and James Madison was president of the United States. His sister, Sarah, was nine, and life was hard enough in frontier lands and frontier times, but it was more so for the Lincolns. Southern Indiana was the new frontier during that time, and its population was still scarce, but opportunities abounded, which is what Thomas Lincoln was looking for.

They staked their claim on a 160-acre plot and quickly set about to build a cabin as winter approached. Thomas was an able carpenter, and he often had little Abraham in tow, helping him with the chores. In time, Thomas made a name for himself in the vicinity and began taking on carpentry work to keep up the family and the homestead. Thomas was a good carpenter. His honesty and integrity compelled him to produce work that was meticulous and well-crafted. Abraham watched and learned and soon was able to everything with wood, from picking the tree that needed to be felled to designing the furniture and assembling the final product.

Even without trade school and formal education, wood and carpentry became second nature to Abraham. Woodworking was one of the two loves of his life. Just like his father. His second was reading. Even though he did not have much formal education, he taught himself to read and became a voracious reader. The following is a list of the consequential books he read in his lifetime.

Autobiography of Benjamin Franklin by Benjamin Franklin

Ancient History by Charles Rollins

Robinson Crusoe by Daniel Defoe

Complete Works of Edgar Allen Poe

Decline and Fall of the Roman Empire by Edward Gibbon

Geometry by Euclid

Fanny, With Other Poems by Fitz-Greene Halleck

Sociology for the South by George Fitzhugh

Poems by Henry Longfellow

Commentaries on American Law by James Kent

An Authentic Narrative of the Loss of the American Brig Commerce by James Riley

Joe Miller's Book of Jests by Joe Miller

Mormonism by John Hyde

Liberty by John Stuart Mill

Journals and Debates of the Federal Constitution by Jonathan Elliot

Analogy of Religion by Joseph Butler

The Life of George Washington by Mason L. Weems

Poems by Oliver Wendell Holmes

Lives of Emperors by Plutarch

The Theory and Practice of Surveying by Robert Gibson

History of Illinois by Thomas Ford

Poems by Thomas Hood

Poems by William Knox

Lessons in Elocution by William Scott

Complete Works of William Shakespeare

There are two things of note from this list. First, this is not the full extent of his reading list. There were other books that he surely must have read. These are just the books that he kept safely and treasured them. They followed him from Illinois to Washington, D.C., and were later passed to his son Robert Todd Lincoln.

Second, it is also said by a number of different sources that Lincoln had memorized almost all the poems that he was exposed to in the books that are on this list. Poetry was the tonic that seemed to sooth his vexed mind when the days grew dark in his mind.

There is plenty of evidence that even though he didn't attend school because it was either too far away or there was no reliable transportation to get him that far, his parents did give him the encouragement that prompted him to read. He did more however.

There are numerous anecdotes about his endeavors to find books. The early to mid-eighteenth century was a period not known for its easy availability of books. It was hard to find one and one of the reasons why Andrew Carnegie started building more than two thousand libraries across the United States starting in 1883. But at this point while Lincoln was still a young adolescent in Kentucky and then in Indiana, few libraries were available.

He typically did not know if a book on a particular subject existed. He would just be interested in a subject and then would ask a teacher in town or someone he knew was educated, and they would suggest a title or two. He'd then go on a sort of treasure hunt to look for that book until he found it. Once he got the book, he would write down quotes or entire sections from it in his own notebook or on paper. He would then return the book. Lincoln made a list of all the books that stuck him, and when he had the opportunity, he would purchase a copy. He had a sense of desire to be able to find more knowledge by sheer curiosity and self-awareness. It was a display of total awareness because it is hardly common to find a person who knows what they do not know and finds the information to fill that void.

Lincoln also had the habit of visiting the drugstore or the general store wherever he visited. Whenever he traveled, even when he sailed down the Mississippi River to New

Orleans, he stopped at places that sold books and looked for what he could afford. What he couldn't afford, he waited until an opportunity presented itself.

During the time he would chop wood for work, he would spend his free time reading his law books or the state's constitution, and when he worked at the grocery store, he would spend the quiet hours lying on the counter and reading whatever book he had just borrowed, bought, or something he had already read. Whenever the store owner would stock books (which rarely happened), he would carefully read those, too, and make sure he did not crease them for anyone who eventually bought them.

When Lincoln got to the White House, the South had already seceded, and when the war eventually erupted, he would find solace in the list of books that he thought were his best sources of comfort. He still made time to read even in the midst of heavy workloads, meetings, strategy considerations, and spending time with his family. Reading was his form of meditation.

Books aside, Lincoln was given to reading as a natural extension of his intellect. He read every bill that came to his desk for his signature. He read every report and every analysis. In the midst of all this, he was also a hopeless romantic. Putting aside his chiseled features and his lanky stature, he was soft on the inside and just wanted to hear the kind words that he took the trouble to utter to others. Words moved and soothed him. It wasn't after a long marriage that Mary Lincoln had come to understand this side of him. For a large portion of their marriage, her vocabulary, her tenor, and her tone were not of the same flavor as Lincoln, which was deeply saddening for him, but he never said a word about it.

Chapter 6 - Young Adulthood

In 1816, the Lincolns moved to a small community in Perry County. It was on the banks of Little Pigeon Creek in southern Indiana. This was virgin country and another piece of land that the Lincolns had come to that was frontier land. They seemed to always be on the leading edge of American expansion, just as little Thomas had remembered his father doing when he was five years old. Thomas Lincoln seems to have been in a psychological loop that kept him always trying but never really succeeding.

Lincoln was now seven years old and having a great time exploring the country. He enjoyed the family's move from Kentucky to Indiana. They left Kentucky in the beginning of summer and used the warm weather and easier conditions through the forest and mountain trails. It took them the whole summer to make the journey.

Lincoln would later remember this trip as one of his most pleasant. It was filled with adventure, his parents were with him, he spent time talking to his father, and as the case with many children, he just loved being on the road. It was the thrill of the unknown since this was the first time he had been outside Kentucky.

In the nineteenth century, out on the frontier, being a seven-year-old was almost like being a man. When Lincoln and his family reached Indiana, it felt almost like a world away in some aspects but felt no different in other aspects. The work, however, was tougher than usual. The land they settled on was densely forested and required clearing, which Thomas and Abraham did by themselves at first.

The family was accustomed to frugality, and the tight situations they faced in the wake of the move to Indiana was not something that was too stressful for the them. They had their muskets and all the wood they needed. So, hunting and cooking what they hunted kept them fed. What they needed to do was clear the land and use the lumber to build a cabin. Until that was done, they spent the nights in tents while the weather was still not too cold. By the time winter came, they hadn't finished the house, and much of it was still laid bare for the elements. But Abraham was still happy with all that was happening. He was starting to feel like a man, and the world was his playground.

Their first winter passed with the settling in process. It was colder than what they had been used to, and the chores were a welcome activity because it kept them active and warmer. Abraham fell asleep every night before his head could hit the pillow, totally exhausted from the chores of the day.

The entire family would be up at dawn. On most mornings and the nights that followed, they would be without light. Candles were a luxury, but the roaring fire that Thomas would build to combat the cold that entered the house was enough to give them the light they needed.

That first winter seemed to last forever. When spring finally arrived and the land began to thaw, the Lincolns got back to work and began putting a barrier to their home so that they could be sheltered from the elements. Abraham had much to learn, and he watched intently and did exactly what he needed to do to learn every ounce of skill from his father.

The days rolled into seasons very rapidly and especially so for a family having to pull together out on the leading edge of a westward-pushing frontier with no services to rely on. Out in the wilderness, there were no stores one could rely on and no drugstore to provide relief. Each man and his family had to rely on their resourcefulness to be able to live.

Getting sick in the outdoors is also a dicey affair. Simple ailments can be dealt with by placebos telling the mind to make itself well, or some concoctions can indeed have an effect, but some problems need expert help. Nancy Hanks Lincoln, Abraham's mother, was in need of such help.

She died from an illness related to the milk she had consumed. It was something that was common at the time in frontier towns, where services were initially scarce, and each family fended for themselves. The milk sickness, as it was referred to, was fairly common and involved contaminated milk of a cow that had grazed on snakeroot.

Mrs. Lincoln had kindly gone to attend to a neighbor's sick family, where she contracted it herself and died shortly thereafter. Her death was, among the rest of the family, the hardest on nine-year-old Abraham, who was close to his mother.

His mother had been his academic inspiration, as it was she who had introduced him to the benefits of learning, even though she and her husband were not able to read and write. With her passing, it became a silent household, as Thomas Lincoln found it too hard to manage a family alone and not have the counsel and aid of a woman in the home. At the time, he became president, Lincoln wrote that he owed all that he had become to the guidance and love of his mother.

Being carpenters, the two Lincoln men felled the necessary timber from their land and whipsawed the planks needed for the coffin and laid Nancy Lincoln in the ground under the shade of the thick forest that surrounded the Lincoln homestead. Lincoln did not stop crying the whole time.

The absence of a softer touch in the Lincoln home, especially someone to guide young Abraham and be an example to the elder Sarah, prompted Thomas Lincoln to return to Kentucky in 1819 with the sole intention to find a wife to take back to Indiana. When he returned, he found Sarah Johnston, the lady that he had once wooed but was unsuccessful in courting before he had met Nancy Hanks. But this time fate dealt him a different result with Sarah Bush Johnston, as the man she had married had also passed, and she was a widow with two children of her own. This time she was more amenable to his advances, and they were married, and she returned with him to Indiana.

Not only was she a courageous woman, but she was also kind and loving, and she easily integrated the household, taking Sarah and Abraham under her wing and guiding them as her own.

The home routine with a stepmother and the carpentry that he performed with his father and the avalanche of reading that he could fit into his busy schedule maintained a stable life for Lincoln at this point. By the time he was nineteen in 1828, he was already six feet four inches in height and slender from the hard life he lived as an active frontiersman.

John Quincy Adams was president at this point when another catastrophe struck the Lincoln family. Abraham's sister, Sarah, passed away during childbirth at the age of twenty-one. This second loss was devastating to him but combined with the loss of his mother ten years earlier and the eventual loss of his son while he was president were the three personal losses that steeled his character and brought focus to his mind. A lesser man would have allowed the loss to dictate his actions, but Abraham Lincoln was not an ordinary backwoods frontier man. He was someone who had greater aspirations for his contribution and higher ideas for all mankind.

Chapter 7 - Spreading His Wings

Wanting to spread his wings and increase the household income, Lincoln found work in town, and it happened to be with the richest man in the area—James Gentry. The task was simple. Lincoln was to accompany Gentry's son on a flatboat barge carrying supplies down the Mississippi River to New Orleans. The adventure was one that appealed to him, and the river, the boat, and the trip left a deep impression on his young and adventurous mind.

There was one other event on that trip that disturbed him enough to leave a lasting impression. When they reached New Orleans, while still on the flatboat, Lincoln observed for the first but not the last time the auction of slaves. The entire scene and the indignity of the buying and selling of humans disturbed him deeply and left a scar that never left him. The emancipation of slaves has been accredited to Lincoln, and it was a major part of his life, but liberating millions of people from the shackles of abuse does not assuage the horrors that preceded it.

On that trip, he discovered that he was a natural when it came to navigating the river and handling the barge. He was naturally made whole again by the open air that immersed him. He conducted his responsibilities exquisitely and went beyond the expectations of the man who hired him. It was always a characteristic of Lincoln to give more than was expected.

When he returned to Indiana, he continued to work odd jobs for Gentry's store, which also happened to be the place locals would gather and discuss the hottest topics in politics at the time. This is the first documented instance of Lincoln's interest in politics, and it suited him well. His interest in reading and the desire to increase his oratory powers paid off, as he was able to articulate his points better than the typical customer at the store.

This slide into politics was purely by accident, and he started to get a view of policies and positions from a grassroots perspective. It was an opportunity that he didn't appreciate at that time to be critical to his future successes. The more he listened to the different perspectives, the more it brought about his own views and polished his own thoughts on the matter. The more he thought about different issues, the more he began to take positions on matters of the day, but he was still far from diving into politics.

Back home, Thomas Lincoln had begun to do well in his business. Father and son had seemingly left their darker days behind and embraced the virtues of industry by putting their mind and backs to good use.

With Thomas Lincoln doing well in his business and Abraham Lincoln doing well with his repertoire of odd jobs, the Lincolns' stay in Indiana seemed to take on an air of prosperity. Between his odd jobs, his continued reading, his expanding social circle, and his love of the river, he was at the pinnacle of his youth.

As time passed, the river was more enticing to the younger Lincoln, and he started to work on other river-based opportunities. He eventually yielded to his enterprising spirit and built his own scow that would ferry passengers from the shore to riverboats sailing on the river.

By the time Lincoln was twenty-one, it was 1830, Adams was still president, and there was a threat of another breakout of the milk disease. Lincoln Senior did not cozy up to those prospects and decided to move to Illinois, a non-slaveholding state.

The Lincoln family moved to Illinois in March 1830 and settled by the Sangamon River, just south of today's Decatur. The family built a log cabin and fenced off close to ten acres of land, which they then farmed. With the earlier experience of navigating down the Mississippi River, the younger Lincoln set about finding a job in the area that would use his boating and navigation ability.

Soon after he turned twenty-two, Lincoln moved to New Salem. His time in New Salem was occupied initially with odd jobs to survive when he came upon Denton Offutt. He assisted Offutt with building a cargo barge when they couldn't find one to take Offutt's supplies down to New Orleans by the river network. The Sangamon River that Lincoln was intimately familiar with led to the Illinois River and then to the Mississippi River, which gave them direct passage to New Orleans.

Lincoln and three others offered to build a flatboat, which Offutt agreed to and paid each man $12 a month. Lincoln built the flatboat, which was eighty feet long. It proved sufficient to handle all the goods that Offutt was planning to have shipped down to New Orleans and to bring other goods back on the return trip.

The problem was that the barge ran aground in the Sangamon River. Lincoln put his back into it and with considerable effort and toil eventually freed the boat laden with bacon and supplies headed south. Lincoln's design for the flatboat was eventually patented, and until today day Lincoln is the only president in history to hold a patent under his name.

Offutt liked what he saw in Lincoln and offered him a job as his assistant in a new store that he was planning to open. It was hard to find a person who was as honest as he was, with that much integrity, and who was also willing to work for a fair wage. New Salem was a new frontier village at the time, hardly even three years old, with a population of less than a hundred people. It has since vanished from the map, and all that stands in its place is Lincoln's New Salem built in memory of the president.

As one with any notion of frontier living could comprehend, the town was filled with travelers who were headed west across the northern route. It wasn't one of the major trails westward, but it was sufficiently busy to warrant the expansion of a frontier post, and that expansion happened rapidly, as did the expansion in other areas of Illinois. The primary pastime among the men here was a toss-up between drinking whiskey and cockfighting. Lincoln, however, managed to remain strict in his abstinence from spirits save one or two occasions at most.

One such occasion that is a popular anecdote told about Lincoln in his youth was the incident where he lifted overhead a barrel of whiskey and proceeded to drink directly from it. The story was more a testament to his unassuming strength given his tall but slender stature. Otherwise, Lincoln was a teetotaler.

Between the time of the offer and the store actually opened, it took some time and so, once again, Lincoln took on odd jobs. Here he met Mentor Graham, a schoolmaster and went to work for him as a clerk. As the clerk, he came into contact with other residents of the area and became popular among them. He also worked as a rail splitter and took on various boating jobs on the Sangamon.

It took Offutt about a year to finally get the store set up, and Lincoln went on to work at the store, and this opened up his fortunes by increasing the number of people he came into contact with. The time at Offutt's store gave him two important opportunities: (1) it allowed him to come into contact with the community at large, and (2) it allowed him the time to read and brush up on language and politics.

It was here at the store on the counter that Lincoln would lie on his back and read. It wasn't just grammar that he worked on; in his free time, he also worked on his arithmetic and read Euclid's treatise on geometry. It is not a book that has the reputation of being easy reading. Yet, it was Lincoln's interest to understand this branch of mathematics from the man who was instrumental in its development.

The time he had spent meeting all those people contributed to his popularity, which he gained from his eloquent disposition. That, in addition to his infamous fistfights that happened to protect the store against bullies and thugs who were terrorizing the town's businesspeople, imbued on him an air of righteousness. On top of all this, his experience with the Sangamon River and boatmanship down the Mississippi River gave him numerous ideas of how the town could benefit from increasing the navigability of the Sangamon River. All these individual and seemingly disjointed matters directed him to become a candidate in the election for state legislator.

This was not to be, however, as his campaign to run for office was interrupted when he joined the 31st Regiment of the Illinois militia that year when there was an Indian uprising. The Indian chief Black Hawk had tried to resettle east of the Mississippi River, but the attempt was misconstrued by the settlers, and the volatile situation soon led to the entry of other tribes, and a full-blown armed conflict ensued.

In Illinois, Lincoln's company had elected him captain, and in the four months of the Black Hawk War, Lincoln experienced the life of the militia but without seeing any battles. It so happened that one Jefferson Davis was also in the war at the same time as Lincoln. He would go on to become the first, and last, president of the Confederacy. Lincoln's most notable incident during the war was when his company caught a member of the tribe and were about to hang him when Lincoln stepped in to stop the hanging.

When the war ended, Lincoln returned and threw his hat once more into the election for the state legislature. He announced his candidacy with this short speech:

"Fellow Citizens, I presume you all know who I am. I am humble Abraham Lincoln. I have been solicited by many friends to become a candidate for the Legislature. My politics are short and sweet like the old woman's dance. I am in favor of a national bank. I am in favor of the internal improvement system and a high protective tariff. These are my sentiments and political principles. If elected, I shall be thankful; if not, it will be all the same."

This was, essentially, his policy position statement. His position also included the advocacy of laws that stopped usury and laws that improved education. It happened that these principles reflected those of the Whig Party.

The Whig Party was one of the four major parties during the nineteenth century in the United States. Its founder, Henry Clay, was one of Lincoln's role models, and we can take two things from this fact. Clay's view of America was one that either appealed to Lincoln's puritanical values or was one that molded his values. In either case, his education and usury planks of policy were taken directly from Henry Clay.

The problem was that the Whig Party didn't have much footing in Illinois at the time, which was mostly supported the Democratic Party and the presidency of Andrew Johnson. The point to note is that while it is not certain how he came to adopt Clay's points of view and the foundation of the Whig Party, it was in direct opposition to the people who were predominantly around him in southern Illinois and Illinois as a whole. As such, his candidacy for the state legislature in 1832 failed.

What's interesting, though, is that while his views were totally different from most people's, he did manage to get most of the votes of his immediate neighborhood, suggesting that his likability among the people who knew him dominated the outcome more than his policy, which they opposed.

With the election loss and without any money in his pocket, Lincoln was attracted to the study of law. When he was younger, he had read books on state law, but he realized that law was central to the country, the states, and the harmony and prosperity of the people. His desire to read law increased over time, and he would devour books on the subject whenever he could. However, his priority at the time was to find work and support himself, and among the things he considered becoming the town's blacksmith, but that didn't happen. Instead, he used his good credit and honesty to purchase half a share of a store in New Salem. The other share was sold to a Mr. Berry for credit as well.

This, however, didn't go well in any way. It actually ended very poorly for Lincoln, who ended up taking fifteen years to pay down the debt that he incurred. The idea of a general store in New Salem was not new, and there were other stores, including the one Offutt opened that eventually went out of business. In this case, the partners who sold the store to Lincoln and Berry were also not doing well and saw the proverbial writing on the wall. That was the reason why they were willing to let it go on credit. Two things sealed the fate of the endeavor. The first was that Berry drank the liquor that was in inventory, and the store was not selling as much as it needed to keep things going. In the end, Lincoln and Berry sold the failing store in 1833 to two other entrepreneurs, but they couldn't handle the burden of a failing store and instead disappeared. That left Berry and Lincoln fully liable for the outstanding sums to the original owners. Before long, Berry died from alcohol abuse, which put the full value of the outstanding debt on Lincoln's shoulders.

That was the last time he invested his time and reputation on a business. Finally, after saving and working at various jobs and becoming prosperous, it took him fifteen years to fully pay the original sum that was agreed to. He could have sought bankruptcy protection from the courts, but he felt that would be dishonorable and decided to pay it all off over time.

His desire to pay off his debt even though it could have been pared down or totally abolished was something that earned Lincoln the epithet of Honest Abe. It was almost a character flaw the level to which he would take his honesty, and it was the same trait that probably made him stand on the side he did when it came time to fight the Civil War. His loyalty to the Constitution the way he saw it made all the difference in the world. While life was certainly important and the blood that spilled in the mud across the country was fully in his mind, his ideals, loyalty to the Union, and adherence to the Constitution made him who he was.

His penny-pinching days in the wake of the New Salem store affair stuck with him, and it seemed that for all the poverty that he had faced growing up he was never one to desire wealth. He felt that wealth was a distraction and something he didn't need. The only thing that he spent money on and even then in a limited fashion was his hats.

Poverty affects people in different ways when growing up. In some cases, poverty brings about a deep desire to become wealthy so that the pain of poverty can seemingly be avoided and remedied. Then there is the consequence of poverty, where one gains strength from knowing that poverty is not extinguished by being wealthy but by not desiring unnecessary, or in the words of Lincoln, "superfluous needs."

Whatever the problem, Lincoln's desire to advance in the world of politics was beginning to gain traction, and his eloquence began to match his ambition. His ideals were starkly different from the locality where he came from, and the typical voter was not fully educated in the nuances of legislation or its ramifications. One of those ramifications came about in terms of the financial impact that different actions brought and was something Lincoln was not totally suited for. Unfortunately, that was exactly what the Illinois legislature was grappling with—economic issues. The Whigs and the Democrats had a battle on their hands concerning economics, and as much as Lincoln tried to jump in, he just did not have the economic sense to contribute positively. Economics, finance, and accounting just didn't come naturally to him. Even his greatest admirers and fans considered him weak in this area, and so did he.

Politics didn't pay the bills, and so he needed to find a way to support himself, and it was by happenstance and word of mouth that he was offered a position to be the assistant surveyor by John Calhoun (not to be confused with John C. Calhoun, former U.S. vice president).

Calhoun was the county surveyor and a lawyer by profession. He was also a staunch Democrat as were many others in southern Illinois. The two men debated furiously over politics, but they also had a high regard for one another. Back then it was easy to have a difference of opinion among gentlemen and yet retain the necessary respect. Upon securing the job, he then sought the assistance of Mentor Graham, who pointed him in the right direction to find information and learn about surveying. Most of his surveys that can be found were ones that are evidence to Lincoln's accurate nature and high standards of work.

He advanced from being a surveyor to becoming postmaster of New Salem, and by the time 1834 rolled around, he decided to run for office again. This time instead of giving speeches to a sea of listeners, he decided to capitalize on his strength, which was to meet and chat with as many constituents in his district as possible. The plan worked, as they liked him more than they disliked the Whig Party.

In his second attempt for a seat in the Illinois State Legislature, Lincoln was able to pull off an upset win. On August 4, 1834, when Lincoln was twenty-five years old, Andrew Jackson was president, and the Illinois state capital was located in Vandalia, Abraham Lincoln won his seat with 1,376 votes.

Upon winning, Lincoln felt the need to prepare for the job, and since the job of being a legislator was all about knowing the law, and, more importantly, crafting the law, he used his time before heading up to Vandalia to study the means to craft law and to understand the law itself. He borrowed what he needed from John Todd

Stuart, a fellow Kentuckian and lawyer, and he purchased what he could from auctions.

The first session of the legislature began on December 1, 1834, and ended on February 13, 1835. Between the time he was elected and the time he left for Vandalia, Lincoln managed to become familiar with the language of legislation and understand the platform of the Whig Party that he championed. He took his time, but he was able to get a good grasp of drafting legislation, and he mastered the technicalities that are peculiar to drafting bills. When the session ended and he returned to New Salem, he had made $158.

When he got back to New Salem, he returned to his job as postmaster and continued his surveying responsibilities while he pursued his endeavor to become a lawyer. Reading occupied most of his time, where he made the effort to master complex documents and memorizing relevant passages.

Chapter 8 - First True Love

"Character is like a tree and reputation like its shadow. The shadow is what we think of it; the tree is the real thing."

Abraham Lincoln

Much of Lincoln's adult life was characterized by loneliness. Between his "nerdy" qualities, his silence, and his awkward physical features, it was not easy for him to be sociable. As much as he was easily liked among members of his same gender, he was rather alienated by members of the opposite sex. You could think of Lincoln as the tortoise in the tale of the tortoise and the hare. He was slow but sure, and he was the same way in relationships as well.

Not to be mistaken, Lincoln was not a shy person in general or afraid of the opposite sex. He just preferred to not be engaged in conversation with them whenever possible. If confronted by a lady, he was always polite, chivalrous, and courteous. Deep inside, however, he had insecurities about his appearance, which was a direct result of his impoverished youth. He and J.P. Morgan, a man born almost three decades after him, shared the same path inters of self-conscious debilitation and ambition all wrapped up in one. Both were silent men, and both were highly driven. The point here being that he was highly self-critical of his appearance.

However, as we all know that no matter how shy one is or how gregarious we can be, there comes a time that even the most cloistered of hearts will fall in love. As did Lincoln. His first love, and only true love, was one Miss Ann Rutledge.

Ms. Rutledge happened to be the daughter of a store and inn. She, too, hailed from Kentucky, which provided Lincoln with some semblance of familiarity and some memory of maternal origin. It was common to find Kentuckians across the border in Indiana, especially those who wanted to return to a more civilized life.

Lincoln arrived in New Salem, Kentucky, in 1831. He was an awkward twenty-two-year-old who was looking to make a living on his own. He didn't have a home in New Salem and chose to live at an inn—the same inn owned by Mr. Rutledge, Ann's father.

Lincoln first saw Ann a few days after arriving at the inn and was instantly attracted to her. He was clearly smitten by her looks and swept away by her demeanor.

He described her eloquently as someone of exquisite beauty, charm, and grace—all qualities that Lincoln seemed to cherish. She was, according to him, the prettiest of God's creatures that he had ever seen or would ever see in the future. She was blessed with uncharacteristic auburn hair and deep blue eyes, standing about 5'2". Her slender silhouette and fair complexion were atypical of the frontier community that Lincoln was used to.

She was known and loved by all in the area, with a bevy of suitors hoping to intersect the rest of their lives with hers. Lincoln was extremely attracted to her and hoped to marry her. According to William Herndon, Lincoln's law partner, he had found some documentary evidence that spoke of Lincoln's heartbreak and that Ms. Rutledge was the love of his life. It was not something that former First Lady Mary Todd Lincoln was too pleased to hear. Considering Lincoln's meticulous journaling and Mr. Herndon's integrity, there is not much doubt that one could ascribe to the possibility that Lincoln did feel strikingly for Ms. Rutledge, who died of an illness. It was recorded that after her passing Lincoln was standing near her grave and commented to a close associate, "My heart lies buried there."

When they first saw each other, he was prevented from making much headway for a number of reasons. He didn't believe that he was ready to make a commitment, but that was not the real problem, which was that he had low self-esteem and saw himself unworthy of someone so exquisite.

To complicate matters, it came to be known that she was in love with someone. She eventually got engaged to him, and all seemed lost to Lincoln. It seemed as though he had missed his chance, and this fed into his already diminished self-esteem. He was heartbroken.

She was engaged to one John McNamara, who was from the East Coast. He struck Lincoln as a suspicious character, but he said nothing of it since it could be misconstrued, and it was not proper to impugn another man's character on less than solid evidence.

McNamara made close friendships and developed a life in New Salem under a false name—a fact that proved Lincoln right but only after McNamara had left town suddenly. His sudden departure came as a surprise to everyone and devastated Ann. He had received news one day from someone in another town and then disappeared.

It turned out that even some of her close friends were suspicious of him, but she was blinded by her infatuation. Eventually, she faced the truth and came to grips that he was just stringing her along. It broke her heart, and it was said at the time that the disappointment led to her eventual demise.

In her heartbreak, she sought solace in the arms and kindness of Lincoln, who did all he could to nurse her back psychologically to her old self. Some days he made headway, but on other days it was just a backstop to a slide in reverse. But he was patient and read to her when possible, walked with her when she was able, and loved her unconditionally throughout.

Lincoln displayed such powerful empathy during his time with Ann. It was the first time that his highly sensitive personality would be put to good use instead of constantly overwhelming him. This time he could feel what she felt and managed to say the right things to pull her out of it.

She gradually returned to health, and she knew, as did the rest of New Salem, that it was because of Lincoln that she had found a renewed sense of life and a restored faith in love. It was also a side of Lincoln that no one knew or expected from a man so gruff in appearance and so difficult on the eyes. What his external appearance lacked, however, he more than made up for in empathy, kindness, and heart.

He had loved her from the beginning. For her, the love was organic. It developed over time and through the kindness Lincoln had so genuinely expressed and the gratitude Ann so deeply felt. Eventually, she and Lincoln were engaged, and after sufficient time had passed, it was rumored that she found out the truth as to why McNamara had left her—he had a family elsewhere and had returned to them. The final revelation of that news ignited the hurt that Lincoln had managed to quell. The return of the sadness was too much for Ann. This time she descended into such deep depression that her body began to fail. She died not too long after that in 1835 without formally marrying Lincoln.

Her death shattered Lincoln's heart and devastated his mind to an unspeakable degree. He had spent almost four years loving her and pouring his soul into her well-being, and she vanished just as she was beginning to return his love. This event altered Lincoln, who was already in a position that could not understand the loss of those close to him. He had lost his mother and saw the erosion of his father. Then he lost his sister, and the world had turned dark for him. It had made him retreat even further within. It was seeing and getting to know Ann that pulled him out of the depths, and now with her gone, the depths had a stronger pull on him.

In the shadow of her passing, his friends began to worry about him and how quickly he descended into such depression. He lost more weight from an already slender frame. He grew more pale, and he looked and behaved as if he were dead himself.

Things turned bad so fast that close friends worried about his health and even his sanity. It became common knowledge that Lincoln had gone senseless. He could be seen walking about mumbling to himself, totally disheveled and unkempt. He lost his job and began to lose all sense of time and accountability. He even began to run out of money. The Rutledge family was not pressing him to pay for lodging, as they understood his situation and were grateful to him for raising their daughter from the depths.

When things started to get out of hand, a Mr. Bowline Greene, who was a close friend, took him to a secluded location away from things that could remind him of the late Ann Rutledge and saw to his recovery. He spent months by Lincoln's side helping him get back on his feet. In that time, the two grew closer. It was a friendship that Lincoln would never forget, and he deeply appreciated Mr. Greene's efforts in raising him from the pit of despair.

The time away from Rutledge's inn and the familiar surroundings that would remind him of Ann, along with the outdoors and the soothing comfort of a friend, did much to help Lincoln strengthen his mind and put the past behind him, although it deeply altered the state of his psyche. Ann would always be the woman he loved foremost. Even in the White House, he often entertained thoughts of her that would spring up when things took a turn for the worse. It was a bittersweet distraction from some of the dark days of the White House.

Just as he was regaining his hold on life, Mr. Greene, who was instrumental in lifting Lincoln out of his depression, passed away, dealing a severe blow to Lincoln's already fragile state of mind and emotion. It is understandable that by this point Lincoln had started to believe that he was a magnet for bad omens and ill will. There was just so much death around him, and each time the extraction was from within his soul.

Lincoln spent the next few months shuttling between the graves of Mr. Greene and Ms. Rutledge, sobbing at the loss that he felt in his bones.

Chapter 9 - State Legislator

"This is a world of compensations; and he who would be no slave, must consent to have no slave."

Abraham Lincoln, April 6, 1859

Lincoln was a state legislator for four two-year terms starting in 1835. He was elected as a member of the Whig Party, which in itself is startling since all of Illinois was strongly Democratic. The formal naming of the Whig Party by Senator Henry Clay was the same year in which Lincoln won his first election and that saw a changing of the tide in the power that the current party system had in Washington and across the states and the new territories.

Early in his career as a legislator one of the significant acts he pursued was the relocation of the state capital to Springfield. He and other legislators, referred to as the Long Nine (since all of them were extraordinarily tall men), were in favor of moving the capital to a location that was the geographic center of the entire state. This was significant during the time of Lincoln because transportation was not something that we see or think of in today's terms. Today, we can board a flight, catch a train, or drive on interstate highways, state roads, and otherwise well-paved asphalt roads. In 1836, the only means of travel was the use of horse carriages on dirt roads that turned to mud after a heavy downpour.

Travel was arduous, and the need for representatives to travel to and from their constituencies and the need for citizens to come to the capital was a real concern. The idea to move the capital to Springfield signified the clear-eyed nature of Lincoln's view on facilitating democracy.

Springfield grew rapidly once Lincoln had moved the state capital over, and the city was expanding with heavy carriage traffic, shops, fashion, the arts, and entertainment—everything you would expect to find in a growing city. One other aspect of the city was also immigration—not just foreigners coming from Europe but also citizens from neighboring states, such as Kentucky, Indiana, and Virginia.

During the time Lincoln was in the Illinois State Legislature, he was part of a fraternity of pretty raucous reps, but one could never accuse them of being ambitious. It is best to keep in mind that Illinois was not part of the original colonies that formed the United States. Illinois Territory had petitioned the United States federal government to enter the Union and was admitted on December 3, 1818, nine years after Lincoln was born. By the time Lincoln was in the Illinois assembly, it was a body that was merely eighteen years old and fairly inexperienced, but they had vigor and ideals that were obvious from the start. The one core and common fact about the men who won the elections was that they "contained the blood and fire of the frontier." This included such men as Democrat Stephen Douglas, a looming figure in early nineteenth century American politics.

Lincoln's attitude in the assembly was one of seriousness and efficacy. He maintained a silence that implied a reflective and contemplative demeanor, and he didn't take part in any unnecessary ramblings; rather, he continuously observed. In short order, in contrast to the rest of the assembly, his manner was apparent, and the Whigs, who were in the minority, were unanimously looking to him to lead them. They even voted in lockstep to make him Speaker of the assembly. That, however, did not come to pass, as the Democrats were always the majority in the legislature.

During this time, the main concern that occupied the state legislature was the allocation of resources in this newly formed state. There were a significant number of public works projects that were debated and taken up in this frontier state, which was the gateway to opening up the northern part of the Louisiana Territory that stretched from the Gulf of Mexico to the Canadian border.

This was the period when Illinois took up a large amount of debt for its public works. This was common across the colonies and Eastern states. There was significant interest in lending money to the states because they now had the power of taxation, and taxation of the citizens of the state meant that they had a large and predictable revenue base to be able to extend sufficient credit.

In those days, the United States didn't enjoy AAA credit as it does today, and there were no rating agencies to administer those ratings. Instead, you had men acting as financial brokers, such as George Peabody, shuttling back and forth between America and the Old World selling debt instruments at a rapid pace. However, a number of states were inclined to stop payment of interest and eventually cut back on paying back the debt they took on. The main cause for all this was overleveraging state income and the subsequent fall in the economy in the early to mid-1800s. A number of states eventually stopped paying the interest on the notes, and many willingly went into default.

The Europeans, many of whom were the investors in these state papers, lost a large amount of money on the financing of infrastructure projects in the United States, but there were a few exceptions. Many of the states eventually paid up, which included Illinois, and this was done at the behest and insistence of Abraham Lincoln. It may have been late, but the Illinois state government eventually fulfilled its debt obligations after suspending debt payment in 1840. This was done in no small part due to Lincoln's strenuous efforts.

It is rather misguided to think that Lincoln was the kind of person who was laid-back in his magnanimity and silent to the point of being weak. He was neither. His silence was about understanding the opponent, and his desire to be in government was to be able to bring about change and develop the Union beyond what it was at the time while maintaining his puritanical values.

His affinity to the Whigs and his later disappointment with their alteration of principles and his eventual attraction to the new Republican values as outlined by Hannibal Hamlin were not something that he was convinced off or learned to see the virtue in. No. They were the manifestation of the person that he was inside. Take, for instance, the issue with Illinois debt that the governor and the legislature were planning on defaulting on. In that period of debates, Lincoln fought hard to convince the majority party that defaulting was not good for the state and against the moral fiber of the new country. They eventually listened to him and were convinced by his points, and so when the time came, they suspended the payment of interest but eventually paid it off in full. That has Lincoln's nature in its soul.

When Lincoln first arrived at the new state capital in Springfield, he visited a store to prepare for his move for the assembly's sitting. His first stop was to acquire bedding and other related articles. His reputation had preceded him, and they trusted him even before he set foot in the store. He eventually found out that all the things he needed to purchase amounted to $17. He didn't have enough to pay for it; in fact, he had very little money. The store owner instantly agreed to give him all the goods on credit. This caused him grave consternation, which the store owner could see in his face. The point is that it mattered what character the man behind the legislation happened to be. If you have a man who is corrupt, you get a country that follows suit. If you have a man like Lincoln, then you have a state (when he was a legislator) that paid its bills, albeit late.

Along these lines, Lincoln had deep thoughts and ideas on social philosophy, which have been documented by accounts retold by his friends and confidants. Many of his ideas that he formed reading Clay's words and the planks of the Whig Party, as well as from his own experience in law and being in the courts, led to thoughts he would have in the White House. One such thought was the abolition of slavery.

To be clear, you cannot extricate the story of the sixteenth president of the United States from the evolution of slavery without distorting what it is to be America. One must also take into account

Lincoln's age at this point. He was fairly young, and if you could add to that minimal formal schooling on his part, reduced childhood socialization, and the preponderance to read, you will have what we easily label today as being a "nerd." That is in no way being disrespectful to a great man but rather a description of the man who looked beyond the technology and social issues of the day and laid the path of a vibrant future, keeping in mind that what he did was alter the course of the country.

Before being president and as president, Lincoln had two major issues on his mind: (1) his heart and soul were in the unity of the Union, and (2) he believed in the literal meaning of the Declaration of Independence in its broadest interpretation. The notion that all men were created equal by one God struck his Puritan upbringing like a gong, and it was very important to him that slavery was not something that should be part of American values.

Even though the men who were responsible for American independence and the man who wrote the Declaration of Independence were all slave owners themselves, Lincoln was not inclined to define the term "men" in the "All men are created equal" statement as limited to the Pilgrims who arrived by transport vessels and not include the men and women who arrived shackled in slave ships. To him, "all" was absolute, and the idea of slavery vexed him deeply.

The Civil War that was fought right in front of his eyes was not a battle between the North and the South. It was fought because of the two ideals of America that he held to be true and to be great—unity (through the Union) and equality (through the Declaration of Independence). These factors were not inseparable, but it was exactly what was being ripped apart at the seams. Lincoln said,

"All such questions must find lodgment with the most enlightened souls who stamp them with their approval. In God's own time they will be organized into law and thus woven into the fabric of our institutions."

Top this off with being in the state legislature and then becoming a capable lawyer and you see an academic and cerebral side of Lincoln that one almost always forgets after being introduced to his humble and backwoods upbringing. It would be a mistake to discount Lincoln's position on the misconceived notion

In his speech in Peoria, while making his case against the Kansas-Nebraska Act, Lincoln talked at length about the issue of slavery and the manner in which the U.S. Congress had decided early in its history that slavery would not expand beyond the new territories:

"Mr. Jefferson, the author of the Declaration of Independence, and otherwise a chief actor in the revolution; then a delegate in Congress; afterwards twice President; who was, is, and perhaps will continue to be, the most distinguished politician of our history; a Virginian by birth and continued residence, and withal, a slave-holder; conceived the idea of taking that occasion, to prevent slavery ever going into the north-western territory. He prevailed on the Virginia Legislature to adopt his views, and to cede the territory, making the prohibition of slavery therein, a condition of the deed. Congress accepted the cession, with the condition; and in the first Ordinance (which the acts of Congress were then called) for the government of the territory, provided that slavery should never be permitted therein.

Thus, with the author of the Declaration of Independence, the policy of prohibiting slavery in new territory originated. Thus, away back of the constitution, in the pure fresh, free breath of the revolution, the State of Virginia, and the National congress put that policy in practice. Thus, through sixty of the best years of the republic did that policy steadily work to its great and beneficent end. And thus, in those five states, and five million of free, enterprising people, we have before us the rich fruits of this policy . . . But now new light breaks upon us. Now congress declares this ought never to have been; and the like of it, must never be again. The sacred right of self-government is grossly violated by it!"

The point that he was constantly making, and it was not limited to the speech in Peoria (part of which is quoted above) dated October 1854, was that much of the land beyond the original states was to be free, but Congress itself was looking to alter that promise and change the fate of the territories. The issue at hand for Lincoln was not that they originally wanted to change the state of slaves in the original states, but he didn't want to expand slavery into the rapidly westward expanding lands and territories. But that is exactly what Congress was implying in passing the Kansas-Nebraska Act—in direct violation of the Missouri Compromise.

Chapter 10 - Marriage and Life After

It was 1836, and Mary Owens was visiting her sister when Lincoln noticed her. Ms. Owens was previously married to someone who had died some time earlier. Her status now made her eligible for marriage, and the lady's sister had half-jokingly suggested that Lincoln pursue Ms. Owens. In the blink of an eye, it seemed that Lincoln was now engaged, and he half-heartedly pursued her in an obligatory, yet unenthusiastic manner.

It was all an apparent misunderstanding that started off perhaps as a possible wish on the sister's part, but it dragged on excruciatingly until the point when he actually proposed—again, out of obligation—and Ms. Owens politely declined. She later said that it didn't seem possible to have a happy life with Lincoln, even though she did say that he was an intelligent and honest man. She didn't feel that there was, in today's vernacular, any chemistry between them.

The response to her refusal was mixed on Lincoln's part. In letters that were in Lincoln's own hand, he repeatedly gives two distinctly opposing points of view. On the one hand, he expresses relief, and on the other he expresses regret.

This is critically indicative of Lincoln's frame of mind and his character. It is typical in people of conflict like this that there are two parts of him that are in active play. The first part is that he is a person who is highly driven by the right way to do something. Even though he wasn't really interested the relationship, he was dragged along by his own desire to do what seemed to be the right thing.

On the other hand, he was driven by his lack of chemistry, and he was undoubtedly still grieving over Ms. Rutledge. Overall, it was a painful time for him that was a cocktail of events from the time surrounding Ms. Rutledge. That was the recurring theme in Lincoln's life. It's as though there were two sides of him that he needed to resolve, and it always manifested in his earthly life.

The break was saddening but not devastating. It was now 1838, Martin Van Buren, the founder of the Democratic Party, was in the White House, and Lincoln was coming up to his second term in the Illinois State Legislature. One of Lincoln's closest allies in the assembly was a man by the name of Ninian Wirt Edwards. He was the son of the only governor of the Illinois Territory before it became a state. Ninian was married to Elizabeth Porter Todd, Mary Todd's sister.

The Todds were from Kentucky, Lincoln's birthplace. Elizabeth Porter was the first to move to Illinois in search of better prospects, and she was supposed to scout the area and then send word to her younger sister Mary Todd about whether or not she should make the trek northbound. Illinois was a lot better than Kentucky in Elizabeth's assessment, and she invited her sibling to visit.

Mary Todd left Kentucky in 1839 and arrived in Springfield to stay with Elizabeth. Ms. Todd was twenty-one years old at the time and weighed a slender 130 pounds. She was well educated and had a strong family background. The most important aspect about her was that she was an eloquent and unrelenting talker.

Talkers usually get comfortable with silent audiences, and silent people usually feel comfortable in the presence of talkers. And so it was a meeting of well-paired opposites when Lincoln first laid his eyes on her when he visited his friend's home where she was staying.

Initially, Mrs. Edwards had discounted the possibility of any chemistry between Lincoln and her sister, thinking that the pair were not suitable for each other because of their seemingly opposite nature. She liked Lincoln, but she also thought he was a little strange.

It was Mr. Edwards who was looking out for his good friend and thought that it would be interesting to pair him with his wife's sister. Because of Elizabeth's hesitance, the initial meeting between the two was significantly delayed. Elizabeth was looking for better prospects for her sister but to no avail. Of course, in the end, she was proven wrong, but it made the journey that the two of them had to make to each other's orbit that much more difficult.

That was not the only barrier and obstacle between the two. As if by karma, another suitor approached, this time in the form of Stephen Douglas. Mr. Douglas, a fellow legislator and the man who went on to beat Lincoln in the race for senator from Illinois, was also intensely interested in courting Ms. Todd. Elizabeth was a lot more interested in pairing her sister with Mr. Douglas for the typical reason that he was a lot more handsome and seemed to have better career prospects.

By the time Douglas could make any advances on Ms. Todd, Lincoln had already made her acquaintance and was pursuing her affection in the most aggressive and gentlemanly manner possible. Mary reciprocated.

Douglas, nonetheless, made his advances. However, the approach made by Stephen Douglas was a little jarring for Lincoln, and the friction that was already between them deepened. In response, Lincoln decided to withdraw his engagement with Ms. Todd. It was not something that was necessary, but it goes to show the level of Lincoln's feel of inferiority. Lincoln by all counts was someone who had a diminished self-esteem.

The relationship between Lincoln and Douglas was something that was deeper than just two opposing legislators. Douglas was everything that Lincoln had wanted to be. While Lincoln had to fight tooth and nail to get it, Douglas had it handed to him, almost on a silver platter. That was not the sole reason, though, why Lincoln begrudged him. It was also and more so because of the intellectual and moral differences they had. Douglas was a Democrat with slavery as one of his main positions. Douglas had drafted and introduced the Kansas-Nebraska Act, and Lincoln had (long after this association with Ms. Todd had ended) spoken out against it. Their differences came to a head during the Lincoln-

Douglas debates, where they argued their points about the way the country should go forward. One of the strongest lines in his debate was, "He [Stephen Douglas] is blowing out the moral lights around us, when he contends that whoever wants slaves has a right to hold them; that he is penetrating, so far as lies in his power, the human soul, and eradicating the light of reason and the love of liberty, when he is in every possible way preparing the public mind, by his vast influence, for making the institution of slavery perpetual and national."

The debates between Lincoln and Douglas before the Senate election in Illinois was the catapult that shot Lincoln onto the national stage. While ultimately losing to Douglas and seeing him leave for Washington as the senator from Illinois, Lincoln was disappointed. Upon defeat he said,

"The fight must go on. The cause of civil liberty must not be surrendered at the end of one or even, one hundred defeats. Douglas had the ingenuity to be supported in the late contest both as the best means to break down, and to uphold the Slave interest. No ingenuity can keep those antagonistic elements in harmony long. Another explosion will soon come.

"I am glad I made the late race. It gave me a hearing on the great and durable questions of the age, which I could have had in no other way; and though I now sink out of view, and shall be forgotten, I believe I have made some marks which will tell for the cause of civil liberty long after I am gone."

With Douglas making the advances that he was not comfortable with and withdrawing his engagement, Lincoln displayed the character of a man who wanted his failures to be on his say-so and not at the rejection of others. Much of his life felt that it was beyond his control, and many of his losses seemed to be that way. From the time he lost his beloved mother, then his dear sister, and, of course, the loss of his beloved Ann, a lot of what Lincoln felt was the lack of control of his happiness. This is partially the reason why he decided to withdraw his engagement. Upon writing his letter, he showed it to one Joshua Speed.

Joshua Speed was a close friend, and in some later writings has been described as Lincoln's lover, but there is no evidence of this, and at the time homosexuality was not an acceptable lifestyle, yet it did exist in the periphery. A lot of analysis in the post-Lincoln years was rife with this speculation. It drew circumstantial evidence from Lincoln's constant travel away from Mrs. Lincoln and by the stories of the way that Speed and Lincoln shared the same bed for an extended period of time. It must be stated, however, that many men used to share a bed in those days, and it was not always homosexual men. In any case, what we can be certain about is that Lincoln and Speed were very close friends, and he wrote the letter to Ms. Mary Todd intending to break off the relationship.

After writing the letter, he showed it to Joshua Speed, who told him that it would be better from him to approach the recipient in person and that sending a letter by messenger would not be the gentlemanly thing to do. Hearing the thought of appearing ungentlemanly vexed Lincoln, but he decided to talk to her at the first opportunity.

The whole idea of the breakup was really a mixture of misunderstanding and the pressures that he was facing at the end of his second year of his first term in the state legislature. The bills that he had supported in the minority were not going well. His good friend had recently passed away, not to mention Ann Rutledge's recent passing and his most recent rejection from Mary Owens. There was, as you can imagine, much that occupied him.

Ms. Todd cried upon hearing Lincoln's decision to break off the engagement, and so Lincoln kissed her and tried to talk her into feeling better. His way of consoling her really was a way of renewing the engagement—a fact that Speed brought to his attention when Lincoln recounted the events that transpired.

On January 1, 1841, a bridal party assembled, but the groom seemed to be missing. When his friends went to find him, it was as though he was in a state of confusion. It was such a bad state that his friends took turns watching over him and didn't allow him to be alone. It seemed that he was at the cusp of a severe manic-depressive episode.

There is a written record in his own hand of the events of the day in which he writes of "the fatal 1st of January, 1841," and how he had broken down considerably. He writes again to another friend, "Whether I shall ever be better I cannot tell; I awfully forebode I shall not. To remain as I am is impossible. I must die or be better, as it appears to me." In today's psychological terms, he was in such a depressed state that he even seems suicidal.

It was around this time that Speed journeyed with him back to his home in Kentucky, where Speed and his mother nursed Lincoln back to mental stability.

From there on, some time passed, and Lincoln was not in his mentally depressed state any longer. Speed had since married after some pushing on Lincoln's part. His business in law was also progressing well when the path was rejoined with Ms. Todd's. The path that came together wasn't all the fruit of happenstance. There was some external tinkering by a mutual friend.

It was around the time when he gave his speech to the Springfield Washington Temperance Society.

"Although the Temperance cause has been in progress for near twenty years, it is apparent to all, that it is, just now, being crowned with a degree of success, hitherto unparalleled.

"The list of its friends is daily swelled by the additions of fifties, of hundreds, and of thousands. The cause itself seems suddenly transformed from a cold abstract theory, to a living, breathing, active, and powerful chieftain, going forth 'conquering and to conquer.' The citadels of his great adversary are daily being stormed and dismantled; his temple and his altars, where the rites of his idolatrous worship have long been performed, and where human sacrifices have long been wont to be made, are daily desecrated and deserted. The trump of the conqueror's fame is sounding from hill to hill, from sea to sea, and from land to land, and calling millions to his standard at a blast.

"For this new and splendid success, we heartily rejoice. That that success is so much greater now than heretofore, is doubtless owing to rational causes; and if we would have it continue, we shall do well to inquire what those causes are. The warfare heretofore waged against the demon Intemperance, has, somehow or other, been erroneous. Either the champions engaged, or the tactics they adopted have not been the most proper. These champions for the most part have been Preachers, Lawyers, and hired agents. Between these and the mass of mankind, there is a want of approachability, if the term be admissible, partially, at least, fatal to their success. They are supposed to have no sympathy of feeling or interest, with those very persons whom it is their object to convince and persuade.

"And again, it is so common and so easy to ascribe motives to men of these classes, other than those they profess to act upon. The preacher, it is said, advocates temperance because he is a fanatic, and desires a union of the Church and State; the lawyer, from his pride and vanity of hearing himself speak; and the hired agent, for his salary. But when one, who has long been known as a victim of intemperance bursts the fetters that have bound him, and appears before his neighbors 'clothed, and in his right mind,' a redeemed specimen of long-lost humanity, and stands up with tears of joy trembling in his eyes, to tell of the miseries once endured, now to be endured no more forever; of his once naked and starving children, now clad and fed comfortably; of a wife long weighed down with woe, weeping, and a broken heart, now restored to health, happiness, and a renewed affection; and how easily it is all done, once it is resolved to be done; how simple his language, there is a logic, and an eloquence in it, that few, with human feelings, can resist. They cannot say that he desires a union of church and state, for he is not a church member; they cannot say he is vain of hearing himself speak, for his whole demeanor shows he would gladly avoid speaking at all; they cannot say he speaks for pay for he receives none, and asks for none. Nor can his sincerity in any way be doubted; or his sympathy for those he would persuade to imitate his example be denied.

"In my judgment, it is to the battles of this new class of champions that our late success is greatly, perhaps chiefly, owing. But, had the old school champions themselves, been of the most wise selecting, was their system of tactics, the most judicious? It seems to me, it was not. Too much denunciation against dram sellers and dram drinkers was indulged in. This, I think, was both impolitic and unjust. It was impolitic, because, it is not much in the nature of man to be driven to anything; still less to be driven about that which is exclusively his own business; and least of all, where such driving is to be submitted to, at the expense of pecuniary interest, or burning appetite. When the dram-seller and drinker, were incessantly told, not in accents of entreaty and persuasion, diffidently addressed by erring man to an erring brother; but in the thundering tones of anathema and denunciation, with which the lordly Judge often groups together all the crimes of the felon's life, and thrusts them in his face just ere he passes sentence of death upon him, that they were the authors of all the vice and misery and crime in the land; that they were the manufacturers and material of all the thieves and robbers and murderers that infested the earth; that their houses were the workshops of the devil; and that their persons should be shunned by all the good and virtuous, as moral pestilences—I say, when they were told all this, and in this way, it is not wonderful that they were slow, very slow, to acknowledge the truth of such denunciations, and to join the ranks of their denouncers in a hue and cry against themselves.

"To have expected them to do otherwise than they did—to have expected them not to meet denunciation with denunciation, crimination with crimination, and anathema with anathema, was to expect a reversal of human nature, which is God's decree, and never can be reversed. When the conduct of men is designed to be influenced, persuasion, kind, unassuming persuasion, should ever be adopted. It is an old and a true maxim, that a 'drop of honey catches more flies than a gallon of gall.' So with men. If you would win a man to your cause, first convince him that you are his sincere friend. Therein is a drop of honey that catches his heart, which, say what he will, is the great highroad to his reason, and which, when once gained, you will find but little trouble in convincing his judgment of the justice of your cause, if indeed that cause really be a just one. On the contrary, assume to dictate to his judgment, or to command his action, or to mark him as one to be shunned and despised, and he will retreat within himself, close all the avenues to his head and his heart; and though your cause be naked truth itself, transformed to the heaviest lance, harder than steel, and sharper than steel can be made, and though you throw it with more than Herculean force and precision, you shall be no more be able to pierce him, than to penetrate the hard shell of a tortoise with a rye straw.

"Such is man, and so must he be understood by those who would lead him, even to his own best interest.

"On this point, the Washingtonians greatly excel the temperance advocates of former times. Those whom they desire to convince and persuade, are their old friends and companions. They know they are not demons, nor even the worst of men. They know that generally, they are kind, generous, and charitable, even beyond the example of their more staid and sober neighbors. They are practical philanthropists; and they glow with a generous and brotherly zeal, that mere theorizers are incapable of feeling. Benevolence and charity possess their hearts entirely; and out of the abundance of their hearts, their tongues give utterance. 'Love through all their actions runs, and all their words are mild.' In this spirit they speak and act, and in the same, they are heard and regarded. And when such is the temper of the advocate, and such of the audience, no good cause can be unsuccessful.

"But I have said that denunciations against dram-sellers and dram-drinkers are unjust as well as impolitic. Let us see.

"I have not inquired at what period of time the use of intoxicating drinks commenced; nor is it important to know. It is sufficient that to all of us who now inhabit the world, the practice of drinking them, is just as old as the world itself, — that is, we have seen the one, just as long as we have seen the other. When all such of us, as have now reached the years of maturity, first opened our eyes upon the stage of existence, we found intoxicating liquor, recognized by everybody, used by everybody, and repudiated by nobody. It commonly entered into the first draft of the infant, and the last draft of the dying man. From the sideboard of the parson, down to the ragged pocket of the houseless loafer, it was constantly found. Physicians prescribed it in this, that, and the other disease. Government provided it for soldiers and sailors; and to have a rolling or raising, a husking or hoe-down, anywhere about without it, was positively insufferable.

"So too, it was everywhere a respectable article of manufacture and merchandise. The making of it was regarded as an honorable livelihood; and he who could make most, was the most enterprising and respectable. Large and small manufactures of it were everywhere erected, in which all the earthly goods of their owners were invested. Wagons drew it from town to town -- boats bore it from clime to clime, and the winds wafted it from nation to nation; and merchants bought and sold it, by wholesale and retail, with precisely the same feelings, on the part of the seller, buyer, and bystander, as are felt at the selling and buying of flour, beef, bacon, or any other of the real necessaries of life. Universal public opinion not only tolerated, but recognized and adopted its use.

"It is true, that even then, it was known and acknowledged, that many were greatly injured by it; but none seemed to think the injury arose from the use of a bad thing, but from the abuse of a very good thing. The victims of it were pitied, and compassionate, just as now are the heirs of consumption, and other hereditary diseases. Their failing was treated as a misfortune, and not as a crime, or even as a disgrace.

"If, then, what I have been saying be true, is it wonderful, that some should think and act now as all thought and acted twenty years ago? And is it just to assail, contemn, or despise them, for doing so? The universal sense of mankind, on any subject, is an argument, or at least an influence not easily overcome. The success of the argument in favor of the existence of an over-ruling Providence, mainly depends upon that sense; and men ought not, in justice, to be denounced for yielding to it, in any case, or giving it up slowly, especially, where they are backed by interest, fixed habits, or burning appetites.

"Another error, as it seems to me, into which the old reformers fell, was, the position that all habitual drunkards were utterly incorrigible, and therefore, must be turned adrift, and damned without remedy, in order that the grace of temperance might abound to the temperate then, and to all mankind some hundred years thereafter. There is in this something so repugnant to humanity, so uncharitable, so cold-blooded and feelingless, that it never did, nor ever can enlist the enthusiasm of a popular cause. We could not love the man who taught it—we could not hear him with patience. The heart could not throw open its portals to it. The generous man could not adopt it. It could not mix with his blood. It looked so fiendishly selfish, so like throwing fathers and brothers overboard, to lighten the boat for our security—that the noble minded shrank from the manifest meanness of the thing.

"And besides this, the benefits of a reformation to be effected by such a system, were too remote in point of time, to warmly engage many in its behalf. Few can be induced to labor exclusively for posterity; and none will do it enthusiastically. Posterity has done nothing for us; and theorize on it as we may, practically we shall do very little for it, unless we are made to think, we are, at the same time, doing something for ourselves. What an ignorance of human nature does it exhibit, to ask or expect a whole community to rise up and labor for the temporal happiness of others after themselves shall be consigned to the dust, a majority of which community take no pains whatever to secure their own eternal welfare, at a no greater distant day? Great distance, in either time or space, has wonderful power to lull and render quiescent the human mind. Pleasures to be enjoyed, or pains to be endured, after we shall be dead and gone, are but little regarded, even in our own cases, and much less in the cases of others.

"Still, in addition to this, there is something so ludicrous in promises of good, or threats of evil, a great way off, as to render the whole subject with which they are connected, easily turned into ridicule. 'Better lay down that spade you are stealing, Paddy; if you don't you'll pay for it at the day of judgment.' 'Be the powers, if ye'll credit me so long, I'll take another, gist.'

"By the Washingtonians, this system of consigning the habitual drunkard to hopeless ruin, is repudiated. They adopt a more enlarged philanthropy. They go for present as well as future good. They labor for all now living, as well as all hereafter to live. They teach hope to all -- despair to none. As applying to their cause, they deny the doctrine of unpardonable sin. As in Christianity it is taught, so in this they teach, that

'While the lamp holds out to burn, the vilest sinner may return.'

"And, what is a matter of more profound gratulation, they, by experiment upon experiment, and example upon example, prove the maxim to be no less true in the one case than in the other. On every hand we behold those, who but yesterday, were the chief of sinners, now the chief apostles of the cause. Drunken devils are cast out by ones, by sevens, and by legions; and their unfortunate victims, like the poor possessed, who was redeemed from his long and lonely wanderings in the tombs, are publishing to the ends of the earth, how great things have been done for them.

"To these new champions, and this new system of tactics, our late success is mainly owing; and to them we must mainly look for the final consummation. The ball is now rolling gloriously on, and none are so able as they to increase its speed, and its bulk—to add to its momentum, and its magnitude. Even though unlearned in letters, for this task, none are so well educated. To fit them for this work, they have been taught in the true school. They have been in that gulf, from which they would teach others the means of escape. They have passed that prison wall, which others have long declared impassable; and who that has not shall dare to weigh opinions with them, as to the mode of passing.

"But if it be true, as I have insisted, that those who have suffered by intemperance personally, and have reformed, are the most powerful and efficient instruments to push the reformation to ultimate success, it does not follow, that those who have not suffered, have no part left them to perform. Whether or not the world would be vastly benefited by a total and final banishment from it of all intoxicating drinks, seems to me not now an open question. Three-fourths of mankind confess the affirmative with their tongues, and, I believe, all the rest acknowledge it in their hearts.

"Ought any, then, to refuse their aid in doing what the good of the whole demands? Shall he, who cannot do much, be, for that reason, excused if he do nothing? 'But,' says one, 'what good can I do by signing the pledge? I never drink even without signing.' This question has already been asked and answered more than millions of times. Let it be answered once more. For the man suddenly, or in any other way, to break off from the use of drams, who has indulged in them for a long course of years, and until his appetite for them has become ten or a hundred-fold stronger, and more craving, than any natural appetite can be, requires a most powerful moral effort. In such an undertaking, he needs every moral support and influence, that can possibly be brought to his aid, and thrown around him. And not only so; but every moral prop, should be taken from whatever argument might rise in his mind to lure him to his backsliding. When he casts his eyes around him, he should be able to see, all that he respects, all that he admires, and all that [he?] loves, kindly and anxiously pointing him onward; and none beckoning him back, to his former miserable 'wallowing in the mire.'

"But it is said by some, that men will think and act for themselves; that none will disuse spirits or anything else, merely because his neighbors do;

and that moral influence is not that powerful engine contended for. Let us examine this. Let me ask the man who could maintain this position most stiffly, what compensation he will accept to go to church some Sunday and sit during the sermon with his wife's bonnet upon his head? Not a trifle, I'll venture. And why not? There would be nothing irreligious in it: nothing immoral, nothing uncomfortable. Then why not? Is it not because there would be something egregiously unfashionable in it? Then it is the influence of fashion; and what is the influence of fashion, but the influence that other people's actions have [on our own?] actions, the strong inclination each of us feels to do as we see all our neighbors do? Nor is the influence of fashion confined to any particular thing or class of things. It is just as strong on one subject as another. Let us make it as unfashionable to withhold our names from the temperance cause as for husbands to wear their wives' bonnets to church, and instances will be just as rare in the one case as the other.

'But,' say some, 'we are no drunkards; and we shall not acknowledge ourselves such by joining a reformed drunkard's society, whatever our influence might be.' Surely no Christian will adhere to this objection. If they believe, as they profess, that Omnipotence condescended to take on himself the form of sinful man, and, as such, to die an ignominious death for their sakes, surely, they will not refuse submission to the infinitely lesser condescension, for the temporal, and perhaps eternal salvation, of a large, erring, and unfortunate class of their own fellow creatures. Nor is the condescension very great.

"In my judgment, such of us as have never fallen victims, have been spared more by the absence of appetite, than from any mental or moral superiority over those who have. Indeed, I believe, if we take habitual drunkards as a class, their heads and their hearts will bear an advantageous comparison with those of any other class. There seems ever to have been a proneness in the brilliant, and warm-blooded to fall into this vice. The demon of intemperance ever seems to have delighted in sucking the blood of genius and of generosity. What one of us but can call to mind some dear relative, more promising in youth than all his fellows, who has fallen a sacrifice to his rapacity? He ever seems to have gone forth, like the Egyptian angel of death, commissioned to slay if not the first, the fairest born of every family. Shall he now be arrested in his desolating career? In that arrest, all can give aid that will; and who shall be excused that can, and will not? Far around as human breath has ever blown, he keeps our fathers, our brothers, our sons, and our friends, prostrate in the chains of moral death. To all the living everywhere we cry, 'come sound the moral resurrection trump, that these may rise and stand up, an exceeding great army'—'Come from the four winds, O breath! and breathe upon these slain, that they may live.'

"If the relative grandeur of revolutions shall be estimated by the great amount of human misery they alleviate, and the small amount they inflict, then, indeed, will this be the grandest the world shall ever have seen. Of our political revolution of '76, we all are justly proud. It has given us a degree of political freedom, far exceeding that of any other nation of the earth. In it the world has found a solution of the long-mooted problem, as to the capability of man to govern himself. In it was the germ which has vegetated, and still is to grow and expand into the universal liberty of mankind.

"But with all these glorious results, past, present, and to come, it had its evils too. It breathed forth famine, swam in blood and rode in fire; and long, long after, the orphan's cry, and the widow's wail, continued to break the sad silence that ensued. These were the price, the inevitable price, paid for the blessings it bought.

"Turn now, to the temperance revolution. In it, we shall find a stronger bondage broken; a viler slavery, manumitted; a greater tyrant deposed. In it, more of want supplied, more disease healed, more sorrow assuaged. By it no orphans starving, no widows weeping. By it, none wounded in feeling, none injured in interest. Even the dram-maker, and dram seller, will have glided into other occupations so gradually, as never to have felt the change; and will stand ready to join all others in the universal song of gladness.

"And what a noble ally this, to the cause of political freedom. With such an aid, its march cannot fail to be on and on, till every son of earth shall drink in rich fruition, the sorrow quenching draughts of perfect liberty. Happy day, when, all appetites controlled, all poisons subdued, all matter subjected, mind, all conquering mind, shall live and move the monarch of the world. Glorious consummation! Hail fall of Fury! Reign of Reason, all hail!

"And when the victory shall be complete—when there shall be neither a slave nor a drunkard on the earth—how proud the title of that Land, which may truly claim to be the birth-place and the cradle of both those revolutions, that shall have ended in that victory. How nobly distinguished that People, who shall have planted, and nurtured to maturity, both the political and moral freedom of their species.

"This is the one hundred and tenth anniversary of the birth-day of Washington. We are met to celebrate this day. Washington is the mightiest name of earth—long since mightiest in the cause of civil liberty; still mightiest in moral reformation. On that name, an eulogy is expected. It cannot be. To add brightness to the sun, or glory to the name of Washington, is alike impossible. Let none attempt it. In solemn awe pronounce the name, and in its naked deathless splendor, leave it shining on."

All this was still going on while he was pursuing Ms. Todd. His spirits were back up at this point, and in an uncharacteristic display of bravado, he managed to insult another Democratic politician. That man, one Colonel James Shields, challenged him to a duel to the death.

This event can be partially classified as comical and even silly. In an attempt to make nothing of it, Lincoln proposed ridiculous term of engagement to the duel. Eventually, the duel did not happen.

Once this matter resolved itself and no duel was concluded and as the year came to a close, marriage finally entered his stars, and Abraham

Lincoln and Mary Todd spoke their vows on November 4, 1842.

The wedding was conducted in a private house under Episcopalian tradition and custom. It was the first such wedding that the residents of Springfield had witnessed.

At the time, Lincoln was thirty-two, and John Tyler was in the White House after assuming the post on the death of President William Henry Harrison.

It is no big secret that Mrs. Lincoln was a well-read woman with a hot temper. Nonetheless, her inclusion in the picture now was one that altered the magnitude of Lincoln's trajectory. It may have not changed the direction, but it certainly energized it. Mrs. Lincoln had indeed a hard life. On the one hand, she had to contend with the sequential death of her children, and then she had to deal with the assassination of her husband. Finally, her only living son, Robert Todd Lincoln, had to be the one to take her to court to have her pronounced as mentally insane. It was a tragic end, but it was not something that was a surprise in many ways.

Perhaps it was the seeds of this insanity that already occupied her faculties when they were first married and then progressed as the calamities piled on. The irony is that Lincoln and his wife were kindred spirits. Both had a significant burden on their shoulders, and both were mentally distraught, but both had the strength of a hundred men and were able to withstand the pressures that were needed to bring the country together.

It was common knowledge that when Lincoln was a lawyer and needed to travel the circuit of courts, he would find the excuses he needed to not come home when he had off days. He found every excuse to stay away from the home front and from Mrs. Lincoln.

Chapter 11 - Lincoln's Angels & Demons

"Don't interfere with anything in the Constitution. That must be maintained, for it is the only safeguard of our liberties. And not to Democrats alone do I make this appeal, but to all who love these great and true principles."

Abraham Lincoln

It was not polite to discuss one's psychological state in the nineteenth century. It was taken as disparaging and rude. This was a time when psychology was not fully understood or seen as a medical issue. Mental health is no more disparaging today than cancer would be. It is what it is, but by identifying it and understanding it, it makes the discussion more comprehensible.

In Lincoln's case, there were numerous instances and symptoms that pointed to a psychological profile that would explain much of his behavior. There is also credible evidence, eyewitness accounts, and analysis that show that many of his motivations and decisions were made under the cloud of a tumultuous mind.

To understand Lincoln, this mental state must stand front and center. It cannot be swept under the carpet in the hopes of maintaining a legacy that we think should be. Lincoln was one of the most influential presidents in this county, and regardless of whether or not he was battling mental issues will not make that fact any different. What it will do is also highlight that he was strong to overcome them when he needed to and human, just like the rest of us, to succumb to it when he did. Either way, truth deserves the light of day.

To be clear, Lincoln was not crazy or psychotic. He displayed symptoms and consequences of severe depression. His condition is not surprising in hindsight but was not understood or even contemplated in real time. There was a chance that he was genetically predisposed or environmentally disadvantaged because of the frontier circumstances that he faced early in life and because of the almost impoverished childhood that he endured.

These monumentally difficult and extended periods, from what he was born into to the relationship he shared with his father, the losses of those he loved in his family, and the existential difficulties he experienced in his youth, were all depression-inducing events. If Lincoln were alive today, he would be diagnosed clinically depressed. There are many credible anecdotes of his behavior and reports that chronicled his strange behavior in private and often in public. For instance, when he was nominated as the Republican candidate for president, as the crowd jumped in jubilee and euphoria, Lincoln navigated his way to the platform in a sullen and almost dazed way to greet the crowd. His speech that followed was articulate but bereft of any jubilee whatsoever. Eyewitnesses at that nomination event described later that he did not smile easily and would not be able to see the sunlight at noon.

Lincoln's mental state was a dichotomy because he was not always forlorn and sulking. He hated people and to be in their company, but when he was in their midst, the clouds would lift, and he would be charming, articulate, and effective. The people around him would raise his spirits. Once they left and when he was alone again, he would descend into a deeper state of depression.

Whatever he did, the accomplishments he was responsible for, and the energy that he had to do big things, were purely motivated by cognitive discipline. Once he knew what he needed to do, regardless of how he felt, he would apply the energy needed to get it done. In this manner, he was unique. His energy was monumental in its ferocity and exemplary in its tenacity. He would be able to stay up for hours and read the incoming status telegrams from all the front lines of battles. He would still continue to manage and administer other areas of the country while this was happening. It wasn't just the war that he managed. It was the financial and legislative aspects of governing that were critical in his mind.

The power of his discipline and the ability to guide a mind already fraught with pain is nothing short of exemplary. Most people with his level of depression would recoil and retreat into their private space and shut out the world. This is anathema to being the quintessential politician. By virtue of the electoral process, it is necessary for politicians who are people persons to be better suited for the job. Lincoln was not this in the least.

Lincoln was not a natural politician. He was disciplined. When circumstances demanded it, he would be as outgoing and vivacious as the situation demanded but not an ounce more. He was able to go out and engage with people and convince them of any position that he saw to be right or one that would help his cause.

It is highly likely that his depression had a deeper cause. No doubt his environment contributed to it and no doubt his life experience contributed to it as well, but the one thing that explains his susceptibility to it and his ability to read his immediate surroundings well would be that he was deeply empathic. Lincoln had all the earmarks of someone with a high EQ—the measure of the emotional quotient.

In other words, Lincoln had high levels of natural empathy for all things and individuals around him. It is like someone who is highly sensitive to a wide range of frequencies is able to hear sounds the rest of us can't at low volumes the rest of us are unable to. In the same way, high-EQ individuals are sensitive to all things around them. They are able to pick up the slightest hint of things and the nuances of all that is going on. This often renders them overwhelmed and often in tears. Lincoln had that symptom, too, as he was often in tears for things that most people would not give a second thought to.

The opposite side of that same sensitivity manifested in the way he interacted and engaged with people around him and the crowds in the audience. He could pick up on what they were thinking and feeling, and he would be able to read the room well enough to be able to mold his message in a way that they would respond well to.

He was also highly sensitive to the desires of people, and he was able to use his insight to choose his methods and his words to tell them exactly what they wanted to hear to get the result he wanted. Eventually, when he was done with them, they would do as he asked.

His empathy was also able to draw energy from the crowds. Because he could tell them what they wanted to hear and they would feel good about it, that would then infect his demeanor, and he would start to feel good about himself and the way the talk was going. The crowd and President Lincoln would feed off each other.

That engagement energized him and put him on his best footing, but as soon as the back and forth was done and each side went their own way, he could only sustain that euphoria for a moment or two before slumping back down under his dark clouds. On one side of the engagement was the man who was vivacious. On the other side was the sullen and silent man who did not like going out to meet people until he did it. He would prefer to stay alone, read, or just be silent dealing with the demons inside his head.

When that nomination event was over, his friends found him sitting alone in one of the many chairs that were there. He was amidst darkness and the smell akin to a sweaty saloon the morning after a brawl. Lincoln sat there quietly looking even more sullen. His only words to his friends were that he was feeling gravely ill. He was having an episode where depression was racking him from the inside, and he could not bring himself to exit the predicament. This depression only escalated throughout life without any help or natural circumstances to curtail it. The only thing that kept him sane was the discipline to do the right thing for the country as he saw fit.

It was this right thing, that even though the this is in the book diverges from the common wisdom that Lincoln was the emancipator of the slaves and there couldn't have been a racist figure in the makeup of his body and soul, the said thesis wants to paint the picture that is supported by all the facts and not just ones that support a statesman of pristine substrate.

When caught in uncomfortable or stressful predicaments, he would punctuate the time with jokes, inappropriate for the situation, and comments that would elicit laughter from the neighboring crowd and for him. It was one of the ways that he could kick-start any change in his mood. Those were the times when it was easy to understand that things had gone too far, and they went too far too often.

The person he spent the most time with in his life ended up being Mary, his wife. She was also the person who would and could drive him to the deepest depths of his depression. Before their son passed, her tenacity and constant fuel for his ambition would drive him to feel inadequate. After becoming president, she was there to push him in assessing the war in a certain way, but soon after their son passed, her dark clouds only deepened his. Mary was a powerful character and a domineering personality in Lincoln's life.

She was the one person he would never have a cross word with or perpetuate a conflict. Some suggest that his love for her was so deep that he chose to remain silent rather than prove his point just so that it would not hurt her. They would debate, occasionally they would argue, but the times when he would press his point until she acceded were rare.

Mrs. Lincoln was also said to harbor an unstable mind, and Lincoln himself was fully aware of it. It was part of his own burden to carry. Psychologists have been kind in their labeling of Lincoln, calling him chronically melancholy. There is even suggestion that his marriage to Mrs. Lincoln was also a factor in his mental deterioration.

These factors, whatever they were that sparked the depression, ironically, also gave him the strength he needed to endure something as catastrophic and drawn out as the Civil War.

Besides his state, he had a mind-set that was quite different from what we would consider rational thought. This in no way suggests that he wasn't a great president—he was. It is merely drawing a distinction that shows that one's path to greatness is not what one is used to thinking.

Lincoln had displayed a sense of destiny in all his actions. He believed strongly that he was meant to accomplish great things, which he did. This sense of destiny may have also been what countered his melancholy states when they struck and drove him to take action when action was demanded.

If one believed in destiny, it could be said that belief was one of delusion. One could then argue that there is a fine line between delusion and greatness. In Lincoln's case, it seems that his strong moral grounding together with his relentless nature were the combination of qualities that resulted in accomplishment. A sense of destiny is not a delusion. Lincoln was never going to be a regular president or someone who just got to office, administered the country, and left at the end of his term. Lincoln stepped into the office of the presidency with that knowledge, and everything that he attempted was tinged with that mind-set. It was what saved him from his own melancholy.

Lincoln had faced many defeats in his life. There were many political defeats and even more personal defeats. In the time between leaving Congress and deciding to run for the presidency, he felt lost. He had lost his sense of purpose. He thought that jumping back into practicing law would be able to alleviate this hollow and life lacking direction, but law practice was even less invigorating than he had imagined. The last time he had practiced law he was on the upswing. He had gone from store clerk and surveyor to lawyer, so the upswing was positive, but when he left Congress, he went from drafting the law to practicing it, and that was a downswing.

This downswing served to aggravate his depression. The last time he was a lawyer the upswing kept him elevated in mood, and the responsibility of keeping clients counseled kept up his cheer. He was also single at the time, and life hadn't taken such a big bite out of him just yet. This time around he had to see the same work but sitting from a different perch. He missed Washington and the ability to advance himself.

There were three stages to Lincoln's depression. The largest of the three was the state of constant fear he was in. His fear was that of being ridiculed and of not being intelligent. He always carried a chip on his shoulder about not being the man that he imagined he would turn out to be. In actual fact, Lincoln was smarter than the average nineteenth-century American. Not only did he know how to read in a society where literacy rates were so low, but he had also taught himself to read. Not only was he smarter than the average settler, but he was also more hardworking.

Lincoln was also naturally partial to long-term outcomes than to short-term benefits. He could see that he was playing the long game, and he settled in for the slog that it would take to accomplish things that stretched to the horizon. But that compounded the stresses on his mind because he would have to spend motivation on an effort but hardly got paid with the sense of accomplishment until much later. The gratification for the work done took some time to come back, and this resulted in eroding his self-esteem.

As this happened, he learned that he had to put up with it because of his "destiny." In regular minds, the moment self-esteem, a decidedly noncognitive feature of the mind, erodes, the person's motivation diminishes, and objectivity reduces. For people who are highly disciplined, they think their way out to do what they have to do, and then they do it even though all the while they are in a terrible state of mind—sad and melancholy.

The fear component of his depression did not lead down a path that is regularly traversed by most patients of depression. In Lincoln's case, by virtue of wanting to reach his destiny, he used the main aspects of his depression to fuel him on. It is worth noting that there was no classification of depression in the 1850s. If one faced a string of symptoms, the best they could do is to say they fell ill. In the same way, there was no way someone could classify EQ and empathy.

Those who are diagnosed with high EQ or are said to be empathic or have highly sensitive personalities can then understand that the reason why they feel a certain way has an explanation for it, and they can move on with their lives. Even if they are not able to feel at peace, at least they are not racked by questions. Lincoln did not have the benefit of this diagnosis. All he knew was that he felt very strongly about many things, and he could not express them adequately or address them sufficiently to be able to make them go away.

Instead, Lincoln used what he could and learned to sort the chaff from the wheat. This also took tremendous focus, and he was able to do that. His tremendous ability to apply his mind meant that he had to direct a lot of energy to his thinking and his brain in general. It was one of the reasons why he would get tired and move into deeper states of depression. Besides that, he had been malnourished as a child, which had left some permanent damage to his metabolic system.

Energy management for the president was challenging, and the constant fluctuation in energy that his brain received altered his mood and deepened his depression.

A side effect of that—when the brain is insufficiently energized—is a constant state of panic, anxiety, or otherwise a general state of fear. Fear was a constant companion to Lincoln, but it turned out that this was a plus for him.

As mentioned, fear in most people is debilitating, and they eventually end up not doing much. Of course, not all people are like that, and Lincoln was such a person. He would persevere amidst the fear that was palpable in him, which is further proof of his mental discipline.

There were two stages of fear in his life. The first was that he was not good enough. This fear caused him to try harder. This is the same fear that diminished his self-esteem but also powered him. Once he learned to read and read law on his own, he then feared that he would not be able to do more than that. His fear was one that would grip him to the point that he would frequently get panic attacks. To get over that, he then aspired to do something with the law and to become better than he was. Lincoln was the epitome of the man who uses his fear to climb to higher levels of success. Each level he climbed resolved an old fear and then reinstated fear in a new form.

Once he had learned the law and had written the law as a legislator, he then had the fear that he would not be able to do much after retirement. Between this fear and the boredom during his second pass at a law practice, he began to have more ambitious thoughts.

There were low points in his law career. This happened in the first pass (before his time in Congress) and in the second pass (after his time in Congress). His law partner once commented that Lincoln's melancholy was the worst he had ever seen. It was one that was all-consuming. His depression never abated, but he never stopped doing better.

Lincoln had made it a habit to convert his inner demons into his outer angels. He had converted his challenges to wins and pains to accomplishments. This required the second aspect of his mental makeup—the ability to engage. His ability to engage in the individual tasks that needed to be accomplished so that he could get the final outcome of his choice is legendary.

It is not common to consider that one of the greatest presidents of this land, one of four atop Mount Rushmore, and the only president to preside over a civil war in this country, was given to fear. In fact, he may have been the only president in history who was afflicted and almost debilitated by it.

But the story of Lincoln would not be complete if the aspect of his fear were not transmitted, and it would be accurate to leave the story at fear's feet. The real story is that he was a man who overcame that fear, and it was that discipline to overcome the fear and to clear the mind's fog while gripped by that fear that made this man legendary.

Chapter 12 - Spiritual Center

Lincoln understood more than anything else that the job of the presidency was a place of moral leadership. There is certainly a number of administrative duties and responsibilities that it carried, but when it comes down to it, it is a force like no other that can raise the hearts of man to war or thrash it in the ash heap of history.

Lincoln's spirituality intersected with his intellect. His intellect was built by him, not by the private schools and universities back in England. It was founded on and built by his personal reading of the great writings of the time and about great men that preceded him.

He learned to read, and then he learned what to read and whom to read about. One of Lincoln's most profound experiences began with the Christian Bible. As surprising as this may seem, since it was obvious that he was eventually agnostic, he was a child of deep Christian values who had heard so much of the Bible and the incorrect interpretations of it.

He himself was subjected to the incorrect and skewed representations of the Bible. His powers of reasoning eventually shook him out of it. It is more evidence that Lincoln was intelligent enough to be able to think for himself and work things out without being tutored, taught, or influenced. It was a benefit of his inherent silence. He was not influenced by his backwater surroundings.

Not many people have been able to separate themselves from the influence of their environment. This is especially true in the congregation and how the early frontier Christian thinking would have influenced him but didn't because he floated to the top like oil in water. His first experience with the Bible was not pleasant or positive. He didn't understand the intention and the deeper meanings, and he was confused and gravitated away.

In time, his curiosity led him back to the Bible later in life and allowed him to dismantle the pedestrian interpretation of it and come to understand the true nature of its teachings. That second run at it opened his eyes and helped change the trajectory of his life. You can see the difference this made in the way he spoke to the Temperance Society.

Lincoln was not a jovial man, but he did not have a mean streak in him. He was fairly serious and down to earth, but he was thoughtful and kind to those who engaged him in conversation. He also had Stoic characteristics of conversation. He spoke only when spoken to unless he was campaigning. He also did not speak about things he did not know about. Lincoln was the quintessential gentlemen. To a new acquaintance, none of his demons would surface—only the angels they powered inside.

He spent his time observing rather than pontificating. He spent his mind thinking rather than plotting pleasures. He spent his silence in two ways. One was constructive, the other destructive. His destructive side indulged in deep and dark thoughts of peril and pain. It was part of the negative manifestations of his depression that was rooted within him from a very young age. The second was spent in constructive cognition of the nature of things.

The key to traversing the path toward enlightenment is to be able to contemplate the knowledge that is absorbed through books and observation. It takes time to assimilate these thoughts to a point that they are actually beneficial. Taking things literally and not spending any time deciphering only results in taking away the opposite of what is intended.

For an autodidact like Lincoln, he had stumbled upon the greatest gift that was in his arsenal—the ability to make sense of what he observed and what he read without a third-party interpretation of the matter. That made his self-schooling more effective than any of the schooling he could have attended in his youth.

As for his moral grounding, it was based on deep, old-world Christian values. His ancestors who arrived on these shores were Puritans, and his parents were dyed-in-the-wool, hardcore

Baptists. Lincoln himself was not a practicing Christian. Neither was he atheist. He was more agnostic later in life, and, in fact, he had rejected Baptist teachings and local interpretations of its original intent. He also rejected much of any of the church's teachings and thought them misguided and self-serving.

One of his profound speeches on temperance given to the Springfield Washington Temperance Society makes his inner thoughts on religion and piety clear. Here he lays out his thoughts on the matter that was not common in those days and to an extent today. Aside from his speeches, his actions and his letter have shown us his adherence to Calvinism and the doctrine of predestination that affected his thoughts and actions.

An excerpt from his speech to the society is as follows:

"In my judgment, it is to the battles of this new class of champions that our late success is greatly, perhaps chiefly, owing. But, had the old school champions themselves, been of the wisest selecting, was their *system* of tactics, the most judicious? It seems to me, it was not. Too much denunciation against dram sellers and dram drinkers was indulged in. This, I think, was both impolitic and unjust. It was *impolitic,* because, it is not much in the nature of man to be driven to anything; still less to be driven about that which is exclusively his own business; and least of all, where such driving is to be submitted to, at the expense of pecuniary interest, or burning appetite. When the dram-seller and drinker, were incessantly told, not in accents of entreaty and persuasion, diffidently addressed by erring man to an erring brother; but in the thundering tones of anathema and denunciation, with which the lordly Judge often groups together all the crimes of the felon's life, and thrusts them in his face just ere he passes sentence of death upon him, that *they* were the authors of all the vice and misery and crime in the land; that *they* were the manufacturers and material of all the thieves and robbers and murderers that infested the earth; that *their* houses were the workshops of the devil; and that *their persons* should be shunned by all the good and virtuous, as moral pestilences—I say, when they were told all this, and in this way, it is not wonderful that they were slow, *very slow,* to acknowledge the truth of such denunciations, and to join the ranks of their denouncers in a hue and cry against themselves.

"To have expected them to do otherwise than they did—to have expected them not to meet denunciation with denunciation, crimination with crimination, and anathema with anathema, was to expect a reversal of human nature, which is God's decree, and never can be reversed. When the conduct of men is designed to be influenced, *persuasion,* kind, unassuming persuasion, should ever be adopted. It is an old and a true maxim, that a 'drop of honey catches more flies than a gallon of gall.' So with men. If you would win a man to your cause, *first* convince him that you are his sincere friend. Therein is a drop of honey that catches his heart, which, say what he will, is the great highroad to his reason, and which, when once gained, you will find but little trouble in convincing his judgment of the justice of your cause, if indeed that cause really be a just one. On the contrary, assume to dictate to his judgment, or to command his action, or to mark him as one to be shunned and despised, and he will retreat within himself, close all the avenues to his head and his heart; and though your cause be naked truth itself, transformed to the heaviest lance, harder than steel, and sharper than steel can be made, and though you throw it with more than Herculean force and precision, you shall be no more be able to pierce him, than to penetrate the hard shell of a tortoise with a rye straw.

Such is man, and so *must* he be understood by those who would lead him, even to his own best interest."

This was partly to blame for his bouts of depression. Lincoln would fairly often feel that he was destined for greatness, but he was unable to make it to that point. He felt that way after the loss in the Senate race against Stephen Douglas.

In this manner, we can think of him as a fatalist not to the point of being morbid—but he did believe that he would be killed ahead of his time. That feeling of an early death tied into his feeling of destiny for something great that he would achieve. The thought that it was his destiny to die early made him invincible because it happens to be the one thing that saddened him but also propelled him. A man without his acceptance of impending death could not possibly bear the burden of the decisions that needed to be made during the worst war that has ever happened to Americans on American soil.

The Bible alone was just the starting point because it was the document that was most often pointed to when he was a child to lend credibility to his parents' words and to the words of whoever invoked it as their witness. They may not have been accurate, but it was still invoked, and in time he needed to see it for himself. Nonetheless, it was not the only source of his intelligence. In fact, having a thorough misunderstanding of the Bible propelled him to one of the greatest truisms of knowledge acquisition—question everything. Which he did. That was how he learned and accumulated an increasing level of intellect that gradually evolved into wisdom.

It didn't stop there. Lincoln had a list of books that he read and made every endeavor to further read the books or sources that his heroes read as well. For instance, not only would he fill his mind with words written by Jefferson, but he would also go further and read some of the books that Jefferson thought to be important.

Aside from the books that he used to learn to read, books that taught him grammar to write, and the books that he used to learn his math, there was an interesting list of poetry, fiction, and history. Once he learned to read, Lincoln had a voracious appetite for anything that was in print and consumed it all.

There was also an interesting aspect to this. He seemed to have the ability to commit the reading material, verbatim, to memory. Lincoln was known to be able to quote chapter and verse of whatever source material he was referring to and be able to belt out pages of poetry whenever he needed to. Many of the speeches he wrote during campaigns and delivered on stumps could be recited from the teleprompter in his mind. He did have notes in front of him, but he didn't need to refer to them too often. That was his style of delivery. He spoke to the audience, not at them. He felt that it was better to engage them so that he could catch their real-time feedback to his tone and content.

As his readings progressed, he began reading law books and such. Then he also came across the works of Benjamin Franklin, George Washington, John Adams, James Madison, and his favorite, Thomas Jefferson.

The more he read, the more he found that it strengthened his reasoning, his arguments, and his eloquence. He realized that the shortcomings of his life were made right once again by the act of reading and by the diligence that it required.

The mind that began to develop in the shadow of Lincoln's joy of reading was one that was able to find meaning in all things around him and purpose in himself. It increased the power of his psyche and tipped him toward the belief that a truly spiritual center was cultivated by the total removal of the ego.

Within this thinking lay the problem of his reduced self-esteem and his eventual poor self-confidence. This is the discrepancy that many historians find when trying to understand Lincoln. On the one hand, he was highly effective; he was also well read and highly motivated, but he was also silent and depressed. The missing clue to reconcile this inconsistency was his lack of self-esteem coming from the fact that he believed strongly in the demolition of the ego. He believed that would lead to better understanding of the world around him and the nature of the bigger picture. This was one of the most powerful decisions that he made in his personal life, and it paid off.

By relinquishing his ego, he was able to learn more than his inherent environment would have allowed. Most people are the product of their environment, especially the environment they do not actively choose. No one chooses where to be born and to whom to be born to. The chances of doing well increase substantially when one is born into a good neighborhood with affluent parents. The opposite of that is to be born into a poor family with no possibility of education and no contact with the outside world—the way Lincoln had been. Only few rise to the top when they originally come from that situation, and they do that by relinquishing the ego that is painted by false narratives and, more commonly, by fears. While Lincoln himself was racked with fear, the fear he had was about what he could not achieve and what others thought of him if he didn't achieve, but he managed to find his way into the light and pull himself out of meager conditions. His fear was about not amounting to anything and to be left behind by the narrative of history. He was, however, not afraid that he may die trying. In fact, toward the middle of his life, he started to realize that he would one day be killed and had premonitions about that.

Throughout his life, the continuing suppression of his ego made a big difference in how he treated those around him and how he learned from them. In many circumstances, he knew more than those he was listening to, but he still extracted all he could from their perspective. He may have ultimately not executed matters with their advice, but he gave them a platform. The benefit was more his than theirs because in listening to everyone but not being swayed by everyone he was able to make informed decisions. One of his characteristics that became apparent is that whenever he was low on self-esteem, he would not be able to distinguish between his thoughts and the advice he got from his advisors.

Such was the case during the dark days of the Civil War. In that time, it worked against him because the war was something that he was shocked with. While the blood in the mud bothered him, it was the ripping of the fabric of the Union that dominated his concerns. He was afraid that history would forever label him as the man who split the Union, the antipole to men like Washington and Jefferson.

Lincoln may not have been religious, but he understood the tenets of religion and was deeply spiritual. Religion and spirituality can be confusing subjects and mistakenly thought to be interchangeable. In Lincoln's case, religion was about the dogma that needed to be followed, while spirituality was the nature to be godlike. Lincoln chose the latter.

The nature of Lincoln's self-esteem and ego were renewed as his intellect grew. The more he understood the greater scheme of things around him, the more he was humbled. The more he was humbled, the more he learned. The more he learned, his insight grew. This removal of the ego was evidenced by the fact that he would listen to his advisors, generals, and confidants intently in all matters of politics, governing, and war.

The psyche of a man who could take the insults of his own cabinet members and the generals of his armed forces had two overlapping catastrophes dismantle it. The first was the secession. Lincoln took this personally. He was already weakened by low self-esteem.

The second was the war that broke out. He was put in a position to choose between killing men of the Union or preserving the Union. This was a hard decision to make. Having been put in that position wore on him until it was difficult to overcome, and he retreated into a shell.

When he regained his focus, he was able to stand up to the generals, who by this point had hardly any respect for him. He took it all in stride until they crossed the line or went too far. When that happened and he no longer had any use for them, he would discard them unceremoniously.

Thurlow Weed had this to say of Lincoln: "He sees all who go there, hears all they have to say, talks freely with everybody, reads whatever is written to him; but thinks and acts by himself and for himself." This is further magnified by the fact that he had no firm belief in religious providence—only that of destiny. You can see this time and again in the speeches, as in the one referenced above delivered to the Temperance Society. You will also see it in his second inaugural address:

"Both [sides] read the same Bible and pray to the same God, and each invokes His aid against the other. It may seem strange that any men should dare to ask a just God's assistance in wringing their bread from the sweat of other men's faces, but let us judge not, that we be not judged. The prayers of both could not be answered. That of neither has been answered fully. The Almighty has His own purposes."

This character profile created an inevitable tragic ending to an intense man, one who benefited others greatly but was the chief cause of his own unhappiness. Having said that, it must be stressed that there was no hatred between Lincoln and his wife. In fact, on good days, Mrs. Lincoln was an excellent homemaker and the spark that lit the fuse to go after his destiny. Mr. Lincoln's biographer was meticulous in his chronicling of Lincoln's life even to the point of annoying Mrs. Lincoln with matters that did not please her, such as the chronicling of Ms. Rutledge and the level to which it affected her husband.

A good place to start for us has been his law partner's biography of him titled *Herndon's Lincoln*. Herndon is honest, yet admiring of a man who didn't change the landscape of legislation but sought to alter the way men thought of other men, the way we thought of the Constitution, and the way we thought of the

United States. It is safe to say that no man of the street with regular morals and placid wit would have been able to do the job and achieve the results that Lincoln did. It required a little abnormality of mind to be able to perform this abnormally gargantuan task.

In assessing his state, we see that he was a man driven by morals that he understood in the way he understood it. His goal of not creating an affinity to alcohol at a time when alcohol was a commonplace beverage and when the use of time to engage in unproductive matters was acceptable, we see that Lincoln would have none of those. There is no indication that he was allergic or became ill in any way when consuming alcohol, but nonetheless he stayed away from it. We see that his approach to women was one of absolute respect and courtesy. There was nothing about him that degraded or thought less of a woman. In fact, he placed women on a pedestal, and he was honest enough to tell Mary Owens that he would not provide her with a comfortable life but would still like to marry her. He was brutally honest and didn't hide what he thought.

His thinking was neither rash nor typical. His thoughts were based on his ideals, beliefs, and state of mind.

Lincoln was given to silence. In other words, he thought before he spoke, but it was significantly more than that. His silence was more than what one would assume thinking to be. He was a very deep thinker. There are two aspects to his thinking that are worth noting. The first was his ability to focus and direct his conscious thought.

Lincoln's ability to hold a thought from inception to conclusion is legendary. That was a strong ability in and of itself without even thinking about his ability to see things through to completion. It's how he taught himself to read, learn law and how to legislate, and learn to become familiar with political issues. It was also how he stayed strong in trying times. But it wasn't just that. He was able to subject a large amount of his thinking to the subconscious, which is evidenced by his "out of the box" thinking and his ability to spend hours in silence and then coming up with solutions that just were not available to those who think in the conscious mind.

There was definitely a mental issue in the Lincoln family. If you remember how his father Thomas was subjected to the horrific killing of his father (Lincoln's grandfather).

What is not commonly known is that his stepmother told him early in life that he should never decide to become president just in case he was to be assassinated. Either she was psychic or this was all really a self-fulfilling prophecy on Lincoln's part after being planted with the seed of death early in life. It is reasonable to think that Lincoln had already been planted with the seed long before he was married, and his wife's mental issues were part of his.

Lincoln read extensively. Not as much as Jefferson, but they indeed had some common reading material between them. Among Lincoln's reading list that formed part of his character and gave credence to a soul that was in search of spirituality was a list of books that stood as the foundation of a learned mind.

Lincoln needed to understand the basis of slavery if he was to understand the point that Jefferson was making and what the other Founding Fathers were trying to implement during the genesis of the country. For this Lincoln took the essays of Leonard Bacon on slavery as his primer and his guide. Leonard Bacon was a pastor in the North. He had eloquently written about slavery and balanced the writings with his view on abolition.

Chapter 13 - National Politics

"All this talk about the dissolution of the Union is humbug -- nothing but folly. We WON'T dissolve the Union, and you SHAN'T."

Abraham Lincoln, July 23, 1856

At the end of his fourth term in the Illinois Assembly, Lincoln had decided not to run for any other office at the state level. He had started to set his sights at the federal level and believed that he would be able to extend his calling and do a good job for the people of Illinois and those in the expanding United States.

While he planned his national strategy, he had a family to take care of, so he pursued his law career, partially to put food on the table and also because he enjoyed the career.

In 1846, he stood for and won the seat from Illinois to the U.S. House of Representatives. It was his first and last term in Washington as a congressman, and while his accomplishments may be slight, it gave him a good introduction to national politics. His seat was under the banner of the Whig Party, and it came at a time when the embers of war were being lit at the southern border with Mexico over the annexation of Texas. Lincoln opposed the war and the whole idea of the annexation that was designed by the White House.

This was a highly unpopular view. Much of the nation and the politicians in Washington supported it, while Lincoln kept voting against every vote that came up in the House that had anything to do with the Mexican-American War.

The problem he had with waging the war in the annexation process and the way that the war was sparked put him on the opposite side of most of the country. This was not the first time that he had taken a position that was different from the majority, and being that he was still in the Whig

Party, who were themselves in the minority, his views were not accepted.

The one thing about him that everyone still agreed upon was that he was honest, and his honesty never came into question. That may have even worked against him because they knew that he was standing on the point against the Mexican-American War, and that it was a position that he truly believed in. That could then mean just one thing. It was misunderstood that his opposition to the Mexican-American War was rooted in diminished patriotism. This was not true.

Lincoln accused President Polk of deception in waging war against Mexico as can be seen in his address to Congress excerpted below,

"The President, in his first war message of May 1846, declares that the soil was ours on which hostilities were commenced by Mexico; and he repeats that declaration, almost in the same language, in each successive annual message, thus showing that he esteems that point, a highly essential one. In the importance of that point, I entirely agree with the President. To my judgment, it is the very point, upon which he should be justified, or condemned. In his message of December 1846, it seems to have occurred to him, as is certainly true, that title—ownership—to soil, or anything else, is not a simple fact; but is a conclusion following one or more simple facts; and that it was incumbent upon him, to present the facts, from which he concluded, the soil was ours, on which the first blood of the war was shed. Accordingly, a little below the middle of page twelve in the message last referred to, he enters upon that task; forming an issue, and introducing testimony, extending the whole, to a little below the middle of page fourteen. Now I propose to try to show, that the whole of this—issue and evidence—is, from beginning to end, the sheerest deception."

This was not the first or the last time that he had expressed this opinion, and it started to become a thorn in everyone's side. It even got to the point that his biographer, whom we have quoted and used as research for this book many times, one Mr. William Herndon, who was also his law partner and close friend, eventually turned on him over the issue. Lincoln was very much alone on this matter except for some support of the Whig Party.

He took on the nickname "Spotty Lincoln" when he demanded to know exactly how the war had begun. It was important to him because he suspected that President Polk had engaged in underhanded tactics in sparking the war. No doubt General Zachary Taylor had done well in the war and was regaled as a hero on his return only to be eventually elected as president, but Lincoln doubted the conditions that resulted in the war that conveniently saw the Union win.

It turns out that Polk was a shrewd battle planner and had instructed Taylor to position his forces in a way that pinned the Mexican army. In their panic and stress, they misunderstood the intentions of General Taylor's camped army and attacked. This was enough reason for President Polk to wage a full-scale battle that was key in the annexation and eventual inclusion of Texas into the United States.

Lincoln eventually goes on to hint that President Polk is dishonest. He said to Congress,

"I am now through the whole of the President's evidence; and it is a singular fact, that if anyone should declare the President sent the army into the midst of a settlement of Mexican people, who had never submitted, by consent or by force to the authority of Texas or of the United States, and that there, and thereby, the first blood of the war was shed, there is not one word in all the President has said which would either admit or deny the declaration. In this strange omission chiefly consists the deception of the President's evidence-an omission which, it does seem to me, could scarcely have occurred but by design. My way of living leads me to be about the courts of justice; and there I have sometimes seen a good lawyer, struggling for his client's neck, in a desperate case, employing every artifice to work round, befog, and cover up with many words some point arising in the case, which he dared not admit, and yet could not deny. Party bias may help to make it appear so; but, with all the allowance I can make for such bias, it still does appear to me that just such, and from just such necessity, is the President's struggle in this case."

The more he pressed his point, the more Congress and the political elite of Washington at the time began to gravitate away from him. Eventually, Lincoln's term in office was up, and he had already decided not to run for a second term. He returned to Springfield, where Mrs. Lincoln and the children awaited his return. But he didn't return right away. He remained in Washington for a few months. Some say that his previous reason for not returning home due to Mrs. Lincoln's treatment of him caused him to stay away this time. That could be, but there was also another reason. He was doing his best to campaign for the presidency of Zachary Taylor, the general who had triumphantly won the Mexican-American War.

In his own words, Lincoln was trying to protect as much of the Wilmot Proviso as he could and not have the incoming president veto it. He was afraid that Taylor's Democratic opponent would step over the Wilmot Proviso and to them, even not knowing that Taylor would or wouldn't, he still took the gamble that Taylor would not, and so he fully supported Taylor. Besides, Taylor was of the same party as Lincoln at the time. He was the last Whig to ever become president and the last Southerner until 1912.

The conundrum was palatable since the Mexican-American War was something Lincoln had not supported and in fact was part of the reason why he had been all but ostracized in the capital.

With that, his stint in Washington ended, and after campaigning for Taylor, he left on a tour of the Northeastern states in what was labeled as a speaking tour. In some sectors of historical analysis, it was deemed that this was Lincoln's version of a listening tour. Instead, it was a prelude to his candidacy for higher office.

That was the first time he went on a speaking tour in New England. It was 1848, and after the tour he returned to Springfield and continued to develop his law practice. He was eventually admitted to the bar and the Supreme Court in 1849.

During his time in Springfield, he kept himself occupied with numerous endeavors of the law, and it is also when he designed and patented his design for the flatboat, which we referred to earlier in the book. (It was U.S. patent No. 6469A.)

The United States was a hot bed of activity as all this was happening to Lincoln. The territories in the West were rapidly opening up, and Lincoln was offered the governorship of the Oregon territory. The Oregon treaty had just been signed with the British three years earlier, and President Zachary Taylor had seen fit to offer the governorship to Lincoln. By this point, Lincoln's views on slavery and their place in the U.S. Constitution was growing significantly stronger, and he wanted to pursue that route instead of heading out west to a new territory. He declined the offer.

The following year in 1850 Lincoln's third son, William Wallace, was born on December 21. Lincoln was exhilarated and stayed home during the few days after the birth to look after his new son. The tragedy that ensued, however, when William was eleven years old and living with Lincoln in the White House was one that hit too close to home for him.

His son died from typhoid fever in February 1862 just a year after the Lincoln family had moved into the White House and less than a year since the Civil War had begun. The link between William's death and the Civil War was the dagger that pierced Lincoln's heart so deep. The Northern army was camped by the Potomac River not far from where the White House drew its water. The contamination from the encamped horses and men (from the waste that washed into the river) had contaminated the water to such a high degree that it caused the infection in young William.

After William's birth in Springfield, Lincoln continued working as a lawyer, traveling around the state and the country. He brought two cases to the U.S. Supreme Court between 1849 and 1852. The first was Longworth vs. Lewis, and the second was Williamson vs. Barrett.

By the time 1853 rolled around, Mrs. Lincoln was pregnant again and gave birth to their third son, Thomas Lincoln, who later died in 1871 at the age of eighteen possibly from cancer, but it is not conclusively known. He died after his father was assassinated, but before his mother was institutionalized.

By 1854, members of the Whig Party had begun to meet regularly looking for a new platform. Lincoln was among these men who were all in favor of creating a new national platform that could take up the expansion of slavery issue and advance it. The best vehicle to do that in politics was through the party mechanism, and since the Whigs were losing out in popularity and the Democrats were advancing, the antislavery Whigs decided that it was time to fire up a new party, so they began meeting, and in 1854 the Republican Party was born. It was March, and Northern Democrat Franklin Pierce was in the White House. By May, the Kansas-Nebraska Bill had been signed into law. It was the spark that lit a fire in Lincoln's soul. If he had any machinations for higher office before, they paled in comparison to this bill coming into effect.

Instead of considering the presidency, he decided to return to Washington as a senator from Illinois and threw his hat into the race. Lincoln stood as a member of the newly formed Republican Party against the incumbent Illinois senator, Stephen Douglas. Unlike today's elections for the Senate, the senators in Lincoln's time were chosen and voted on by the state's assembly. In Illinois, Lincoln would have had to be chosen by his former colleagues at the Illinois Assembly to be able to represent the state in the Senate.

On the national stage Lincoln was hardly known at this time, but he was known well enough at the assembly, and he had a good chance of winning the election. Douglas, on the other hand, had been a rising star in national politics and had wide name recognition. In the runup to the November election in 1858, they conducted a series of nine debates held in nine constituencies across Illinois. It's good to remember that there were no televised debates back then, and the debates allowed a great number of people to attend and the newspapers in those areas to carry the substance of the debate.

The nine debates came to be known as The Great Debates of 1858 or as we have also come to know them as the Lincoln-Douglas debates. Lincoln pretty much knew that he wouldn't have a chance to win because most of the State Assembly consisted of Democrats. It was good, though, that he participated, which centered around the issue of slavery and its expansion into the new territories. This is where the famous line was uttered during the debates:

"That is the issue that will continue in this country when these poor tongues of Judge Douglas and myself shall be silent. It is the eternal struggle between these two principles—right and wrong—throughout the world. They are the two principles that have stood face-to-face from the beginning of time, and will ever continue to struggle. The one is the common right of humanity and the other the divine right of kings."

He ultimately lost the contest, and Stephen Douglas was sent back to Washington as the senator from Illinois, but the debates raised Lincoln's profile from a veritable unknown to becoming a force of the North. His position on slavery and its expansion became the soul of the Northern cause, and his vehemence and resolve became the bane of the South.

It was only on a speaking tour that he stopped at New York's Cooper Union. His speech at the Union was deliberate and hard hitting. It was aimed at three specific groups, and it hit its mark effectively and masterfully. By this point, Lincoln had brushed up his skills as a master orator, and he eloquently targeted the people of the Northeast, the people of the South, and to the new part of the Republicans.

After the Lincoln-Douglas debates ended, Stephen Douglas returned to Washington, and Lincoln did not know what to do next. It was the second time that he had lost an attempt to get to the Senate. It was Mary Lincoln that prompted Lincoln to aim higher and not give up. Much has been written about Mary Ann Todd Lincoln most of which is unappealing and abrasive. But that is to be expected if you consider that she had been through more than her share of suffering and was expected to keep her grace under the scrutiny of the Washington elite when she first entered the White House. It is important to remember that she was a daughter of the South that fully and wholeheartedly supported her husband's views. But her loyalty to the Northern cause was always suspect because of her Southern heritage.

She was well aware that her husband was more than just a simple backwoods man, and she supported him even before they got married. It broke her heart when he had broken off the engagement, and it broke her heart again when he didn't show up for the wedding on January 1, but all was forgiven, and she was the energy behind his solitude and perseverance.

Chapter 14 - Politician

For as difficult a life that he had endured in the early part of his life, Lincoln had managed to emerge into the public eye with the sense and instinct of the consummate politician. In private, his thoughts would lead into darkness, but being in public would alter the landscape of his mind.

Lincoln used the energy of the people around him to transform his inner demons and elevate his persona to something that was larger than life. He did not plan on doing this, but it was a skill that came naturally as the forces in his life molded his fate.

In that respect, Lincoln was a product of his time and place. It was a time of emerging differences that swelled in the subterranean minds of the once-colonies-now-country, where the freedom of all was the force that pulled at the seams of a country stitched with high ideals but a weak understanding of morals.

The central moral issue at the time was not just about the slavery of men, women, and children, but the moral issue that plagued the country was a little more sophisticated than that, and it was plain and clear to Lincoln's mind.

The central moral issue was about the treatment of mankind over the greed for profit. What Lincoln clearly understood and stood against was the manner in which the fabric of morality was being frayed by greed and indifference to human life.

On Lincoln's part, there was the element of political calculation that drove many of his decisions and much of his thinking. It came naturally to him—a chameleon in the truest sense of political adaptability.

While moral outrage powered his heart, political instinct drove his actions. He knew when to speak truth to power and when to pour bespoke honey into the ears of the electorate.

This was on top of his natural linguistic ability that infused his speeches and colored his writing with poetry— poetry that projected the soul of his ideals and the consistency of his intent. This translated into a quality of trustworthiness that vibrated in the timbre of his voice and resonated in the hearts of his audience. It was hard to dislike this awkwardly tall man with a face seemingly chiseled by an unskilled carpenter.

During one of his campaigns for elected office, as he was making his case to the attendees, a fight broke out amidst the crowd between two men diametrically opposed on some topic.

Lincoln halted, jumped off the podium, and briskly made his way to the ongoing fisticuffs. Upon arriving, he effortlessly pulled the two men apart and cross-examined them as to the cause. It turned out that the men disagreed with each other about the topic of Lincoln's speech. One was in Lincoln's corner, the other decidedly on the other side.

By the time Lincoln was done with both, he had gained a new supporter. In his brief contact with these men, he had managed to pour that honey potion he was so famous for and warmed the hearts of both, the advocate and his antagonist. If only Lincoln were able to speak to every person in the South like that the immorality of racism and stain of slavery would have been omitted from the tomes of American history.

Lincoln's fabric as a politician was a complex weave of personal trials and sufferings, with the interest in the academic approach to better understanding. As much as Lincoln strove to learn, it was not the academics that interested him. It was the development of the mind and the assimilation of knowledge that animated his actions.

Understanding this point is crucial for understanding Lincoln and the shape of his mind. In the mid-nineteenth century, there were a small number of grade schools, even fewer high schools, and only a handful of institutions of higher learning. Not only was it cost-prohibitive to attend school, but the closest one could sometimes be half a day's walk, which made it impractical to attend, especially since there was a mountain of chores to help with at home or on the farm.

There were other reasons beyond cost and convenience as well. It was sometime a matter of opportunity cost. Even if the schoolhouse was next door and there were no chores to attend to, the time at school took away from being at a job to earn that extra penny that helped put food on the table.

Going to school helped in learning some math, reading, and writing. Everything else was geared at being able to get a job in the future. Being a farmer didn't need that. It wasn't until just after Lincoln's time did the idea and concept of academic advancement enter the mainstream.

Without the systemic pressure of getting an education or at the very least to be part of the paper chase, boys grew into men without the benefit of organized learning. Each was left to his own devices to put food on the table in any way they could.

Lincoln had undergone all of this at this time. There was no need for an education. He just needed to paddle his barge, handle a saw, and make change behind the cash register. Yet, his interest in language catapulted his ability to communicate, his ability fueled his desire to improve himself, and his desire traced his arc across history. He was truly self-made.

The backdrop to all this was the pain that colored his thoughts. In his metamorphosis from frontiersman to politician, he still lived a life trapped by many of the same responsibilities that all young adults had. Despite the challenges, he found the time and the will to advance his reading, develop his grammar, and perfect his communication before he picked up a copy of the Illinois constitution and the subsequent law books that put him on track to understand the law. This was the beginning of a life that would pit career against morals. It was the spark that lit the awareness that not all laws were just.

They say that a man is the vessel that contains the sum of his past and his vision of the future. In Lincoln's vessel, the two were diametrically opposed. One was dark, the other enlightened.

However lofty his ideals, it is only fair to remember that Lincoln was the quintessential politician. The honey potion he trickled into the ears of his audience was made of one part poetry, three parts hyperbole. He was still, nonetheless, Honest Abe. The sobriquet reflected the measure of his moral vessel without mitigating it by how easily he bent the truth in exchange for a ballot.

A competitive streak navigated aggressively within the shadows of Lincoln's intellect. He was not a man who would be bested by a situation or a person. He did whatever he needed to do and went wherever he wanted to be—and he was relentless.

That same inherent tenacity saved him from his own demons later in life when he transitioned from politician to statesman.

His first presidential campaign was won by a fluke. The gods were smiling on him, and the three other candidates split the popular vote to give him the Electoral College, but it was not always like that when he ran for Congress.

He made it a point to canvass the constituencies and speak with hordes of constituents over the course of the campaign no matter how far-flung the travel to do so. He would win super majorities of the votes. In one instance, he won 297 out of 300 possible votes. He was dogged in his campaigns and took time to talk to each man, woman, and child about the issues that plagued them and offered a consoling word to whatever their plight may have been. Politics was indeed a calling for young Abe.

America is a land of laws. It always has been since its inception. Founded on the word of a consensus between thirteen states in 1776 and articulated in Jefferson's Declaration of Independence, it was an aspiration cast in the desire of a perfect union and bound together by the toil of men.

Those words that gave rise to a country of laws, which brought forth a nation of diversity that became the bastion of freedom and prosperity, were rooted in righteous morality.

So it was apt then when the nation found itself standing at a moral fork in history, that providence dispatched a man of righteous fabric fluent in the law and steeped in political instinct to shepherd it.

The individual, the country, and the shepherd were all presented with a choice. The choice, rarely presented as binary, was fortunately so this time. It was only the second time in this experiment of self-governance that the soul of the collective was asked to choose. It was not merely a choice between slavery and abolition, white and black, rich and poor. It was, plainly and simply, about good and evil.

To be clear, all that is not righteous cannot be deemed evil until a point comes in the unfolding of events where equity, humanity, and civility are forsaken. Such was the case in the years leading up to the Civil War.

Each person had to look within, the country had to make its choice, and Lincoln had to find the strength to vanquish evil simply by doing what was right regardless of the cost.

As history unfolded from the Potomac to the Mississippi River, it became painfully clear to Lincoln that it was no longer just about the law, the vision of the Founding Fathers, and the economic foundations of the country. He realized that it was about the battle for the moral fabric of the country and its future.

That was the choice that faced Lincoln, but it was wrapped in a complex web of externalities. When it is a simple choice between good and bad or when it is a clear-cut issue, most Americans do the right thing. But when the issue is wrapped in layers of interconnected issues and prejudices, self-serving circumstances, and personal hardships, it does not just become difficult to choose right from wrong. It becomes hard to even see what is right.

What started out as an imperative to survive, with memories fresh of how countless families lost farms or worked themselves to the bone, there was a string of hardworking men and women who needed farmhands to work the farm that they owned or would be unable to feed their families. There were large plantations owned by wealthy families and who would not be able to be price competitive or worth the full extent of the farm without the slave labor they had. More importantly, most of the poorer farmers or less substantial plantation owners always carried a large debt to the slave traders. If they lost the slaves, they would owe money to the traders and not have enough hands to work the farms to pay down that debt. They could be out on the street. The problem was systemic. None of this is to excuse the morality of the situation but to

There was another problem as well. By the time Lincoln was born in 1809, indentured servitude had evolved into outright slavery and been that way for two centuries. The practice had spread wide across the land and deep into the culture of the colonies. The burden of the path slavery took lies partially on the shoulders of the slave trade industry. Slavery did not happen overnight.

Beyond the surface of the visual suffering, which was horrendous in its own way, there was a more fundamental and painful issue that drove the minds of those who endured it and understood the consequences. A country that acquiesced to the temptation to corrupt the soul would have been forever damned.

The battle between forces of freedom and of slavery, dignity and greed, North and South was all that and more. It was, in final measure, about the fundamental matter of seeing God in all man—something that had long been forgotten as the desire for a strong labor force powered the personal economy and fueled national growth.

Lincoln was a figure of the nineteenth century. Born in 1809 and assassinated in 1865, he was of a generation that emerged from the pivotal years of the eighteenth century—a consequential chapter in the country's history to say the least. It saw the gelling of a new nation, from many, one, and the battle for independence. It also saw the aggressive ramping up of industry. In the eighteenth century alone, an estimated eight million new slaves were brought into the country. The average price of a slave was $2,000 in the year 1750. In today's dollars, that's about $80,000. With eight million brought in, that makes the slave industry worth $640 billion between 1700 and 1800. That's an average of $6.4 billion a year. From a quantitative economic perspective, applying the relevant multipliers, it is sufficed to say that the direct implication of slavery was that it injected billions into the economy. But that is just the revenue that the traders make.

The real value in slavery came from a workforce that generated 80 percent of the GDP. Drilling down, the GDP in the North needed fewer slaves and had a cost-competitive position because of the prevalence of mechanization. In the South, the percentage of GDP propelled by slave-heavy industry was higher, and the cost distribution was more toward the slave than any mechanization. Industries in the South were not given to the mechanical advancements of the day and were still very much dependent on manual labor.

Slavery became the engine of the South. Without slaves, every single farm, every single farmer, and the entire economy that had been built on the back of slaves would collapse. Freeing the slaves meant losing their investment and possibly their farms and livelihood. They could not see past their own fear of hardship in the absence of slavery.

That fear propelled much of the South toward self-preservation. Consequently, as most politicians do, they capitalized on that fear.

There are two rails slavers relied on in their defense. The first was that they did not treat slaves poorly. The second platitude was that they were better off on the farm in America than they were in the village they came from. None of these, of course, were even remotely true, but the point is not if it's true but the mind-set of the slaver. It was a deep and ingrained mind-set that pervaded the colonies and the states. They didn't see themselves as slavers of an entire race of people but as liberators. It was further fueled by the politicians and their fear-mongering.

The first time Lincoln saw a slave auction the indignity of the event overwhelmed him. His perspective of the institution of slavery was not influenced by growing up with slaves, which served to effectively desensitize the heart to the plight of indignity. He and his family had always worked their spread by themselves, and he had gone on to work for others or managed his own business.

Layered on top of this was his strict interpretation of the Constitution and the Declaration of Independence. He learned and resonated with the truism made famous in Jefferson's Declaration that "all men are created equal." His sense of morality, predating his introduction to the document, combined with his intellectual development in the law cemented the character of a man and the integrity of a future statesman.

It was unshakable. Nonetheless, being steadfast in one's morals is one thing, but moving the deep mind-set of a country toward something that goes against their self-interest is altogether different. Had it not been for the Civil War, would the issue of slavery been justly and sufficiently addressed?

Chapter 15 - Electoral Math

In the days after the 2016 election, the topic of electoral math, popular vote counts, and the Electoral College came to the forefront of national politics. It remains obvious that before that election most citizens were not fully knowledgeable or consciously aware that the greatest democracy on earth had a very undemocratic way of electing the president.

It was consequential in 2016, and it was consequential in 1860. Everyone today knows that governing such a sprawling and populous country is complex. Having it as a democracy is even more so because there are many different layers of officeholders at the county, state and national levels. The framers of the Constitution wanted to distribute the levers of control in such a way that every center of power would be able to hold another center of power in check. They wanted to make sure that they steered away from the monarchical concentration of power in both the absolute sense, where the power was vested by convention or legacy, and in the practical sense, where one office gained so much power that the other branches of government slid into obsequious acquiescence.

To keep the powers fragmented and distributed, the elected offices were decided to be performed differently. Each district was given one representative who would go to Washington to voice the concerns of that small group of people. The counties would also elect a representative to the state capital. That state legislature would then choose two people to be senators who would go to Washington to form the Senate. Each state would get two regardless of population. Note that U.S. senators today are elected in a statewide contest instead of being chosen by the state legislature as was the case in Lincoln's time.

To isolate the momentary popularity of the time, elections were staggered. Representatives were elected every two years, while senators were elected every six. That means a momentary sense of appreciation of a party or the hatred of the same would not mean that the diversity of the office bearers would be wiped away in a whim. The Founding Fathers were cognizant of keeping the "whim" factor out of governing politics.

Then, of course, is the factor of the presidential contest, which is held every four years. The difference is that the president is not elected in the same way as the representatives of the Senate. The president is elected by the Electoral College.

This is where the confusion lies and where there is a misunderstanding of how American elections work. The framers decided that the president, who has a pivotal responsibility in the administration of the country and the deployment of its assets, is not directly elected by the people of the country. They are elected by a special group of people that number the same (almost) as the number of representatives to the U.S. Congress in that state. For instance, if State A has twelve representatives in Congress and two in the Senate, then it has fourteen Electoral College votes, but the persons in the Electoral

College are different from the people who were elected to Congress or the Senate. It is these people in the Electoral College who would cast their vote for who becomes president.

It is common fallacy among today's electorate that the Electoral College must go to the popular vote in the state. That is not so in almost half the states. The Electoral College in many states is not compelled by law or the Constitution to vote in the same way as the will of the people in that state. In other words, Candidate X could get fewer of the counted ballots voting in his favor, and the Electoral College could still give all the votes to the candidate it chooses.

That's in the worst-case scenario.

But on the other hand, the way it actually works is that the Electoral College casts its vote according to the will of the people of that state. Whoever gets the majority of the vote, even by one, gets all of the Electoral College votes (in all but two states currently).

The key to understand here is that the majority of the vote does not mean the will of the people. In a straight fight where 100 percent of the constituents vote for one other the other candidate, then someone is going to get more than 50 percent of the vote (as little as 50 percent + 1). But what happens when there are four candidates? That would mean (hypothetically) that if two candidates get exactly 25 percent, then one of the candidates only needs to get 25 percent + 1 of the vote to beat the fourth candidate and collect all the Electoral College votes.

A candidate could ostensibly win 100 percent of the Electoral College by winning a little over a quarter of the state's votes. That is by no means the will of the people.

In the case of Lincoln's first-term election, that is approximately what happened. Lincoln was not the favorite to win. He was a latecomer into the Republican convention, while the favored to win at the time was Hannibal Hamlin, but by virtue of smart politicking on the part of the Lincoln's campaign manager, Lincoln catapulted to the head of the line and scooped up the nomination. Hamlin got the second most number of votes. In the early days of the Union, the vice-presidential candidate for the ticket was chosen by the vote tally. The one with the most votes got the nod for the top of the ticket, while the second got the nod for the vice presidency.

Hamlin was the true champion of the slavery question. He wanted the Republican Party to be the champion for this cause, but this clashed with Lincoln's ultimate goal. It is one for the reasons why Lincoln did not support Hamlin for his second term. It was Hamlin who had the support of the radical arm of the Republican Party.

The Republican Party had split in the middle of Lincoln's first term since the war was going poorly. The Radical Republicans who had full support of the liberal North wanted to distance themselves from Lincoln and his losing war effort. It was also the reason why he had received such criticism from the publications that were Northern liberal in nature.

The personal relationship between Lincoln and Hamlin was also fraught. There were frequent outbursts and friction between them. Hamlin always believed that Lincoln was not doing enough to set the question of slavery to rest. Lincoln had always used the issue of slavery to his benefit but was really looking to consolidate the power of the federal government instead of emancipating the slaves.

By the time the Republican Convention occurred, the party had split, and the Radical Republicans had nominated their own presidential candidate. Lincoln had chosen to take on Andrew Johnson, a war Democrat, to be able to shore up a wider base.

Between the nomination of 1864 and the election at the end of that year, the tide of losses had been stemmed, and the fortunes of the Union effort had turned. And along with it the popularity of a war president who was now winning. The Radical Republican candidate then stepped down and endorsed Lincoln for a second term, who then went on to win the election that November.

There are a number of issues regarding Lincoln's term as president. It must be noted that the effort that is being put into bringing to light that he was not the great Emancipation president is not to disparage his name but to set the record straight that his intention was to unite the country first and not to alter the position of slaves. This does not make him a bad person or a bad president. In his letter to Horace Greeley, he explicitly writes, "My paramount object in this struggle is to save the Union, and it is not either to save or destroy slavery. If I could save the Union without freeing any slave, I would do it."

Chapter 16 - The Presidency

"You say you will not fight to free negroes. Some of them seem willing to fight for you; but, no matter. Fight you, then exclusively to save the Union."

Abraham Lincoln, August 26, 1863

Lincoln's first course of business was to tour some of the states in the South. He stopped in Kansas in 1859 en route to other areas in the West. By early 1860, Lincoln made his second New England Speaking tour, although it didn't really start off that way. He was actually on his way up to the Philips Exeter Academy to see his eldest son, Robert Todd. Young Robert had just failed his entrance exams for Harvard, and Lincoln traveled to meet with him and offer courage and heart.

On his way, though, he decided to stop in New York to give a speech at the Cooper Union. That speech made such a big impact on the attendees that word spread of the content of the speech and of Lincoln's position. It was February 1860, and President Buchanan was in the White House.

As you can imagine, the speech revolved around slavery. The Cooper Union Speech was one that was based on an earlier speech that he had given at a church in Brooklyn, New York, some months earlier. Lincoln had done considerable research into extracting the intent of the Founding Fathers as to what their position would have been when it came to slavery.

He didn't need to look far.

The materials he had studied of the original signers of the Constitution showed that a slight majority had explicitly intended that slavery was not promoted in the Union. The rest, who were also against slavery, were not fully vocalizing their principles because they didn't want to offend their major donors, who were wealthy slaveholders. They agreed with the morality of the matter but had insufficient conviction to stand by it. Nonetheless, the original draft of Jefferson's Declaration of Independence explicitly made reference to the abolition of slavery. Lincoln had picked up on it and understood that the genetic makeup of America was not one that included slavery because it went against the core of American values of equality and freedom. To believe in the idea of America precludes participation in the institution of slavery.

What was lost on most people of the period and even today to a large extent is that America is not just a land sandwiched between two oceans. America is an ideal—a Utopian prototype that is significantly more intangible than it is tangible. It is more than its infrastructure, entertainment, and commerce. It is based on principles, practices, and pursuits instead of feudal patronage, vassalage, and enslavement.

It doesn't matter how much land is acquired or how we acquired it. It is not about how bravely we fight or how eloquently we energize our collective spirits, but the moment it is no longer based on ideals, it is no longer America. It is just a strip of land.

Among the founding ideals and principles, equity stands out as the basis of all else and strongly remains as the underlying current of all that is quintessentially American. Whether it is freedom of speech, religion, or assembly, whether it is the pursuit of happiness or the equal protection of the law, the thread that makes America America is equity.

During his years spent learning the law and then practicing it, he fell in love with the intellect and the compassion that characterized the framers, the Founding Fathers, and the deep thinking that was necessary to give birth to the nation. That is also the reason why he did not see the country as an extension of any practical religion. America was not born Christian. It was born free.

There were other facets of history that also prompted his position. He came to realize that when the Continental Congress met to debate and vote on the declaration the original draft that included the issues on slavery was part of the debate. It was decided during the debate to exclude the language on slavery because there were constituencies that were not willing to sign on to independence if it were included for the simple reason that slavery was allowed and in fact started by the British. It was something that bothered Jefferson.

The research that he had undertaken was to find the intent of the Founding Fathers and to seek guidance from the spirit of their intention. He found it, and it resonated with him that to be able to expound equity, and therefore freedom, supporting slavery would be untenable.

His long travels that took him across the states and territories, from the shores in the east to the plains in the west, gave him an opportunity to read and contemplate his findings.

On this particular trip to see his son, he was asked to stop in New York on the way and deliver a speech. By the time arrived to deliver the speech, the Young Men's Republican Union had decided to sponsor the event, increased the number of attendees, and moved the venue to cooper Union in Manhattan.

It was 1860, and Lincoln had not yet declared his intention to run for the presidency. Mrs. Lincoln was pushing the cause at home, and he was contemplating it on his travels. There were even rumors circulating that he might. The Young Men's Republican Union wanted to test his mettle and determine if they could find a candidate in this ex-congressman from Illinois, which is why they took over and sponsored the event. It was an audition of sorts, specifically by the New Yorkers so that they could understand his views, his character, and his abilities.

Most New Yorkers at this point had not seen or knew what he looked like. At first glance, it is widely reported that those who saw him thought very poorly of him. They had made the mistake of judging him from his awkward appearance. They were almost aghast at his appearance—lanky, too slender, and almost pale in complexion. He did not look presidential by any means, and they were collectively disappointed by his countenance.

In an illustration worthy of the phrase "do not judge the book by its cover," the room was spun on its head by the eloquence and intelligence of the man. The longer he stood there, the more he filled his suit and assumed the posture.

By the time he was a quarter of his way through the speech, the crowds were hooked on his every syllable. They were on their feet clapping, shouting, and asking for more. Every punctuation in his speech was met with explosive cheer and approval. The room was transformed as if by a spell that touched each heart and mind in attendance. They could no longer see the lanky and skinny "unpresidential" ex-congressman speaking. Instead, by the sound of his voice and the content of his mind, they saw a charismatic leader on fire before them. That fire of enthusiasm was infectious, spreading across the whole room and up that day and then in the days that followed up and down the Northeast corridor. It was the baptism of fire they needed to be converted, advancing him to the front of the line for the Republican nomination.

It will always be considered as the kindling that fired up the Republican Party.

"Who were our fathers that framed the Constitution? I suppose the 'thirty-nine' who signed the original instrument may be fairly called our fathers who framed that part of the present Government. It is almost exactly true to say they framed it, and it is altogether true to say they fairly represented the opinion and sentiment of the whole nation at that time. Their names, being familiar to nearly all, and accessible to quite all, need not now be repeated.

I take these 'thirty-nine,' for the present, as being 'our fathers who framed the Government under which we live.'

What is the question which, according to the text, those fathers understood just as well, and even better than we do now?

It is this: Does the proper division of local from federal authority, or anything in the Constitution, forbid our Federal Government to control as to slavery in our Federal Territories?

Upon this, Senator Douglas holds the affirmative, and Republicans the negative. This affirmation and denial form an issue; and this issue—this question—is precisely what the text declares our fathers understood "better than we."

Let us now inquire whether the 'thirty-nine,' or any of them, ever acted upon this question; and if they did, how they acted upon it—how they expressed that better understanding?

In 1784, three years before the Constitution—the United States then owning the Northwestern Territory, and no other, the Congress of the Confederation had before them the question of prohibiting slavery in that Territory; and four of the 'thirty-nine' who afterward framed the Constitution, were in that Congress, and voted on that question. Of these, Roger Sherman, Thomas Mifflin, and Hugh Williamson voted for the prohibition, thus showing that, in their understanding, no line dividing local from federal authority, nor anything else, properly forbade the Federal Government to control as to slavery in federal territory. The other of the four—James

McHenry—voted against the prohibition, showing that, for some cause, he thought it improper to vote for it.

In 1787, still before the Constitution, but while the Convention was in session framing it, and while the Northwestern Territory still was the only territory owned by the United States, the same question of prohibiting slavery in the territory again came before the Congress of the Confederation; and two more of the 'thirty-nine' who afterward signed the Constitution, were in that Congress, and voted on the question. They were William Blount and William Few; and they both voted for the prohibition—thus showing that, in their understanding, no line dividing local from federal authority, nor anything else, properly forbids the Federal Government to control as to slavery in Federal territory. This time the prohibition became a law, being part of what is now well known as the Ordinance of '87.

The question of federal control of slavery in the territories, seems not to have been directly before the Convention which framed the original

Constitution; and hence it is not recorded that the 'thirty-nine,' or any of them, while engaged on that instrument, expressed any opinion on that precise question.

In 1789, by the first Congress which sat under the Constitution, an act was passed to enforce the Ordinance of '87, including the prohibition of slavery in the Northwestern Territory. The bill for this act was reported by one of the 'thirty-nine,' Thomas Fitzsimmons, then a member of the House of Representatives from Pennsylvania. It went through all its stages without a word of opposition, and finally passed both branches without yeas and nays, which is equivalent to a unanimous passage. In this Congress there were sixteen of the thirty-nine fathers who framed the original Constitution. They were John Langdon, Nicholas Gilman, Wm. S. Johnson, Roger Sherman, Robert Morris, Thos. Fitzsimmons, William Few, Abraham Baldwin, Rufus King, William Paterson, George Clymer, Richard Bassett, George Read, Pierce Butler, Daniel Carroll, James Madison.

This shows that, in their understanding, no line dividing local from federal authority, nor anything in the Constitution, properly forbade Congress to prohibit slavery in the federal territory; else both their fidelity to correct principle, and their oath to support the Constitution, would have constrained them to oppose the prohibition.

Again, George Washington, another of the 'thirty-nine,' was then President of the United States, and, as such approved and signed the bill; thus completing its validity as a law, and thus showing that, in his understanding, no line dividing local from federal authority, nor anything in the Constitution, forbade the Federal Government, to control as to slavery in federal territory."

By the time he had left New York, word of his performance and his ideas had spread. Even though he was on his way to see his son, he ended up stopping a total of nine times along the way to repeat his message, each time to progressively larger crowds. He ended each speech to thunderous applause with these words,

"Wrong as we think slavery is, we can yet afford to let it alone where it is, because that much is due to the necessity arising from its actual presence in the nation; but can we, while our votes will prevent it, allow it to spread into the National Territories, and to overrun us here in these Free States? If our sense of duty forbids this, then let us stand by our duty, fearlessly and effectively. Let us be diverted by none of those sophistical contrivances wherewith we are so industriously plied and belabored—contrivances such as groping for some middle ground between the right and the wrong, vain as the search for a man who should be neither a living man nor a dead man—such as a policy of 'don't care' on a question about which all true men do care—such as Union appeals beseeching true Union men to yield to Disunionists, reversing the divine rule, and calling, not the sinners, but the righteous to repentance—such as invocations to Washington, imploring men to unsay what Washington said, and undo what Washington did."

Three things caught the attention of Northerners, Southerners, and the territories with this speech.

1. The first, obviously, was that the Constitution was not promoting slavery in its intention. He proved that the individual signers were not intending slavery by virtue of their past behavior and their silence on various bills that they were involved in crafting and voting on. By that he enforced the idea that the Union was never intended to bless the idea of slavery.

2. The second, and this is more important but often missed, is that he was exerting the federal government's power over the states. This was almost more concerning than the issue of slavery.

3. The third, and this was related to the issue of slavery, was that he truly saw those that looked different from him as equals. After two hundred and fifty years of being around slaves and lording over them, many had forgotten that those they called slaves were human and deserved equality.

For those who were listening to the speech, its content resonated perfectly to the way the North had evolved since '76. The South had gone one way and the North the other. In time, it was two worlds driven apart by unique climate profiles, which drove unique industries and advancements, which drove unique self-preservation issues. The South grew dependent on the slave population, while the North did not.

The crowds he stood before proved insatiable. They wanted to bask in the glow of his words and understand the content of his character. They had caught a glimpse of both that afternoon at the Cooper Union. He energized their imagination and animated their involvement in the crusade against the expansion of slavery into the new territories. In return, their enthusiasm empowered him with the confidence he needed to push forward toward his destiny and to overcome whatever his hesitation was to make the decision.

By the time he arrived at Exeter Academy, word of his speeches at the nine stops along the way from New York had traveled far and wide at the speed of wildfires during an Indian summer. It had also made its way down south to fall on the ears of staunch Southerners and slaveholders, wealthy and poor alike.

While the North jumped in jubilation, the South winced at what was being contemplated and what that implied. They were not strangers to abolitionists or their talking points, but this was different. This time there was a conviction in the heart and tenacity at the lips of the chief proponent. What's worse was that he was right. The Founding Fathers and the framers of the Constitution did not envision slavery. The South had grown used to the forbidden fruit, and now it was almost impossible to consider a world where there was no slaves.

After visiting Robert, his solitary time on the long journey back was spent in contemplation of a presidential run. Word was out by that point that he would have to go up against Stephen Douglas, his old nemesis, if he were to enter the race.

Based on his eventual writings and thoughts chronicled by those around him at the time, it is clear that he was suspended in the chasm of indecision for some length of time. On the positive side, he was encouraged by the crowds that cheered him and his wife who motivated him. In his own mind, he had a duty to the country to set it on the course of righteousness.

On the other side of the chasm was the darkest of voices within him that feared the process, feared losing, and feared the penetrating daylight of a national campaign.

Even though Lincoln had done well in previous contests, it was only because of his personal charm—as seen during his speech at the Cooper Union in Manhattan. It was the same when he won his seat in Congress—by meeting almost everyone in the district and charming them with his eloquence and calm. That would, however, be impossible to replicate across the country. It would not be possible to meet every single constituent for a national contest the same way it had been in those district contests. Lincoln understood this limitation.

He also knew that his position on a number of things, as morally and legally accurate as they were, were not popular positions in a large part of the South. It would be almost impossible to get any traction in the South. Stephen Douglas was significantly more popular and more presidential. He also had policies that app

Another aspect of Lincoln's decision was based on who was behind him in the effort. He would not have been able to pull off a nomination much less the election if it were not for a grassroots effort, which had to be orchestrated, and only the new Republican Party was able to pull that off.

During the Republican Convention that year, which was held in Chicago between May 16 and May 18, 1860, the favorite to gain the nomination was Senator William Seward. Lincoln's last-minute nomination was a surprise to all but a few supporters. His Cooper Speech had catapulted him to the front of the line. Even his surprise entry at the last minute was able to garner the support necessary to become the nominee.

All this was not just because of his speeches and growing popularity but also because of a highly able and witty campaign manager, who steered the strategy from before Lincoln had made the decision.

Behind the scenes, a lot of horse trading followed the planning. Lincoln had agreed to give out Cabinet positions and keep Hamlin as his vice president.

There is a misunderstanding of what the Republican Party stood for, especially in today's context. Even the word "Republican" is rooted in the word "republic" and stands for a central federation. The Republican Party of Lincoln's day was liberal (as much as it could be in the mid-nineteenth century). Conversely, the Democratic Party, which Steven Douglas belonged to, was the conservative party of the day.

The core push of the Republicans back then was for a centralized system of governance. They believed that the efficacy of being one nation rather than a grouping of states loosely brought together was more efficient and would be stronger. But the solution brought with it other problems. It also meant that the states would no longer be able to control their own destiny, which was something that had been fought long and hard for just a century earlier.

The Republican Party was not looking at it from the perspective of the consolidation of power but from the fact that there were shared interests that could be combined to provide better economies of scale. Think about the military today, where its budget is greater than the combined budget of two dozen of the largest military forces in the world. That kind of economies of scale could not be achieved if the states had chosen to keep control over their own military and not have one national defense complex.

In the same vein, there were other shared issues that provided greater utility than standing individually. The Republicans, under Lincoln, saw this as the driving force of their endeavor, but this would not sell in the North, the South, or anywhere else in the young country at the time. The one thing that all the states were united on was that states' rights were paramount within a federal context.

There is a countervailing argument to the states' rights issue that rose in the antebellum period. The first was not entirely honest, and that was that the South was actually more interested in having a stronger federal government. Alternative historians argue that it was in the best interest of the South that the federal government was stronger so that they could enforce the rights of the Southern states to have runaway slaves that escaped to the North to be returned to them. This is an argument that makes no sense whatsoever. This argument is not disputing the states' rights argument; instead, it is confusing states' rights with enforcement of one state's law in another.

With this out of the way, it is clearer to see what the path of using slavery as a proxy war would be. There was also the fact that the South was trying to weaken the hold of the federal government because it was electorally disadvantaged. In the years leading up to the Civil War, there were more antislavery congressmen thane pro-slavery congressmen by virtue of population distribution. The South had a smaller population and an even smaller voting constituency since millions of slaves that were in the South didn't vote.

Population density gave the Northern states more say in who would be president and the advantage in distributions in Congress necessary to pass legislation.

The issue of slavery would then become the key to advancing the benefits of Republicanism (in this case, mending central government control).

The Republicans represented the notion that being one country was better than being what is merely a union of states, and for that they needed to bring the country closer together. This was a view that at the time was controversial and not reflective of the reality at the grassroots level.

That changed over time, and today the Republican Party is no longer the party of Lincoln. It is the party of conservatism. There is certainly nothing wrong with that. It just goes to show that the values Lincoln championed should not be confused as being conservative. As history clearly shows, they were liberal. It has just become convenient for the present crop of Republican politicians to brand themselves as the party of Lincoln.

Lincoln's goal as president was to champion the legislation to abolish slavery and return the United States to its righteous path. It was also to build the mind-set of one nation rather than a federation of states. In a twist of fate and a case of "be careful what you wish for," he got both when the South declared that if the Republicans won, they would secede from the Union.

Another matter that escapes public awareness is that presidents under the system of the U.S. government do not have structural control over legislation. That still sits with the legislative branch of government. The president's job is to enforce the laws that are already on the books and advance the country within those laws in a way that he sees fit.

Strong presidents have pushed members of their party to prioritize their agenda and election promises. Sometimes that has worked; sometimes that has backfired. In an alternate history, if the South had not seceded and the country had not plunged into a civil war, it would be difficult to see how it would have been to legislate what Lincoln envisioned.

The rest, as they say, is history. From there Lincoln went on to win the general election that year in part because he was a good candidate standing up for a strong cause that lit the base. More importantly, though, the reason why he beat Stephen Douglas is simply because the Democratic Party had split that year, and the vote split between him and John Breckenridge. That allowed Lincoln to win the electoral votes and ascend to the presidency.

Chapter 17 - Lincoln's War

Lincoln's whole life was a war filled with battles at every point of consequence. He had to battle for everything he never acquired or wanted. He had to battle for the women he loved, do his job, and to learn. If war was his life and battle was his way, then strength of mind was his artillery. His strength of mind was legendary but often not spoken of in great detail.

Lincoln's battles were not something most people could have fought much less won the way he did. His strength came from his weakness. We have seen that weakness in the chapter on his spiritual center and other areas of the book.

The critical aspect of his time in office was derailed because of the secession of the South. Had that not happened, Lincoln had other plans for his legacy. The main push behind Lincoln's presidency would not have been to abolish slavery in the South but to prevent the new territories from coming in as slave states. Lincoln did not intend to abolish slavery because that would upset the apple cart too much.

Lincoln wanted to quickly expand to the west and advance the revenue of the nation to build the infrastructure in the East and North. For that he needed the country to be a powerful tax base, and for that he could not have abolished slavery.

To be clear, he did not support the indignity of slavery. He supported industry and a strong tax base, which, in turn, was driven by slavery. Before secession he never insisted that the South stop slavery, but they did not like the idea of the new states not to be slave states.

In the Republican Party, there was the notion that even the South should be free from slaves. Lincoln was not part of this platform. When he took on Andrew Johnson as his running mate in 1864, the battle between him and his previous vice president, Hannibal Hamlin, was exactly about this issue. Hamlin wanted to push the South into becoming free. What made it work out the way it did was because a war had already started, and the war took precedence over the freeing of slaves or any other matter.

Chapter 18 - Second Term

For most of the Civil War that began just three weeks after his inauguration and lasted until a few days before he was assassinated, it was a war that initially seemed righteous. But as the bodies began piling up beyond the imagination a country can afford, people began to turn on the efforts of Lincoln. By June of 1863, Lincoln was faced with a tactical and political conundrum.

If he failed, not only would slavery have become commonplace all across the Union, but his efforts to alter the course of history would be forever lost, and his belief that he was meant to do great things would be a lie he told himself. The cost of failure was too high for the country, for the office of the presidency, and for his own mind. Those factors and the possible consequences powered him through his sleepless nights, but with Mrs. Lincoln steadfastly behind him, he leaned into the wind.

From a factual standpoint, the tides had turned at Gettysburg in 1863 and at Vicksburg the same year. If it hadn't happened, Lincoln's approval rating would have been permanently damaged. Before the victories, those in his own party were already gunning for him, and he was despised by even his own generals, who were referring to him in rude and uncomplimentary terms.

Until this point in his presidency and this juncture in the war, Lincoln had been too acquiescent to those whom he thought knew more than he did. He knew what needed to be done but didn't have the strength to do it because the will of this decisions was less than the full measure needed. Lincoln had the resources to end the war the first year, but because of his hesitance and his unwillingness to rely on his own counsel, the North wasted time, resources, and lives.

Each president is the manifestation of the times they serve in. That is the power of a democracy and something that is not fully understood by the masses. The presidential election, if not aided by nefarious external forces, is the sum aggregate of the will of the people. In all the things he says and all the things they perceive in him, and in the troubles that plague the country, he is the manifestation of the solution. It is up to him to use the apparatus of the other branches of government, whether to bring them together, to persuade them, or to veto them, in taking action that is in the best interest of the country.

But to do that, Lincoln had to take full control of the powers that were available to him and to come into himself in the decision that he had to make. Since nothing happens overnight, it took time for him to cascade into a position that allowed him to have full confidence in himself, his assessment, and his solutions.

All he needed was a shift in the way he perceived himself. The question that lies in every one's mind is the events that result in this fortunate shift. It wasn't good prevailing over evil. Lincoln's fortunes didn't turn because he was right. They turned because Lincoln, it turns out, was a master tactician.

What changed was Lincoln's self-assessment and governing style. Up to the spring of 1863, Lincoln was a passive commander in chief, which allowed his generals to run roughshod over him. Generals do not have the benefit of the overall view. They only see areas that they are in charge of. Lincoln had been relying heavily on their input, and he was not inserting his ideas and strategies into the discussions. In fact, in many of the battles they had lost, he realized that his initial instincts and ideas were right, but he had deferred to the generals, and they had instituted it without the full perspective he had. Lincoln's secretary, who was in attendance in all the meetings and taking notes, wrote that Lincoln would give in to the generals' "whims and complaints and shortcomings as a mother would indulge her baby." It had reached such a critical point that those generals stopped respecting and adhering to Lincoln's "timid" suggestions. In the summer that year, all that changed.

The shift in demeanor preceded the shift in strategy. He no longer nudged them or made a suggestion. Instead, he gave them strict instructions, and if they didn't follow them down to the last-minute detail, they were fired. He took charge in sweeping fashion, and the generals snapped straight with respect. Within a month from the time he snapped out of his passive ways, the country started to see a difference in the outcomes of the battles. That one last shift, on his part, altered the trajectory of the war, the composition of the United States, the state of slavery, and the history that might have been. *The New York Times*, which had been relentlessly criticizing Lincoln until now fell in line and was singing his praises. As goes *The New York Times*, so goes the North.

The presidency and the war taught Lincoln a major lesson. Even when you take feedback and suggestions, the final decision is the commander in chief's. As one of his later successors famously said, "The buck stops here." Lincoln had figured that out himself, and the tide had decisively changed.

It couldn't have come at a better time. The tide had turned just as the presidential election of

1864 was coming around. Whatever dissension that existed within the party over the direction of the war had been tamped down, but the issue with slavery still remained as a source of tension between Lincoln and Hamlin so much so that Lincoln decided to pull Andrew Johnson and excluded Hamlin.

By this point, the Republican Party had temporarily altered their name and called themselves the National Union Party. Lincoln had some competition for the nomination, but after the war turned around, he beat any competitor who would stand in his way.

He went on to win the general election, which was held in November 1864, for a second term in 1864 with 55 percent of the popular vote. He carried twenty-two out of twenty-five states that voted that year and accumulated 212 electoral votes.

There was a change in his demeanor and in his outlook. The confidence of his own abilities, which had eluded him and compounded by the depression that he had grown to accept as part of his inner self, had been shattered. Many people who saw Lincoln in the waning days of the war saw a man reborn.

After the reelection, Lincoln went back to the business of running the country and making plans to rebuild. He was prompted to punish the South on many occasions during the war, and he was once again heavily lobbied to do so. Lincoln was resolute in his declination.

The postwar reconstruction of the South and the North to a much lesser degree was always on Lincoln's mind even from the earliest days of the war. Now the time had come, the formal surrender was imminent, and the thoughts of reconciliation filled his mind to a greater degree.

He knew that imposing reparations and penalties would not be a wise solution. The North and South were after all part of one family. Instead, Lincoln saw fit to forget and forgive and alter the course of history by unifying the country and to strengthen the bond between the federal government and the states. It was at this point that he, as part of the reconstruction and reunification, imposed that all states had to abide by the federal antislavery laws. By doing that, he officially elevated the United States of America into the light of freedom for all.

On the afternoon of April 9, 1865, General Robert E Lee surrendered to General Ulysses Grant at Appomattox Court House. The two generals had engaged in battle that morning, but when it was clear to General Lee that his options were nonexistent and that he had been cut off from retreat, he surrendered.

The surrender documents were concluded, and a ceremony to disband was instantly executed with men in the Confederate army returning their weapons before being freed to return to their homes. The Confederate army was disbanded. Lincoln had won the war, and all of the country, North and South celebrated. The celebration was more in the North, but the South was happy that the killing was over with. When it was all said and done, more than 600,000 men died in the line of duty fighting their brothers. It was the most brutal war America had experienced. In comparison, American casualties in World War II were 420,000.

Chapter 19 - John Wilkes Booth

John Wilkes Booth was a bastard, and that is meant literally. His father eventually married his mother only on John's thirteenth birthday. Booth's father, Junius Brutus Booth, was part of a family of popular stage actors who settled in the Baltimore area. Merely saying they were popular really doesn't cut it. They were the leading family name in all of theater and known by high society of the Northeast Corridor stretching from Boston to Washington, D.C. and even down in to Virginia.

Junius Booth was as eccentric as he was popular and was the period's most well-known and well-thought-of Shakespearean thespian. Edwin, John's older brother, was also an accomplished actor in his father's footsteps. John Wilkes, however, was initially a dud when he tried his hand at acting. He didn't have the background and the depth of knowledge that stage actors who took on Shakespeare's plays needed.

His youth was one of privilege in terms of the way he was raised on a large farm and with few things to care about. His youth was as different from Lincoln's childhood as night contrasts day. His family farm was in Bel Air, Maryland, which sits almost exactly halfway between Philadelphia and Washington, D.C.

The Booth clan was as liberal as could be in their politics and most decidedly on the side of the North when the Civil War eventually broke out. All of them were staunchly of the North except John Wilkes. On this matter, he would have severe arguments with his family and was the outcast when it came to this subject.

The patriarch of the Booth clan was a dyed-in-the-wool thespian who represented the intellectual side of the art, while John Wilkes had no such streak. But he was ambitious. He wanted to be as good as his father and certainly better than his older brothers. His ability, at first, fell short of his goals. Even though he was fluent in the language, he couldn't deliver the nuances that riddled the plays he was cast in, and the nuances couldn't fly.

Then he found something that neither his father nor his brothers could offer that he could. It turned out that John was nimble and energetic and brought a very powerful action sequence to the stage, which was something that the audience had not experienced, and he started getting acclaim for this. Even though his popularity rose everywhere in the county, it gained the most in Virginia.

John was indeed handsome and full of energy. He became an instant hit on the stages of Virginia once he started bringing action to his character, and he was, in fact, the first actor in America to be so attractive to the women audience that his clothes were ripped away one day as he walked through the crowd.

He repaid this glowing adulation by staying in the South for consecutively longer stretches of time and slowly began to understand their concerns and favor their politics. Before long he was fully sympathetic to the Southern plight and began to be resentful of the Northern perspective.

As his popularity grew, so did his affinity to the South. As his affinity to the South grew, the more it divided him from his family and increased his hatred toward a president who was taking the country in a new direction by virtue of his policies.

When the unknown Lincoln began campaigning for the presidency, the South had started to dislike what they had been hearing, and when he ascended to the presidency and it seemed that he was able to put his campaign rhetoric to practice, the states in the South that hadn't supported him began fomenting the idea to secede from the Union.

It was around this time that John Wilkes began despising Lincoln and could not bring himself to see an America that Lincoln saw. His hatred grew so deeply that more than once when he was on stage at Ford's Theatre and President Lincoln was in attendance, he would direct fiery speeches or scenes that were part of the play while looking directly at Lincoln. This happened often enough that caused Lincoln to comment a couple of times that he felt Booth was directing some kind of animosity toward him.

It has been constantly studied by scholars that the final act of the assassination would not have been possible if it not for a confluence of events. What started out as an idea to kidnap Lincoln then advanced to the notion of assassinating him because of Booth's state of mind and the events that were happening in the war. The war had ended, and the South had lost, sealing the notion of slavery in the South and shaking Booth to his core. Compounding that was the failure of his oil well in the North that had rendered him broke. If he had waited a few weeks, his other oil well would have begun producing, and he would have been wealthy. We may be reading about him instead of Rockefeller, but his exasperation in his personal life, his loss on the political front, and his hatred of a man who was everything that he was not leading the country put Booth into a mind-set that altered the course of American history.

Booth on his own was not a bad person. Who among us has not made mistakes that we later regret? We regret these mistakes because in the heat of the moment we commit mistakes resulting from poor decisions, which prevent us from seeing the true nature of our actions and their eventual consequences. Booth was no different. In his mind, he had lost everything, and the idea of losing the South of which he was so attached altered his sense of right and wrong. In no way are we trying to justify what he did to be acceptable or right. Regardless of one's politics or the losses we incur in our pursuits does it give us the right to take a life, president or pauper.

Chapter 20 - Last Act

"Now he belongs to the ages"

Edwin Stanton, April 15, 1865

Two days after the surrender at Appomattox, Lincoln delivered a speech, which stresses that his focus would be the reconstruction of the Union, both in the North and the South. America was united again, and he was the president for all, North and South. John Wiles Booth was in the audience listening to the speech as he seethed with hatred and disappointment. At the end of the speech, Booth, who as you will recall had intended to kidnap Lincoln during the war, now advanced his conspiracy and declared, "Now, by God, I'll put him through. That is the last speech he will ever make."

On the evening of April 14, 1865, shortly after 10:00 p.m. while the play was under way, Booth entered the upper-level box that the president and First Lady occupied. At the same time, it was planned that Vice President Andrew Johnson was to be assassinated as well, but Booth's accomplice, George Atzerodt, who was supposed to do the deed, backed out. The other member of Lincoln's cabinet who was to be killed that night was Secretary of State William Seward. He was stabbed, and although he survived, he was brutally disfigured from the wounds to his face. The man who attacked him, Lewis Powell, was hanged for his crimes.

Back at Ford's Theatre, as the Lincolns were in a celebratory mood, Lincoln reached over and held his wife's hand, which in those days was not what polite society did in public. But it was a romantic gesture. Mrs. Lincoln smiled and wondered aloud to her husband what their friends would say if seen to which Lincoln replied in a whisper, *"She wouldn't think anything about it."* As he said this, Lincoln, who was in an extremely good mood, was listening to the play and laughing at a comedic line delivered by Harry Hawk. In that instant, as Lincoln held his wife's hand, the theatre was shaken by the loud noise of the .44 caliber Derringer pistol that discharged the single bullet that lodged in Lincoln's frontal lobe after entering behind his left ear and shattering his orbital plates. He slipped into a coma with Mary Lincoln sobbing uncontrollably by his side.

Soldiers carried Lincoln's comatose body in the rain to a house across the street and up to the first-floor bedroom. Doctors arrived and could see that even though Lincoln was still alive the gunshot was fatal. Lincoln's oldest son arrived less than two hours later and found his father unconscious but breathing peacefully. There was no suffering in the final moments of his death. He was at peace. There were no convulsions and no sounds. By 7:00 a.m. the next morning, it looked more like he was soundly and peacefully asleep. At 7.22 a.m. on April 15, 1865, President Abraham Lincoln passed on to the ages.

Conclusion

We need heroes in our life so that we can aspire to the better angels that they aspired to. It is not about hero worship or a reason to adulate at the feet of a myth. These achievers need to be seen as they are—faults as well as virtues. Only then can their achievements be an example for the rest of us.

This applies to President Abraham Lincoln, the sixteenth President of the United States. Born on April 12, 1809, to an upstanding family under harsh conditions, he grew up in one frontier land after the other until he finally settled down, early in his youth, in Illinois. He had decided to take responsibility for his own fate and to be the cause of his lot in life.

That fate turned out to be something that no one he grew up with would have ever come to expect. Even for Lincoln himself, he did not aim for higher office until after he left the U.S. House of

Representatives after one term. He came to realize that as a congressman, one of many, he was unable to make change or to move the country in any way. Toward the end of his term, he realized that he needed to do more. He had considered the Senate and then the presidency.

Out of the forty-five presidents who have held the office, Lincoln holds the honor of being the only one to oversee a civil war and be the cause of almost half the country attempting secession. Whether he caused the chain of events that led to that or he perpetuated the war by his lackluster performance in the early part of the conflict is not the point of this book. Nor should it be the point of any analysis of Lincoln.

Analyzing Lincoln with the aim of learning from his strengths and identifying the weaknesses one could avoid requires that his life be seen under the light of truth and respect. Lincoln was by all means a regular man and one who was fallible in many ways. He had to live with the visage of one that was not always appealing to others, and that determined the path of his life from his teenage years.

Yet, he persevered. He began to drop his reliance on how he looked to something he could change, which is what he knew. Beyond that he looked to become part of a culture of industry. In other words, he wanted to use his resources of work and stamina to be able to make a name for himself. He did.

The first lesson that anyone could ever hope to extract from his life would be that regardless of where one is born or under what conditions they are born into, there is always a way to climb out of it. We live in a world today that has cultivated obesity and poverty at the same time because we have done away with self-discipline and self-reliance.

Lincoln's life is the antithesis of today's mind-set. He used his mind to think about the big things, and that made him the giant in his days whose shadow was cast onto ours. The widow of the late Martin Luther King once said that "small men cannot do big things." This applied, in reverse, to Abraham Lincoln. He was a big man who was able to do big things.

The Romans have a saying, which roughly translated means, "to conquer the world, one has to conquer his own self." In other words, one has to be able to conquer his own thoughts, his own demons, and his own sins before he can go on to do big things. Lincoln was a big man who could conquer his own mind and go on to do truly great things.

Lincoln had a number of tools to help him in this effort. He found that reading helped, and within the practice of reading, he found that memorizing lines helped take it further. It is one of the reasons why he associated learning and memorization with happiness and intelligence. Over the course of his adult life, he memorized quotes, passages, and entire poems almost effortlessly, and this brought peace and clarity to his soul.

Lincoln's psyche and persona is his own, but it did build on the example and psychology of his father. When Lincoln lost his sister and his mother, he was young and did not know how to react to the catastrophe. Children who are still psychologically developing base their responses to stimuli on the adults who are responding to the same stimuli as well. Lincoln watched his father for clues on how to react to things that happened around them and to them.

What he found was that his father harbored deep depression, stemming from his trauma as a child himself. When death visited the Lincoln household repeatedly, it brought with it a dark cloud to settle over Lincoln Senior. It injected silence into his demeanor and incapacitated the man of the house. For Lincoln Junior, the death of his mother unexpectedly robbed him of both parents, not one. With his mother gone and his father retreating into depression, he was left to grapple with the pain of childhood and the grief of loss without the benefit of a soothing voice or cuddling arms. It was fortunate that Sarah was there for him even though she was not much older than he was, and she was facing the same pain. The siblings grew closer from this shared loss and the unfortunate state of affairs.

Lincoln's depression and melancholy were not just from the events that shaped his life. Those were bad enough to trigger his depression, but the fact that helped it along and aggravated it was that he was also thought to deal with problems in a way that was inverted. The saving grace for him was that he had taken up a pastime that his father had not—reading.

In the course of his reading, he learned to elevate the way he spoke and the way he thought. This overlapped with rules and ultimately the law that society had to operate under. This was of profound interest to him. Law gave him the structure that family and religion could not. Once he began to understand the concept of law and the way societies organized themselves, he elevated his views and started questioning the ways humanity organized itself, and he turned to the Roman books of history. He started to understand the value of freedom and the power of democracy. However, he also saw some of its shortcomings.

In understanding those shortcomings and the latent weakness, he came to appreciate the need for power and unilateral decisions. He began to see the true nature of the presidency. Whether or not the Founding Fathers felt that it was to be used in such a way was another point altogether, but to him it was a stroke of genius.

There have been a few presidents in the history of the United States who have been such a force of will themselves that they single-handedly expanded the power of the presidency and the reach of the office. It was never intended for a king to rule this country and to demand adulation from his subjects. Instead, the country was built to be governed by itself. Be that as it may, the Office of the President, while created by Articles of the U.S. Constitution, does have tremendous latitude in its development, and that gave a handful of men the ability to expand its role.

George Washington, as much as he did for the nation in the Revolutionary War, was not such a president who could expand on the powers of the presidency during his tenure and neither were men such as Jefferson or Adams. Only two men in our history have expanded the powers of the presidency and pushed the bounds of the office. Abraham Lincoln was one of those men.

Historians have been debating the legality and righteousness of the actions of men like Lincoln who have tried to expand those powers. Some have labeled those who have succeeded as usurpers, while others have regaled them as presidential and carved their visage into mountains. Regardless of what men think after the fact, none of them can ever imagine or emulate the intensity of the mind that carries a man from the backwoods of the frontier to the hallowed halls of the White House.

Teddy Roosevelt

The Soul of Progressive America

Teddy Roosevelt

The Soul of Progressive America

A Biography of Theodore Roosevelt
The Youngest President in US History

JR MacGregor

Teddy Roosevelt – The Soul of Progressive America

Copyright © 2021 JR MacGregor

All rights reserved. No portion of this book may be reproduced, stored in a retrieval system, or transmitted in any form or by any means – electronic, mechanical, photocopy, recording, scanning, or other – except for brief quotations in critical reviews or articles, without prior written permission of the publisher.

Published by CAC Publishing LLC

ISBN 978-1-950010-46-2 paperback

ISBN 978-1-950010-45-5 eBook

Introduction

Theodore Roosevelt is the reason why America is what it is today. There is a reason why he is memorialized atop Mount Rushmore, with only three other history-changing men.

Roosevelt began life with unbounded curiosity and a mind like a sponge. Curiosity begat learning, learning begat ideas, and ideas fueled action. Action, obviously, was the soul of change. When sufficient change happened, we are permitted to think of it as a revolution.

Theodore Roosevelt was nothing less than a revolutionary figure in American politics and history. He fueled his energy to do great things with enthusiasm and intellect.

At the center of his energy to move an entire country was the propensity for hard work. He believed in it, he preached about it, and he practiced it. On top of that, he was dedicated to his family and his cause.

The country can only prosper when the man charged with its leadership is righteous. Roosevelt's virtuosity extended from religious adherence to religious fidelity and affective empathy.

His father's wisdom infused his conscience. As a politician who was tempted by a long list of unscrupulous characters, he always held strong. The values placed in his head as a child gave him strength. Roosevelt was schooled at home as a child and constantly under the watchful eyes of his parents until it was time for Harvard. There was no moral relativism or ambiguity in his life's trajectory.

In essence, his character was built from the ground up. So were his mind-set and strength. The strength that he learned from his father allowed him to overcome almost certain death. His childhood was one that was plagued by constant near-death episodes. Doctors were not able to do much about it. It was his father who pulled him out of the depths of suffering by teaching him to place his mind over matter.

Roosevelt loved the outdoors. He was a naturalist in his soul. The affinity to nature spurred his mind. His curiosity fueled his learning. His passion empowered his writing, and his empathy inspired his teaching. In his speeches and his writing, it is plain to see that he endeavored to elevate those around him by filling their minds and raising their spirits.

From those virtues rose the inevitable invocation of equity. The mind that seeks equity can't help but find nature—the ultimate evidence of balance and consequence. Roosevelt began his lifelong relationship with the outdoors when he traveled out of the city to convalesce. He eventually associated being outdoors with good times, health, and spirituality.

The duality of his total persona—the intellectual and the outdoorsman—was represented in how he dressed.

The quintessential wardrobe that came to define Roosevelt was either the three-piece suit and monocle or the khaki safari outfit with a rifle resting on his shoulder.

He accomplished a great deal during his presidency and the decade that preceded it. He did it despite the weight of the conservative faction of the Republican Party hanging around his neck. He remade the country in his image and would have done much more if he had been elected to a third term. The America we live in today is one that reflects his image.

Chapter 1 - Family

There were two presidents, the twenty-sixth and the thirty-second, who carried the name Roosevelt. Franklin Delano Roosevelt is the latter, and Teddy (his grown-up name) was the former. Both men were indeed related. They were fifth cousins.

It's hard to envision what being fifth cousins with someone looks like or what it would feel like to meet one's fifth cousin. A first cousin is when the person's parent is a sibling of one of your parents. Second cousins are when one's grandparent is the sibling of the other person's grandparent. Third cousins are connected by siblings who are great grandparents, and so on. In Teddy Roosevelt and Franklin Delano Roosevelt's case, one would have to go back five generations.

The first of the Roosevelts to arrive in the New World from Holland was Claes Maartinszen van Rosenvelt. Rosenvelt, in Dutch, means "field of roses." As such, coming from Holland, it is likely that wherever Claes hailed from, it had something to do with a field of roses. It is how the Dutch nomenclature worked.

He is believed to have set foot in New Amsterdam (what is New York today) in the 1640s. He married Jannetje Samuel Thomas, and the couple went on to have four children: Christiaen Roosevelt (born in 1650), Elsje Roosevelt (born in 1651), Anna Margaret Roosevelt (born in 1654), and finally Nicholas Roosevelt (born in 1658).

The last common ancestor that the two presidents shared was this Nicholas Roosevelt, who went on to marry Heyltje Jans Kunst and had Jannette Roosevelt (1683), Margaretta Roosevelt (1685), Nicholaes Roosevelt (1687), Johannes Roosevelt (1688), Elsie Roosevelt (1690), and Jacobus Roosevelt (1691). This was part of the second generation of Roosevelts that had taken root in New York. The other parts were children born to the other children of Claes Maartinszen van Rosenvelt. This is where the two prominent branches of the Roosevelt family split. Five generations later one sibling from this family would be the ancestor of Franklin Delano Roosevelt, and another sibling would be the ancestor of Theodore Roosevelt. The former were known as the Hyde Park Roosevelts and the latter as the Oyster Bay Roosevelts.

Johannes Roosevelt, who was born in 1688, went on to marry Heyltje Sjoerts. One of the sons they had was named Jacobus Roosevelt, who was born in 1724. At the same time, Johannes Roosevelt's younger brother, Jacobus Roosevelt, who was born in 1691, married, and one of the children he had was named Issac Roosevelt, who was born in 1726. Isaac and Jacobus (born 1724) were first cousins.

These two first cousins, being located in different parts of the colonies, built families of their own that resulted in several children. Jacobus Roosevelt had several children, one of whom was named Jacobus as well. He was born in 1759. This is the Oyster Bay line. On the parallel track was Isaac's son James Roosevelt, who was born in 1760 and would go on to be part of the Hyde Park

Roosevelts. Jacobus and James were second cousins.

The family they nurtured then brought about Cornelius van Schaack Roosevelt, who was born in 1794 and one of the sons of Jacobus Roosevelt. On the other track, the next generation brought about several children, one of whom was Isaac Roosevelt, who was born in 1790. Isaac and Cornelius were third cousins.

Cornelius, Theodore Roosevelt Senior's father, was born in 1831. While on the other side, Isaac fathered several children, one of whom is James, who was born in 1828. They were fourth cousins.

James married twice. His second marriage was to Sara Delano, and together they had one son, Franklin Delano Roosevelt. On the other track, in Oyster Bay, Theodore Roosevelt married Martha Steward Bulloch, and together they had several children, one of whom is Theodore Roosevelt Jr., the twenty-sixth President of the United States. Franklin Delano Roosevelt and Theodore Roosevelt are fifth cousins.

The familial connections didn't end there because Theodore Roosevelt Junior's brother Elliot Roosevelt had a daughter Eleanor Roosevelt, who went on to marry Franklin Delano Roosevelt. Theodore Roosevelt walked Eleanor down the aisle when she married Franklin.

Teddy's father, Senior, was a strong and foreboding character. He was built for the rough-and-tumble world of the Industrial Age in New York. Senior was the fifth son of Cornelius van Schaack Roosevelt and Margaret Barnhill Roosevelt. The family was one of the wealthy names in New York, having built the family wealth through hard work and street smarts in a city that was growing fast and outpacing all other cities in America and in most of the world. Senior, while growing up in a rich environment, was not easygoing by any means. He worked hard and had a strong sense of urgency in all efforts he undertook. He was a valuable partner in the firm of Roosevelt & Son, which was founded by his father. The company was primarily engaged in trading.

The attribute that was most recognized by his peers, however, wasn't the wealth that he had participated in building. It was more for his kindness. Senior was kind in person and in general. In person, this large and thundering man was a gentle giant. In general, he would seek out ways to be charitable to organizations and people that were in need. He would make it a point to volunteer at least once every week in the pursuit of care for the less fortunate. This included monetary aid and physical involvement in the actions that would result in that end.

As part of his philanthropic pursuits, he sought out hospitals to donate to so that those who were not able to pay for services would be able to receive care. He also started research programs so that doctors would find cures for diseases that were still incurable at the time. He further donated to cultural causes, including museums of art and natural history, to be able to benefit the people of the city.

Senior was born September 22, 1831. When the first sounds of fire were heard around Fort

Sumter on April 12, 1861, Senior was a strong and healthy adult of twenty-nine years. He chose not to enlist and instead, as many rich families did, paid for a substitute. The Draft Act of 1863, by which point Senior was thirty-two years old, allowed for two ways to stay out of conscription. The first was to pay $300 to the federal government, and the second was to pay someone to take his place. Senior chose the latter. He paid a surrogate to take his place in the war and then went on to contribute to the war differently.

He was not the only one who took the path out of conscription. Such men as Andrew Carnegie, John D. Rockefeller, and JP Morgan were just some of the famous names who took advantage of this section of the law.

But the Civil War created a new complication within the Roosevelt family of Oyster Bay. Senior was an ardent supporter of Lincoln and the Union's cause. He was a great fan of Federalism and saw the value of being stronger together. On the other hand, the love of his life and mother to their children was an ardent supporter of the Confederate position.

If there was ever a defining personification of the Southern belle, Martha Bullock Roosevelt, or Mittie, would have been it. It is even thought widely among socialites that the character of Scarlet O'Hara in Margaret Mitchell's Gone With the Wind was based on Mittie. She was a strong personality and one of the prettiest young ladies in New York.

She was also powerfully connected in the South, being the great-granddaughter of Archibald Bulloch, the first governor of Georgia. Her Southern roots could not fit in with the ways of New York, which in the mid-1800s became the driving force of the liberal and New World way of doing things. The South remained ensconced in the gentlemanly strain of life. The two were directly in contrast with each other.

Yet, when they first met on one of Senior's visits to Georgia, they were strongly attracted to each other. Strong women are not always attracted to weak men, and strong men are never attracted to weak women. It takes strong personalities to be able to define each other's strengths and passions, and that balance was struck well in the marriage that Senior and Mittie shared.

The Roosevelts were married in 1853. Their first child, Anna Roosevelt (known popularly as Bamie or Bye), was born in 1855, followed by Teedy in 1858, and then by his younger brother Elliot (Eleanor Roosevelt's father) in 1860, and finally Corine (grandmother to Joseph and Stewart Aslop) in 1861.

Once married they had one other issue that confronted them daily—they had two children out of four who were constantly afflicted with allergies and sounding the alarm almost every day. Even then, the couple had enough mental and physical capacity to keep an eye on the war.

Mattie hailed from the Deep South ideologically and from a family with deep roots and interests in the South. They had originally been of Scottish stock and landed in South Carolina before the Revolutionary War. After the Revolution, they moved to Georgia and accumulated large plantations. The plantations were the engine of the Bulloch wealth. They were undoubtedly a slave-owning family, making them one of the few Southerners who were truly vested in the way the war turned out.

James and Irvine Bulloch, Mittie's brothers, served in the Confederate Navy. James was an admiral and famed for being the man who sailed the CSS Alabama (CSS is the abbreviation for Confederate States Ship) from England to the Confederate states after its completion. His brother Irvine was a midshipman on that voyage. The CSS Alabama was a notorious commerce raider that would sail the eastern coast of the United States attacking Union merchant and naval vessels.

Senior did not participate in the fighting side of the war, but he had decided to contribute to the effort in his own way. He met with Abraham Lincoln and lobbied the federal government to create a wage deduction program where the salaries of those who agreed were sent back home to the family instead of giving it directly to the soldiers. Lincoln agreed, and the War Department instituted the program. It was left to Senior to travel around the State of New York and convince as many soldiers as he could to sign up for the program. Many did. Once that was done, he set up a donation campaign to organize holiday gifts and food for the various companies that were around New York, and he kept meticulous records of the donations and the money spent on the gifts and food. In cases of some shortfall, he would put in his own money to make sure the troops were kept in good spirits around the holidays.

When the War Department instituted the program, it sent the money that was deducted from the soldier's salary to the Union Club in various states. The money for the soldiers from New York was sent to the Union Club in New York. Senior was its treasurer. He took this job without salary and compensation and ensured that all the money that was deposited to the Union Club was disbursed to the families of the soldier. He was given the title of Allotment Commissioner of New York.

It was more of a moral contribution to the war than a physical or a monetary contribution, and this saw him travel frequently at one point during the war. He visited Union forces near and far to give advice and persuade them to do the right thing. It was a highly stressful time for the family. Between the political differences of both husband and wife, the frequent need to travel, Mittie's support of the Confederacy, and the strains of everyday life, the Roosevelts experienced considerable stress.

That strain, however, was no match for the love the two shared for each other and the love they had for their four children. They endured. Soon the war was over, Teedy started to feel better, and business for the Roosevelts was on the upswing. With the war over, as part of the recuperation efforts for Teedy and Corine, the family decided to seek out places where the air was cleaner and cooler. They vacationed all over the world, but before they started visiting foreign destinations, they would frequently visit Oyster Bay in Long Island. The memories of his childhood prompted Teedy to make it his home and thus directed this wing of the Roosevelt family to be known as the Oyster Bay Roosevelts.

On February 9, 1878, Theodore Roosevelt Senior, father, friend, and mentor to the twenty-sixth president of the United States, passed away at the young age of forty-six. At the time it happened, Teedy was away in college. The news shook him to the core. He was close to his father—the kind of bond that can only arise when one clings to someone throughout his youth the way Teedy did with his father. It was the kind of bond that arises when a young man grows up and needs guidance to navigate the world and the problems it throws at him.

Roosevelt never really buried his father. He carried him in his heart everywhere he went. From the hills out in the West to the streets in the East. From Albany to Washington, Africa to Cuba, there was nothing that Teedy would do or undertake if he thought his father wouldn't approve.

"My father, Theodore Roosevelt, was the best man I ever knew. He combined strength and courage with gentleness, tenderness, and great unselfishness. He would not tolerate in us children selfishness or cruelty, idleness, cowardice, or untruthfulness. As we grew older, he made us understand that the same standard of clean living was demanded the boys as for the girls; that what was wrong in a woman could not be right in a man. With great love and patience, and the most generous sympathy and consideration, he combined insistence on discipline. He never physically punished me but once, but he was the only man of whom I was ever really afraid. I do not mean that it was a wrong fear, for he was entirely just, and we children adored him. ... My father worked hard at his business, for he died when he was forty-six, too early to have retired. He was interested in every social reform movement, and he did an immense amount of practical charitable work himself. He was a big, powerful man, with a leonine face, and his heart filled with gentleness for those who needed help or protection, and with the possibility of much wrath against a bully or an oppressor. ... was greatly interested in the societies to prevent cruelty to children and cruelty to animals."

It is difficult to understand the workings of a man like Teddy Roosevelt in a modern-day context. He was the classical conservative but also a modern liberal. Almost enigmatic in irony. He was not infallible nor was he the perfect man. What he was and what this generation of politicians can take from him is having a steadfast loyalty to the truth regardless of the cost that it levied on the present or the consequences that ensued.

Some say that his personal life was filled with tragedy from the day he was born to the day he passed. If Teddy were here, he would disagree. He lived a life that did not waste a second worrying about what he didn't have. He did not shed a tear for whatever left him unexpectedly. He did not reminisce old stories. He kept charging forward. All of life was his San Juan Hill.

Chapter 2 - Life

Theodore Roosevelt Senior and Martha Bulloch Roosevelt were two very strong people who came together and raised a young man with strength of intellect and kindness of heart. Teedy was born October 27, 1858, at the family brownstone on E. 20th St. in the Gramercy section of New York City.

The years he spent at home from the time he was born until the time the allergies and asthma subsided was not laid to waste in the halls of the large mansion. It was put to good use by the tutors that were engaged by his parents who were highly intolerant of ignorance and by the Roosevelt children themselves. While Bammie and Elliot did go to school, Tee and Corinne attended home school.

He became so good at reading books that he was able to devour up to three books in a day and sometimes a book before breakfast. Without getting into a course on speed reading, it is necessary to mention that the ability to speed read is not inherent in anyone. Anyone can learn it. Teedy's ability to read at that rapid rate was because of his ability to focus and that he had a strong mind. Not only did he read, but he was also able to retain almost 100 percent of the content, including pictures and diagrams.

In his older years, Teedy himself had written several books, one of which was an autobiography. In it he shared some strategies for reading and the choice of content. His first strategy, and we should take this seriously, as he is one of the most widely read presidents in our history, is that one needs to read anything he can get his hands on. In other words, as he did, don't just stick to one genre or a few limited categories of topics and styles. Read everything you can.

He also advised to find books that one enjoys, which comes back to the first rule. If you don't read a lot, you will not know what kinds of books you may enjoy.

He also suggested to be honest about the books that one comes to like. If you like books in one specific category but it does not make you sound intelligent or learned, don't feel shy. It is not a competition.

What he talks about in his autobiography gives us real insight into the kind of man he was and further insight into the childhood he had with the books he read.

As his own advice suggests, he liked all books. That was just his nature. He loved to wrap his mind around the intent of the author and the story that was being transmitted. If it wasn't a fiction book, then the purpose of the reading was not to enjoy but to absorb the information that was contained therein. There was always a purpose to his reading.

Once he started traveling, he realized there were worlds beyond New York City and Long Island. He started reading books about faraway places. It is said that it was one of the things that allowed him to expand his imagination, and this allowed him to see things differently from how others did.

More importantly, Roosevelt was a genius in his own right. He was able to retain the content of the reading and then reflect on it and assimilate it. His reading allowed him to transport himself in space and time and to see in ways that others would never bring themselves to. It altered the way his mind worked. Many physicians attribute his incessant reading as the activity that paved the way toward his cure.

The reading took on a greater significance when the family began traveling overseas. It was partly to enjoy the sights and experiences, but it was also to replace the environment that had been part of Teedy's life. They went to a diverse set of locations. From the classic locations, such as London, Paris, Rome, and Switzerland, to contemporary locations, such as Holland, Prussia, Austria, and Hungary, to exotic locations, such as Israel, Greece, Syria, and Egypt.

The towns and cities that most fascinated young Teddy, however, were such places as Alexandria, Giza, and Cairo. The cities had given him a point of reference to some of the books he had read about his hero, Alexander the Great. The layer of experience that started with books and then was augmented with visits to places he read about elevated his mind to the point that it placed him on a trajectory of being able to manifest thought into reality.

Travel elevates the mind and especially for someone as astute as Teedy. The new signs, interesting sounds, and fresh smells of the Old World piqued his senses enough to wake up parts of him.

Achievements

Theodore Roosevelt's achievements span many theaters. He retains the record of being the youngest man to become president. It is commonly thought to be JFK. This is true but for a slightly technical point. JFK was the youngest man to be elected to the presidency. He was forty-three years old. Roosevelt, on the other hand, inherited the presidency upon the assassination of President McKinley. When he succeeded McKinley, Roosevelt was not yet forty-three years of age. He finished out the term and then stood for the office in 1904. At that time he was forty-six.

Even though he was the youngest to sit behind the Resolute desk, he made some of the greatest strides in moving the country to the position of preeminence it stands at today. Theodore Roosevelt's achievements were of long-lasting significance in numerous areas. As soon as he took over from McKinley, he got to work, not wasting a moment. He was already full of ideas. Those ideas combined with his base of knowledge from reading and traveling experiences provided a base to launch. Aside from accomplishing administrative and governmental goals, Roosevelt was able to transform the office of president and refine the actions he took to serve the best interests of the country even if some of them were not popular.

Many of his programs did turn out to be popular, but he was not doing them for the sake of popularity. He was doing them for the sake of the good of the populace. He struck a balance that most presidents have found hard to do.

He was not a stranger to controversy either. It is easy to become controversial, especially when one is not looking at popular opinion or following established practices. It is one of the reasons why players inside Washington were not fond of him. However, he also managed to make simple events controversial because of his simplicity and open-mindedness. One such unnecessary controversy was in 1901 when he invited Booker T. Washington to dine with him at the White House. Another controversy of a more serious nature was when he ended the Anthracite Coal Strike in 1902. That was the good part. The part that became controversial was that he used the military to force mine owners to negotiate a settlement with the striking union workers.

That same year Roosevelt also signed the Elkins Anti-Rebate Act. This was important because large railroads were cutting prices to major commercial customers and transferring the cost to regular travelers. This enraged the railroad companies. He also went on to settle the Alaskan border dispute over the Lynn Canal. He enacted the Panama Treaty in 1904 and issued the Monroe Doctrine—the manifestation of his Big Stick policy.

Roosevelt was a force that swept through Washington in the areas of social and political reform. These and other achievements were overwhelming. Then there was the Treaty of Portsmouth in 1905 when he successfully negotiated the end of the Russo-Japanese War. It was this negotiation that led to him being awarded the Nobel Peace Prize.

He also created the U.S. Forest Service. Remember that Roosevelt was close to nature. He saw the value of preserving it and the need to be enveloped by it. His trip to the West to hunt bison was just another way to spend time with Mother Earth. It was one of his greatest qualities. He then went on to smash the Beef Trust—the three meatpacking giants that formed the National Packing Company. He also went on and indicted

Standard Oil for violating the Sherman Act. He signed the Antiquities Act in 1906 and then the Forest Homestead Act, the Hepburn Rate Act, and the Meat Inspection Act. He made sure that the legislative calendar was always filled to the hilt. He was very involved in the legislative process, constantly coming up with legislative proposals and then keeping an eye on the progress. He also went on to create more national monuments and worked at admitting Oklahoma as the forty-sixth state. During this time, he pushed Congress to come up with the Immigration Act. When 1908 rolled around, he was on to the Employer's Liability Act and designating the Grand Canyon as well as several other national monuments.

Chapter 3 - Mind

Before he managed to unshackle his mind from his limitations, TR was, to put it kindly, weak. The constant shadow of an attack and the difficulty in mustering the needed effort just to make it through the day had resulted in dousing his spirits and curtailing his ambitions. For all that he grew up to be, the beginning that he was endowed with was paltry.

In his later days, TR would look back and say that his youth was timid. He reflected about the state of his mind and his heart, fearful of the onset of the next death-defying act or the next battle for air. The implications of his self-view show the shadow of a man who was towering in his later years but built on a platform of painful struggles. It was like a skyscraper built on a foundation of hay.

Most men would find that debilitating and seek to overcompensate. That, however, is not the track that young TR chose to follow. Instead, he chose to build his strength from within rather than to apply a veneer to his facade. This was of his own volition. His father had told him to build his body, which was not entirely to put on a superficial presence, but it was to make him healthy from within. TR took that a step further and decided to shed his fears by displacing it with strength, much as light displaces darkness.

TR's inner fear was one of mortal consequence. He stood at the fork in his development. One road would lead to constant fear and relinquishing all control. The other would lead to dominance and fearless power over the elements. He willfully worked toward the latter.

The first stage of TR's life, much like that of many men of success and achievement, was one of self-control. That self-control was not just applied to their faculties but to the events that transpired around them. They believe they can control all that happens around them, and in most cases, they are not wrong.

It can be argued that it was these childhood events that contributed to the path that TR eventually took. It was TR's conclusion that if it were not for those ailments and constant bombardments of desperation that his true grit would not have revealed itself. He believed eventually, with much humility, that the true path to a person's greatness goes through the most profound hardships. A simple life will not make a great man. It seemed that the Roosevelts, as wealthy as they were, were not in the habit of lavishing their children with the comforts of wealth and the trappings of power. They raised their family with traditional values and intense study. On the other side of New York City, many decades later, a young FDR would face the same, and he, too, rose to become president.

The transition from victim to victor happened over time. It was not a moment of epiphany like those portrayed in dramatic narrative. His happened over an extended span beginning when he turned fourteen and lasted through that year. The state of his being had weighed heavily on him. His father had done his best to portray the virtues of those with a strong mind, and TR certainly had that. His ability to focus on one thing at a time allowed him to turn away from whatever malady afflicted him at the moment. Yet, he was physically weak. Even with his superior powers of concentration, his thoughts frequently hovered on the fact that he was not strong like all those men he read about in his books.

Remember that he read a lot, and he remembered all of them. More importantly, it made an impression on him. The more he read, the stronger his impressions became. One area in particular that vexed him was how he saw literary characters—how his heroes handled the world around them. They were commanding, strong, and self-sufficient. Until he was thirteen, he was none of those things and decided to alter his course.

After a particularly concerning asthma attack, TR was sent to a lakeside ranch to convalesce. They were in the city, which was particularly disagreeable to him that summer. He was sent by himself by carriage. The journey proved enjoyable at first. Once they left the city and moved deeper into the countryside, his condition, which was already on the mend, improved further, invigorating him. Each spell of asthma would typically bring a sense of weakness, just as each elevation of conditions would bring confidence and delight.

While feeling elevated and amid the wealth of nature, he came across two boys who were traveling the same path. His carriage was built for comfort. Their legs were built for necessity. He was polished and well read, while they were rough and illiterate. They noticed the carriage, only to be surprised that its contents were no older than they were but much paler and unaccustomed to the wilderness. They instantly sensed quarry.

There was nothing mean about them according to TR, but "boys would be boys." The three became acquainted, and soon afterward the bullying started. Fisticuffs ensued, and while it was clear they could impart a severe walloping on their pale counterpart, they were just toying with him. The sharper TR understood this to be a greater insult than if they had just gone all out and beat him up to the fullest extent they knew how. Instead, they taunted him, slapped him around, and otherwise humiliated young TR.

This was the point that altered his trajectory. Nothing changes a boy into a man more than when instincts boil up from deep within. The same happened here. At the end of the episode, TR was none the worse for wear, but his mind had been made up. He was no longer going to find himself at the whim of weaknesses.

His attitude about the event cemented his resolve. Upon his return to New York, after time by the lake, his father set him up with a boxing trainer.

TR's ability to look inward for answers was one of the hallmarks of his presidency. He was often characterized in private as being obstinate and stubborn. He was neither. From that day in the wilderness, he had begun a journey that would raise his independence to such high levels that he knew that he had more insight into almost any matter than anyone around him except his parents. He kept advisors to give him details on a certain subject, but he still took his counsel as to what to do with that data. That is what made him a good president and a strong leader. His reading and rapid assimilation of facts and figures were also important in his decision-making ability.

From his light weight, it was truly surprising to most that he went on to take up boxing seriously. His instructor, one Mr. John Long, who was engaged by Roosevelt Senior for his son, formed a bond with young TR and helped guide him. Besides his weightlifting, boxing proved to be a powerful influence in TR's pliable young self. Instead of gelling int a weak person that incident and the ensuing boxing lessons allowed him to break through his limitations by facing them.

He never became a boxing champion. Although that would have been a fairy-tale ending, he did take part in a competition organized by his boxing coach. He signed up just so that he could be a part of something. He did not think that he would win or even come out of it without getting himself bumped and bruised. For all his encouragement, his coach secretly thought the same. TR was still slender at this point and not yet quick on his feet. The outcome stunned everyone. Once TR stepped into the ring, he was a changed person. His focus, his desire, and his newfound skill found common ground and took down his opponent to win the trophy in his weight class. It was a pewter mug of little retail value, but it was of great sentimental value to TR even after many years had passed.

It stood as the manifestation of vanquished fears and realized hope—a hope that was to be a better version of himself and be strong like the men in his books. That little 50-cent cup managed to hold the tears of a young boy that were traded for accomplishment.

That incident led to improvements in his confidence. By the time he was eighteen at Harvard, he had done well enough at boxing to join the varsity boxing team. He didn't get into any competitions or win any medals, but he was always part of the team and spent his effort as a sparring partner for teammates who would compete. When he finally did become competitive, he won runner-up at the championship being beaten only by the eventual winner, one CS Hanks, who bloodied his nose in an underhanded move.

In his own words, TR repeatedly looked upon his formative years with deep gratitude. The epiphany that his past had everything to do with his success as a man and contributions as a president is something that he repeatedly expressed in his writings. Much of the man he became was due to the challenge he faced in the cradle of his illness.

In his teenage years, he went on to appreciate the skill of hunting. TR was not in it for the killing, nor the hunt. He was in it to be able to elevate his physical skill and ability to outthink and outsmart his target. He developed an instinct for hunting, but he was not physically able to be a skilled horseman until some considerable time had passed. He enjoyed riding. It gave him a sense of masculinity that was generational during TR's time. It was like a teenager getting his driver's license today. Getting on a horse and being skilled at it was almost a right of passage and something that TR set his mind to accomplish and eventually did. Hunting was just part of the passage to the goal.

Just like his boxing, TR's riding took consistent effort to acquire. It was not until after consistent practice that he became an expert horseman during his adventures as a young man.

TR was not the kind of person who is daunted or hindered by anything. Even if something was a steep climb to acquire, he would patiently and consistently keep at it until he achieved some sort of facility with the task. That innate character in him was an engine that others could not turn off. It defined much of his adult career, his governorship, and his presidency.

By the time he was in his mid-teens, his frame had started to thicken. By the time he was in the Oval Office, he had shot all the way up to 237 pounds, a stark contrast to when he was a teenager. His weight had always been a testament to his ability to overcome the meager beginnings. That trophy earned him another accolade. He is in the top five of the chubbiest presidents.

He was not bothered by his portly appearance. It was, in fact, his projection of victory over a condition that caused him to be frail. He wore his pounds as a suit of accomplishment.

Chapter 4 - Law

TR graduated from Harvard College in 1880 two years after his father passed. He was now a man on his own and a man on a mission. His intellect and long years of preparation under the hardship of ailment and stress of ambition pointed him to his next stage in life—the means to provide justice.

In the mind of the newly minted Harvard man, his next step in life would be to tread a path of justice. There was something innately immersed in Teddy's fabric of existence that opened his eyes to notice and his heart to empathize with the disparity of opportunity and the lack of equity in the days leading up to the dawn of the twentieth century.

He was a man of nature, and most students of nature eventually come to realize the harmony between all living things and that there is a natural sense of balance, equity, and symbiosis.

Being from a well-heeled clan, he naturally turned to the power of the law and the potential of the country that was born of that law and embodied the structure of the Constitution. He had grown up being in awe of it and its effect. He naturally confused the law of nature and the law of man. He believed the law of man was the best way to execute the societal forces and to govern them equitably.

This was the core reason why he decided to pursue a course of study that would acquaint him with a deeper understanding of the principles of justice.

He enrolled in Columbia Law School, just as his cousin and later president Franklin Delano Roosevelt did. Both did not graduate from law school, leaving just a year shy from completing their two-year Juris Doctor course of study. Both Roosevelt cousins were eventually awarded their law degrees posthumously.

Both men left law school under different mindsets. The older Roosevelt, the twenty-sixth president, left because he became disillusioned by the structure and effect of American jurisprudence.

Upon entering Columbia Law School in New York, Roosevelt immediately began to dislike the foundational premise of the law. In his words, the law is not about justice. It is an ironic concept to most informed minds that the Department of Justice in the United States, formed just ten years before TR graduated, is about the law. In TR's mind, law was not about justice. The more he read the law and understood its premise, the more he was certain that law and justice diverged in their ultimate goal.

He was especially incensed that something like the premise of caveat emptor—or the more commonly known, buyer beware—was something that did not exude justice in its existence. Instead, it made way for con men to bend the protection of the state to their purpose. It inherently reduced the common man to a target and placed the powers of the state against them.

Roosevelt did not support or side with the common man because it was the noble thing to do but rather sided with them because it was the right thing to do. It was so because the common man had been left out of the loop in the attainment of value. It could be said that TR was an equal opportunity advocate. Where there was a disparity between those who sought protection under the law and those who used the law to place others under their heel, he wanted the government to arbitrate the condition and remedy it.

Roosevelt saw the purpose of the law as righteous but saw legislation that had been enacted to be no different from the decree of the monarchs. His disappointment with the nature of the law was palpable. He felt that the federal framework had been hijacked and skewed toward the rich. Beneath that framework was the basis of law. None of it matched his sense of justice. To him, justice bordered on socialistic tendencies. To be clear, Roosevelt was not socialist. At a speech in New York, he clearly articulated, "The first requisite of a good citizen in this republic of ours is that he shall be able and willing to pull his weight."

It is commonly misunderstood that Roosevelt wanted to provide a socialist environment for the masses and thus become a Populist. That was not his intention because he had repeatedly said that was not the case. Of course, any man can say what he wants to suit the opportunity of the moment. What matters is the action he eventually takes.

Roosevelt was the original anarchist of the nineteenth century—at least in the true definition of the word—not the evolved and more shady meaning of it. Roosevelt did not believe that government was needed to govern the conduct of the citizens but rather to facilitate the advancement of society and to allow the tenets of the Declaration of Independence to take root.

He felt the law should be just but found that was not always the case. This is the reason why he was prompted to quit law school and join the legislature so that he could be part of the body that wrote the laws. At that young age, he had the foresight to recognize that it was not the rules and the laws that were wrong but rather the men who created them. He further realized that one could not reject the law because it was wrong. Instead, one had to go about getting those laws changed.

He appreciated the fact that a society without any laws would be significantly worse off. He was also a patriotic American and based that patriotism on the country that was structured and governed by the rule of law and not the whims of men. Nonetheless, the principles that had become ingrained in American jurisprudence had come to detract from the element of justice and equity in the law.

Take, for instance, the way outside forces dictate the composition of the law-making bodies in government and consequently dictate the laws that those bodies enact. Take it further and one finds that the Supreme Court, the highest court in the land, is not immune to this as well. It can be molded and shaped to favor laws that favor certain parts of society. None of this in Roosevelt's mind was equitable and ostensibly detracted from the intent of the founding documents and the principle of equity and justice. Without equity, there can be no justice, and without justice, there can be no America because America is the manifestation of its Constitutional laws. Without its Constitution and laws, America is just a spot on the map.

The problem that Roosevelt determined was that the cowboy attitude of the frontier and the expansion of the commercial endeavors in America in the post-Industrial Revolution world had turned the country into the playground of the robber barons.

He understood why lawyers got such a bad reputation from practicing law. It occurred to him that it was not the lawyers who trampled on the law. They were just doing their job. It was the way the laws were written that caused the problem. Because of this, his disillusionment, and his lack of trust in the system that was beginning to take shape, he decided to leave law school and go to where he could make the most change—the place where the law is written.

No one can conclude that Roosevelt's sense of anarchy had anything to do with lawlessness. It was all about the law, which he saw as the fundamental tool to advance a civilized society.

By the time he left Harvard and made his way back to the Empire State, he had no need for money. The Roosevelts up to that point and a point much later in history were wealthy beyond average. Teddy's father had bequeathed him with enough resources that he didn't have to work if he didn't want to. He could have chosen to spend a lifetime of leisure, and he would have had enough resources to support himself and his family when the time came. It was a luxury that not many people were blessed with.

It was this contributing factor that allowed Roosevelt to veer off his path to become a respectable lawyer and take some time to set himself up on a different path. The notion that the laws were not doing justice turned him to politics.

In Roosevelt's mind, aspirations of elected office, whether at the country, state, or federal level, should be a secondary endeavor and not the primary mode of sustaining oneself. In other words, he who seeks office would have a backup profession that he can return to when he no longer can be elected or chooses to quit because he is placed in a position of a moral dilemma.

Roosevelt believed that a person who took political office should do so to serve and not to make a living. Of course, this is naive. The counterargument could also be made that a person who had an outside business to run could not possibly be in the position to pay full attention to the matters of his office. It could further be argued that a person who is taking care of said business could find themselves in a position of conflict.

The point of the matter for this book does not rest with the merits of the professional or part-time politician. Instead, the point of the matter is to note the strain of naivete and hint of idealism in this young version of the eventual great president.

Young Roosevelt was indeed naive. It was one of his most profound characteristics. It became the basis for his idealism, which became the basis for his moral authority, and that moral authority became the foundation for his effective presidency—one that the masses agreed with—albeit for the wrong reasons.

In his zest for equality and his ability to not have to work for a living, his path diverged from that of the typical Harvard graduate. Neither did he need to find work nor did he need to continue on an academic path so that he could find a higher paying job later. He could do as he pleased. He still enrolled in law school, but his mind had started to think of politics. A year after he enrolled and found that the law, in an academic setting, was divorced from reality—at least the way he hoped reality would be—he left. Next stop: politics.

Chapter 5 - Politics

The political environment at the grassroots level was markedly different then from what it is today. Joining a party today is almost like signing up at the local gym, if not easier. It was not so during TR's time at the turn of the century.

The only party that was relatively easy to sign up with was the liberal Republican Party—the party that had recently risen in popularity and was now a mainstream organization. They were friendlier to the masses than other parties that had come and gone before them. Even then, becoming a member was not as easy. The party worked like a corporation and took its membership seriously. One had to be introduced, nominated, then approved by existing members.

If Roosevelt wanted to join the Republican Party, he would have to find a sponsor to vouch for him. Roosevelt did not know anyone who could do that.

Roosevelt joked that he had to "jimmy his way in the door." Jimmy in he did indeed. There were two reasons for his choice. First, it was easier to gain membership than other political organizations. Second, it espoused the values of inclusiveness, equality, human rights, and liberal aid to the needy, although that last value could be contentious when describing Roosevelt himself. He wanted the needy to be able to have a fair chance and not have the system rigged against them. To his credit, his gradual ascendancy to the highest office eventually saw him move heaven and earth to even the playing field. That was still some time away. For now, he had to clear the grassroots.

He began his quest by speaking to the people he knew, men whom he had met through his father, contemporaries from Harvard, and their acquaintances among New York's business class—men of money. The response he received for his troubles would have been discouraging to any other in his place. He was laughed at when they heard that he was looking to join a political party.

Unanimously, they told him that the business of political parties was for the plebeian class, and that the men of education and money were above that. It was a surprise but not foreboding turn of events. It had been the mind-set of the moneyed class that political mechanisms were to be left to the rough and gruff of the city. The men of money would provide their say in the form of political contributions when they backed the right candidate who could win the election and once that candidate was installed in office.

Instead of following along, his response to these men of money was highly unusual for the kind of stature Roosevelt descended from. He was incensed by the notion that the rich did not partake in American politics and that the rich stood in the background backing the horse they chose to win. He told them that if they thought they were the moneyed class then those plebeians were the true ruling class because it was they who chose the occupant of the governing offices.

This was an eye-opener for Roosevelt. He had not yet been awakened to the idea that there was a fault line between the business owners and the wage earners in a political sense. It was the epiphany that rang true as he altered the way he dressed later on in his youth and tried to fit in with the common people and tried to understand their troubles and their ideals. He did not discriminate against them because of the way they spoke or the size of their paycheck. His perspective of them as the ruling class gives students of presidential history insight into the mind of one of the most complex men to ascend to that office.

He went on to tell the men who mocked him for wanting to leave the business world and enter politics that he thought it was the noble thing to do. When he called the peasants the governing class, it is clear to any bystander that Roosevelt was fully aware of the essence of the U.S. Constitution, where the power of the government is in the hand of the governed. Of course, this includes the rich, but it doesn't include just the rich to the exclusion of the poor. To expound further on that, since there are more poor than there are rich, then the majority is the side that should influence the outcome of government.

He joined the Twenty-First District Republican Association. They had their meetings at Morton Hall, a large room over the local saloon. The saloon was filled with the locals, who were there to blow off steam after a hard day's work and to shoot the breeze—not unlike what you would find at the neighborhood pub today. Meetings at Morton Hall would be conducted at least once or twice a month. They met regularly and were hierarchical. There were regular members, and there were captains who managed them. All of them had jobs during the day, and they would descend on the saloon most nights.

TR decided that he would spend more time at the saloon and get to know the regular people who made up the Twenty-First District. In the beginning, he stood out like a sore thumb. He would appear with the worse clothes that he could find, but he was still overdressed and too clean to be among men who worked with their hands all day. He didn't get much traction because of his appearance. He was not one of them. So he altered his manner of dress and intentionally wore poorer clothes but not with the intent of being one of the boys, but to be less foreboding and more approachable, without being regular.

This worked and he started to make a few friends. People started to make conversation since he had been at the saloon almost daily. It was exactly what he wanted. The conversation with the moneyed men of Wall Street had taught him that there was a life he did not fully know, and if he was to enter the governing class, he would have to know what it meant.

Teddy rapidly built a relationship with Joe Murray, one of the many lower captains at Morton Hall. It was a friendship that remained powerful over the next thirty-three years. Murray was born in Ireland and then brought to New York at the age of four. He was raised barefooted in the immigrant neighborhood of New York's First Avenue. When he was just about to turn eighteen, he enlisted in the Potomac Army and was part of the troops that brought an end to the Civil War.

He then came back to First Avenue, quickly rising in popularity as a mob boss, being a brave, powerful, dynamic young man. Nonetheless, he was a bit reckless and ruthless. Politics was rough in that district, as with other areas of the country in those days when Tammany Hall held undisputed influence. His neighborhood had been dominantly Democratic. Democrats like Joe and his buddies conducted the typical thuggery for the local Democratic leader on election day. He then rewarded them in return.

Like other higher leaders, this community leader had become smug by prosperity and neglected the grassroots and gangs that had been instrumental in helping him achieve success. He demonstrated total indifference toward the gang's hard work and blatant disregard for his pre-election commitments after an election.

What he did not count on was that Joe Murray was not someone one forgets. Joe explained his objectives to his group and said they needed to be patient. They were then preparing for retribution to be executed the day after the election. They then decided to vote for the opposition—whoever it was on the Republican ticket. In each polling constituency at the time, every participating party had a box near the polling station where party officials administered the ballots of the party.

It was a constituency in which, as a practice, the Republican Party's leader would have his hat over his eyes and his box knocked over scattering his vote. The size of the Democratic majority relied on the appreciation of how much was demanded from bosses. Things, however, unfolded differently that day. With a resolute sense of loyalty, Joe's mob made sure that things went the Republican way.

They retaliated against their rivals when they were only seen as the tough and fighting sort. They delivered justice swiftly and strategically, a version of justice that was part sophisticated. It served as a warning to any Democrat who would go back on their promise to the gangs.

In Joe's mind, as Teddy tells it, it was merely an act of revenge, but the Republican leaders back at headquarters didn't really catch the meaning of Joe's actions. They were shocked to say the least. In attempting to find the reason for this outcome, they proceeded to investigate. In investigating, they found that the man behind all this was Joseph Murray, Teddy's newfound friend. To shed more light on this, they sent for Joe.

There was no doubt in Teddy's mind that the establishment the Republicans brought Joe to was something like Morton Hall. The people who were tasked with getting him there were comparable to folks at Morton Hall as well—hardworking simple folk. In Joe's eyes, however, they represented the higher echelon of society, something that he was not yet up to but aspired to. Joe was introduced to the attendees as the man who swung the vote and told that he held promise. For his efforts, he was given a job at the post office, a prestigious position in the late 1800s.

All this might have meant little to the average man of nineteenth century New York but not to Joe Murray. It meant a great deal to him. Joe was naturally as a straight as they come, which made Joe and TR kindred spirits. He was fearless and steadfast just like TR, and that endeared Joe to him. Joe was a man who could be trusted in any position demanding boldness, competence, and good conscience. He did his duty diligently at the post office and became devoted to the organization he felt had given him the biggest break of his life.

It was some time from that point until he and Teddy met. By then he was steadily climbing his way to the upper echelons he had desired. He even got to the point where he could afford to own a first-class race trotter, a sure sign of financial elevation. Soon after Teddy started frequenting Morton Hall, he met Joe, and the two of them were drawn to each other. It was most likely because of their aligned values and determination to loyalty, honor, and trust. At first, there was an awkward silence, but by the winter of that year, they became good friends. Teddy initially had little notion that Joe and his clan returned the favorable view of him that he had for them. Things became clear when Joe stood behind Teddy's proposal on a matter about street cleaning, and even though they were beaten, it was clear that they saw eye to eye.

As the elections approached the following year, Joe decided that he would like to go for the appointment to the lower house of the legislature. As a total surprise to many and to Teddy especially, he chose Teddy as his partner—the person with whom Joe thought he had the best chances of winning. It was Joe's fight, not Teddy's, but it was Teddy who reaped the most from that decision. At that time, Teddy didn't have sufficient reputation or the expertise to make a play for the nomination. In fact, he never would have thought of even doing so. Thanks to Joe, Teddy Roosevelt got his first crack at elected office.

Once the nominations were completed and Teddy was confirmed to be the candidate on the Republican ticket, Joe and his crew set out to canvass the neighborhood. Once he had their seal of approval, not much needed to be said.

Roosevelt was elected to the legislature in 1881 as the youngest to join the body since its inception. He then went on to be reelected over the next two years. Part of his political persona, which developed across the arc of his career, was to be a force of action instead of words. His eventual idea was to speak less and do more. His ideology was developed from being in close contact with the men in Joe's crew. Over the next two decades, from 1881 to 1900, that philosophy kept getting reinforced in the various events that he experienced until, finally, it evolved into the infamous "speak softly and carry a big stick."

The men in Joe's crew who went around and "convinced" people to do one thing or another had perfected the art of strong-arming their targets. They didn't say much. What needed to be said was said with a big "stick."

In January 1882, Roosevelt was elected to the New York State Legislature representing the 21st

District of Manhattan. He launched his campaign with a rather short note to the electorate.

"Dear Sir, having been nominated as a member of the Assembly for this District, I would appreciate it if you honored me with your vote and personal influence on election day. Very respectfully, Theodore Roosevelt."

Notice that he did not mention any of his credentials, his beliefs on matters of the day, or what he expected to do if he was elected.

He had been elected to the Assembly with the support and help of the "Fifth Avenue Crowd," a group of respected businessmen, as well as the First Avenue Crowd (Joe's crew), who assisted Roosevelt in garnering support from prominent families who lived in the district and the rank and file across town. They ran on his "honesty and integrity" and his "eminently eligible" moral standing for the job. In conjunction with these accolades, Roosevelt went on a saloon-hopping excursion, which his advisors eventually realized was not a good idea for him. Roosevelt was victorious in his bid and elected by a majority of an estimated fifteen hundred votes.

Upon returning east, Roosevelt entered the New York City mayoral race. It was a tough period for him. He had just lost his mother and wife on the same day—November 16, 1884. Mittie had died from typhoid fever. His wife, Alice Lee, died of a disease of the kidney. His psychological condition made him hesitant to join the race. Loyalty to the Republican Party was the only reason he decided to run. Roosevelt believed he had, at best, a slim chance of victory. He confessed to a friend, "The best I could hope for is a decent run." He was running against the Tammany Hall–backed candidate Abram Hewitt, and Henry George, an independent. In the final tally, his assessment proved right. Hewitt won.

In May of 1889, four years after his failed race for mayor, Roosevelt was appointed as one of three commissioners of the Federal Civil Service Commission. Here, he made recommendations to the president about reforms and named candidates he thought suitable for certain positions. It was significantly beneath his potential, but he took it on with vigor and enthusiasm.

In 1895, after serving for six years as the Civil Service Commissioner, TR was made police commissioner. He accepted this role with the same mind-set and demeanor as he did his previous appointments and challenges. During his tenure, he was intolerant of corruption in any form, explicit or implicit. That fortified his reputation and advanced his brand of being a reformer. It became his ideological persona for the duration of his political life and beyond. He served in this role until March of 1897.

He was appointed as assistant to the Secretary of the Navy in April 1897. It's the same position that his fifth cousin came to occupy two decades later. Roosevelt embraced the opportunity to be the Assistant Secretary to the Navy and set about, as he had done before, to apply his intellect and values to the job. He impressed everyone up and down the chain of command. He fervently advocated the construction of a dozen new warships, warning President McKinley of the Japanese intrusion of Hawaiian waters. He didn't stop there, though, going on to outline the various options available to him. This thoroughly impressed President McKinley. TR also advocated that the president send the U.S. fleet into the Mediterranean and told McKinley that he would resign his office and volunteer to fight if America went to war with Spain, which FDR also said.

Roosevelt had consistently advocated conflict with Spain. That conflict boiled to reality on February 15, 1898, when an explosion rocked an American battleship docked in Havana Harbor. The incident killed more than 250 crewmen. Roosevelt had been one of only a few who had advocated conflict with Spain until that incident. In the wake of the explosion, however, the tide had turned. A majority now insisted on retribution.

As Assistant Secretary of the Navy, Roosevelt had been instrumental in preparing the U.S. naval fleet. He had honed the fleet and made sure they were ready for battle. He told Dr. Leonard Wood, a good friend, "I have accomplished everything I can to get our Navy ready." After the Havana Harbor incident, McKinley petitioned Congress for a declaration of war. Congress immediately voted and passed the measure necessary to declare war with Spain. Roosevelt now had his war.

There wasn't any doubt in Roosevelt's mind that he would actively participate in the coming war. By this point, he was pushing forty years in age, yet he had never had any significant military training. This would not, however, stop him from becoming a soldier. His only worry was that the fighting might end before he could become part of it. If he didn't make it to Cuba, he planned to get to some other theater of conflict.

Roosevelt was as giddy as a school kid with his first army figurine set. He was fond of his all-volunteer Rough Rider regiment. It suited his personality since the soldiers came from diverse backgrounds. The First U.S. Volunteer Cavalry was composed of graduates of Ivy League institutions, Native Americans, cowboys, entrepreneurs, and children of Civil War veterans. The soldiers of Rough Riders began training in San Antonio, Texas. They were then sent to Tampa, where, after a strenuous trip, they got under way by ship. Roosevelt quickly realized there was confusion in everything from scheduling to logistics of the intended attack. There was even terrible incompetence in choosing camp locations and even a lack of food and medical supplies.

When the Rough Riders were being deployed, they got word that the Spanish were lying in wait in the waters off Florida, hindering the departure of the troops. It turned out to be a rumor with no basis. The fleet of about fifty ships then got under way, heading for Cuba. The landing in Cuba was fraught with immense challenges. The soldiers tried hard to get from the landing vessels to the beach, and there were casualties during the disembarkation process. Men, horses, and mules drowned in the melee. Roosevelt finally had his chance to shine. He charged up Kettle Hill on Little Texas, his horse, as his men followed close on foot. As the got to the summit, Roosevelt crashed into a wire fence.

He didn't panic or worry. Instead, he dismounted from his injured horse and joined his troops on foot, walking to the summit. The Spanish troops retreated from their position when they realized they were in harm's way and at a severe disadvantage. Roosevelt then switched his focus. He turned to San Juan Hill. He and his men teamed with other units that were on their way up. Once again, the Spanish realized their diminishing position and retreated. For his valor, courage under fire, and nerves of steel, Roosevelt's commanding officer, General Wheeler, proposed he be promoted to the rank of colonel and receive the Medal of Honor.

Roosevelt didn't shy away from this. "I think I've earned my higher rank and medal of honor." He eventually received his promotion to colonel but not his Medal of Honor. That came much later, posthumously in 1999. According to Roosevelt, "San Juan was the great day of my life."

When he returned from Cuba, Roosevelt realigned his focus and looked for an opportunity to reignite his career. It happened that New York's state politics was in disarray, and there was contention between the party bosses and the current governor of the state. There were allegations of impropriety in the governor's administration. To be able to win the election again, they had to be able to put up a candidate who had a flawless reputation and was strong in morals. The party bosses turned to Roosevelt. Not only was he a man with a stellar reputation, but he was also now a man with heroic military experience.

The smell of fresh battleground mud was still on him when his name was thrown into the ring. One of the New York Republican bosses who liked what he saw in Roosevelt and felt that he could get him elected just wanted to make sure that Roosevelt would be someone he could control. He didn't want an idealistic sort of person who would try to change Albany. His advisors, however, noted that he had no other alternative. The two men, Roosevelt and Platt, met and Roosevelt indeed made an impression on the latter, who promised that the party would back his nomination if he so desired. He agreed and soon after he left the meeting Roosevelt was already making plans for his candidacy. He charged up Albany just as he did San Juan Hill. Roosevelt leaned on his military record and battle experience as his election strategy. He even had past brothers in arms show up on the campaign trail to boost this persona.

Roosevelt had his own set of enemies. To them, he was an American imperialist. All this was thrashed out during the campaign. As with all campaigns for high office, mud is slung from all sides. As untrue as it was, he was even labeled corrupt. The outcome was welcomed but nothing to shout about. Roosevelt won with a razor-thin margin—less than twenty-thousand votes. More than a million ballots had been cast in the race for governor that year. It turned out that Roosevelt knew how to play the game of state politics. He gave Platt sufficient comfort that he would not sideline or cross him in any way. The memory of what happened to Joe's candidate all those years ago was obviously still at the back of his mind. He made sure to consult Platt on appointments and worked with him whenever convenient.

It was still early in his administration when Roosevelt wholeheartedly endorsed a franchise tax bill. This meant that the state would levy taxes on state-owned companies operating railroad and streetcar businesses.

Boss Platt was unhappy with Roosevelt's support of this bill, but in his deft maneuvering, Roosevelt pointed out that the passage of the bill would demonstrate the Republican Party's focus on caring for the people. It sounded fine, but, in essence, Roosevelt was just making excuses. Platt understood clearly the footwork at play. Roosevelt showed true brinkmanship handling Platt who could not counter the governor in a meaningful way.

There was indeed no doubt that Roosevelt was a reformer. Aside from the Franchise Bill, he was also instrumental in restructuring state and local civil service; improving the state canal operation; improving jobs for workers; extending the state conservation program; reforming state education, election law, and a ban on transport schemes; and regulating corporations. Roosevelt worked hard to disassociate himself from the political machinery to become governor for all individuals of the state.

As governor, Roosevelt's true intentions were becoming clear. The fog that once shrouded his intentions was lifting. With each legislation that he championed; his true self emerged. At the same time, he was evolving, and his heart grew increasingly steadfast. For those who thought he was socialist, which he was in certain ways, he began to seem like a capitalist. To those who thought he was capitalist, he began to look like a nationalist, and those who thought he was nationalist, he began to seem socialist. He started to make enemies on both sides of the aisle because he was not playing the usual games everyone was used to.

In 1899, he delivered a speech that laid his heart on his sleeve, outlining what he thought was important. The elements of nationalism, socialism, democracy, and capitalism were all rolled into one. For those who only see Roosevelt through monochromatic lenses, this should be an eye-opener.

"In speaking to you, men of the greatest city of the West, men of the State which gave to the country Lincoln and Grant, men who preeminently and distinctly embody all that is most American in the American character, I wish to preach, not the doctrine of ignoble ease, but the doctrine of the strenuous life, the life of toil and effort, of labor and strife; to preach that highest form of success which comes, not to the man who desires mere easy peace, but to the man who does not shrink from danger, from hardship, or from bitter toil, and who out of these wins the splendid ultimate triumph.

A life of slothful ease, a life of that peace which springs merely from lack either of desire or of power to strive after great things, is as little worthy of a nation as of an individual. I ask only that what every self-respecting American demands from himself and from his sons shall be demanded of the American nation as a whole. Who among you would teach your boys that ease, that peace, is to be the first consideration in their eyes-to be the ultimate goal after which they strive?"

Roosevelt was not one to mince words. Every faculty of his consciousness endeavored to speak the truth. He saw all things through the lens of utility and honesty. If there was no need to say something, he remained silent. If there was something to be said, it had to be the truth.

On top of this, he had to mesh his character with the typical politician's skill of speaking with duplicitous intent. Instead of being upset with him, however, the majority of constituents found his honesty refreshing on one hand and inarguable on the other. When one has the truth on one's side, it is hard to argue it.

"You men of Chicago have made this city great, you men of Illinois have done your share, and more than your share, in making America great, because you neither preach nor practice such a doctrine. You work yourselves, and you bring up your sons to work. If you are rich and worth your salt, you will teach your sons that though they may have leisure, it is not to be spent in idleness; for wisely used leisure merely means that those who possess it, being free from the necessity of working for their livelihood, are all bound to carry on some kind of non-remunerative work in science, in letters, in art, in exploration, in historical research-work of this type we most need in this country, the successful carrying out of which reflects most honor upon the nation. We do not admire the man of timid peace. We admire the man who embodies victorious effort; the man who never wrongs his neighbor, who is prompt to help a friend, but who has those virile qualities necessary to win in the stern strife of actual life."

The problem with Roosevelt was not that he pontificated the virtues that were difficult to adhere to. The problem was that he did not grow up under the same pressures and same deficiencies that the audience labored under. To his credit, he saw people as the masters in a democracy. To his wisdom, he tried to shine a light on practices that would elevate the people he spoke to. He was right to do so, but he was wrong to expect that it would make much difference. Man cannot be altered by words alone and certainly not through the words contained in a speech in the course of an evening. This was not the debate stage in Harvard. This was the real world.

While many of his speeches were lost on the people he spoke to, every ounce of the essence they contained is valuable to us one century later.

"It is hard to fail, but it is worse to never have tried to succeed. In this life we get nothing save by effort. Freedom from effort in the present merely means that there has been some stored-up effort in the past. A man can be freed from the necessity of work only by the fact that he or his fathers before him have worked to good purpose. If the freedom thus purchased is used aright, and the man still does actual work, though of a different kind, whether as a writer or as a general, whether in the field of politics or in the field of exploration and adventure, he shows he deserves his good fortune. But if he treats this period of freedom from the need of actual labor as a period, not of preparation, but of mere enjoyment, even though perhaps not of the vicious enjoyment, he shows that he is simply a cumberer of the earth's surface, and he surely unfits himself to hold his own with his fellows if the need to do so should again arise. A mere life of ease is not in the end a very satisfactory life, and, above all, it is a life which ultimately unfits those who follow it for serious work in the world."

Roosevelt was more a philosopher than a politician. To be in a position where he could make a difference, he had to play the game—the politician's Potomac two-step. He knew that to move the progressive agenda he envisioned he had to be able to give in to some of the ways things were done. In the end, however, he was responsible for some of the most profound changes the country had ever seen.

In this speech in Chicago, he strikes a familiar tone. He rests the burden of the state's health on the shoulders of her citizens. He is almost telling a parent how to raise their children. He is not being arrogant. He is actually trying to be helpful. Of course, it falls on deaf ears.

"In the last analysis a healthy state can exist only when the men and women who make it up can lead clean, vigorous, healthy lives; when the children are so trained that they shall endeavor, not to shirk difficulties, but to overcome them; not to seek ease, but to know how to rest triumph from toil and risk. The man must be glad to do a man's work, to dare and endure and to labor; to keep himself, and those dependent on him. The woman must be the housewife, the help-meet of the homemaker, the wise and fearless mother of many healthy children. In one of Daudet's powerful and melancholy books he speaks of 'the fear of maternity, the haunting terror of the young wife of the present day.' When such words can be truthfully written of a nation, that nation is rotten to the heart's core. When men fear work or fear of righteous war, when women fear motherhood, they tremble on the brink of doom; and well it is they should vanish from the earth, where they are fit subjects for the scorn of all men and women who are themselves strong and brave and high-minded."

His speech contains a hint of classical reference, specifically, the words of Plutarch. It may have been intentional, but it was most likely autonomous. It is worth remembering that Roosevelt was well read. He devoured books at the rate of up to three each day. During that time, much of his reading included classical texts on Greek and Roman philosophy. That comes through in his speeches, which is why it is an excellent resource in understanding the man and the president.

"As it is with the individual, so it is with the nation. It is a base untruth to say that happy is the nation that has no history. Thrice happy is the nation that has a glorious history. Far better it is to dare mighty things, to win glorious triumphs, even though checkered by failure, than to take rank with those poor spirits who neither enjoy much nor suffer much, because they live in the gray twilight that knows not victory nor defeat. If in 1861 the men who loved the Union had believed that peace was the end of all things, and war and strife the worst of all things, and had acted upon their belief, we would have saved hundreds of thousands of lives, we would have saved hundreds of millions of dollars. Moreover, besides saving all the blood and treasure we then lavished, we would have prevented the heartbreak of many women, the dissolution of many homes, and we would have spared the country those months of doom and shame when it seemed as if our armies marched only to defeat. We could have avoided all this suffering simply by shrinking from strife. And if we had thus avoided it, we would have shown that we were weaklings, and that we were unfit to stand among the great nations of the earth. Thank God for the iron in the blood of our fathers, the men who upheld the wisdom of Lincoln, and bore the sword or rifle in the armies of Grant! Let us, the children of the men who proved themselves equal to the mighty days, let us, the children of the men who carried the great Civil War to a triumphant conclusion, praise the God of our fathers that the ignoble counsels of peace were rejected; that the suffering and loss, the blackness of sorrow and despair, were unflinchingly faced, and the years of strife endured; for in the end the slave was freed, the Union restored, and the mighty American republic placed once more as a helmeted queen among nations.

We of this generation do not have to face a task such as that our fathers faced, but we have our tasks, and woe to us if we fail to perform them! We cannot, if we would, play the part of China, and be content to rot by inches in ignoble ease within our borders, taking no interest in what goes on beyond them, sunk in scrambling commercialism; heedless of higher life, the life of aspiration, of toil and risk, busying ourselves only with the wants of our bodies for the day, until suddenly we should find, beyond a shadow of question, what China has already found, that in this world the nation that has trained itself into a career of unwarlike and isolated ease is bound, in the end, to go down before other nations which have not lost the manly and adventurous qualities. If we are to be a really great people, we must strive in good faith to play a great part in the world. We cannot avoid meeting great issues. All that we can determine for ourselves is whether we shall meet them well or ill. In 1898 we could not help being brought face to face with the problem of war with Spain. All we could decide was whether we should shrink like cowards from the contest, or enter into it as beseemed a brave and high-spirited people; and, once in, whether failure or success shall crown our banners. So it is now. We cannot avoid the responsibilities that confront us in Hawaii, Cuba, Porto Rico, and the Philippines. All we can decide is whether we shall meet them in a way that will redound to the national credit, of whether we shall make of our dealings with these new problems a dark and shameful page in our history. To refuse to deal with them at all merely amounts to dealing with them badly. We have a given problem to solve. If we undertake the solution, there is, of course, always danger that we may not solve it aright; but to refuse to undertake the solution simply renders it certain that we cannot possibly solve it aright. The timid man, the lazy man, the man who distrusts his country, the over-civilized man, who has lost the great fighting, the masterful values, the ignorant man, and the man of dull mind, whose soul is incapable of feeling the mighty lift that thrills 'stern men with empires in their brains'—all these, of course, shrink from seeing the nation undertake its new duties; shrink from seeing us build a navy and an army adequate to our needs; shrink from seeing us do our share of the world's work, by bringing order out of the chaos in the great, fair tropic islands from which the valor of our soldiers and sailors has driven the Spanish flag. These are the men who fear the strenuous life, who fear the only national life which is really worth leading. They believe in that cloistered life which saps the hearty virtues in a nation, as it saps them in the individual; or else they are wedded to that base spirit of grain and greed which recognizes commercialism the be-all and end-all of national life, instead of realizing that, though an indispensable element, it is, after all, but one of the many elements that go to make up true national greatness. No country can long endure if its foundations are not laid deep in the material prosperity which comes from thrift, from business energy and enterprise, from hard, unsparing efforts in the fields of industrial activity; but neither was any nation ever yet truly great if it relied upon material prosperity alone. All honor must be paid to the architects of our material prosperity, to the great captains of industry who have built our factories and our railroads, to the strong men who toil for wealth with brain or hand; for great is the debt of the nation to these and their kind. But our debt is yet greater to the men whose highest type is to be found in a statesman like Lincoln, a soldier like Grant. They showed by their lives that they recognized the law of work, the law of strife; they toiled to win a competence for themselves and those dependent upon them; but they recognized that there were yet other and even loftier duties—duties to the nation and duties to the race.

We cannot sit huddled within our own borders and avow ourselves merely an assemblage of well-to-do hucksters who care nothing for what happens beyond. Such a policy would defeat even its own end; for as the nation grows to have ever wider and wider interests, and are brought into closer and closer contact, if we are to hold our own in the struggle for naval and commercial supremacy, we must build up our power without our own borders. We must build the isthmian canal, and we must grasp the points of vantage which will enable us to have our say in deciding the destiny of the oceans of the East and the West So much for the commercial side. From the standpoint of international honor, the argument is even stronger. The guns that thundered off Manila and Santiago left us echoes of glory, but they also left us a legacy of duty. If we drove out a medieval tyranny only to make room for savage anarchy, we had better not begun the task at all. It is worse than idle to say that we have no duty to perform, and can leave to their fates the islands we have conquered. Such a course would be a course of infamy. It would be followed at once by utter chaos in the wretched islands themselves. Some stronger, manlier power would have to step in and do the work, and we would have shown ourselves weaklings, unable to carry to successful completion the labors that great and high-spirited nations are eager to undertake.

The work must be done; we cannot escape our responsibility; and if we are worth our salt, we shall be glad of the chance to do the work—glad of the chance to show ourselves equal to one of the great tasks set modern civilization. But let us not deceive ourselves as to the importance of the task. Let us not be misled by the vainglory into underestimating the strain it will put on our powers. Above all, let us, as we value our own self-respect, face the responsibilities with proper seriousness, courage and high resolve. We must demand the highest order of integrity and ability in our public men who are to grapple with these new problems. We must hold to a rigid accountability those public servants who show unfaithfulness to the interests of the nation or the inability to rise to the high level of the new demands upon our strength and our resources.

Of course, we must remember not to judge any public servant by any one act, and especially should we beware of attacking the men who are merely the occasions and not the causes of disaster. Let me illustrate what I mean by the army and the navy. If twenty years ago we had gone to war, we should have the navy as absolutely unprepared as the army. At that time our ships could not have encountered with success the fleets of Spain any more than nowadays we can put untrained soldiers, no matter how brave, who are armed with archaic black-powder weapons, against well-drilled regulars armed with the highest type of modern repeating rifle. But in the early eighties the attention of the nation became directed to our naval deeds. Congress most wisely made a series of appropriations to build up a new navy, and under a succession of able and patriotic secretaries, of both political parties, the navy was gradually built up, until its material became equal to its splendid personnel, with the result that in the summer of 1898 it leaped to its proper place as one of the most brilliant and formidable fighting navies in the entire world. We rightly pay all honor to the men controlling the navy at the time it won these great deeds, honor to Secretary Long and Admiral Dewey, to the captains who handled the ships in action, to the daring lieutenants who braved death in the smaller craft, and to the heads of the bureaus at Washington who saw that the ships were so commanded, so armed, so equipped, so well engined, as to insure the best results. But let us also keep ever in mind that all of this would not have availed if it had not been for the wisdom of the men who during the preceding fifteen years had built up the navy. Keep in mind the secretaries of the navy during those years; keep in mind the senators and congressmen who by their votes gave the money necessary to build and to armor the ships, to construct the great guns, and to train the crews; remember also those who actually did build the ships, the armor, and the guns; and remember the admirals and captains who handled battleship, cruiser, and torpedo-boat on the high seas, alone and in squadrons, developing the seamanship, the gunnery, and the power of acting together, which their successors utilized so gloriously at Manila and off Santiago. And, gentleman, remember the converse, too. Remember that justice has two sides. Be just to those who built up the navy, and, for the sake of the future of the country, keep in mind those who opposed its building up. Read the 'Congressional Record.' Find out the senators and congressmen who opposed the grants for building the new ships; who opposed the purchase of armor, without which the ships were worthless; who opposed any adequate maintenance for the Navy Department, and strove to cut down the number of men necessary to man our fleets. The men who did these things were one and all working to bring disaster on the country. They have no share in the glory of Manila, in the honor of Santiago. They have no cause to feel proud of the valor of our sea-captains, of the renown of our flag. Their motives may or may not have been good, but their acts were heavily fraught with evil. They did ill for the national honor, and we won in spite of their sinister opposition.

Now, apply all this to our public men of to-day. Our army never has been built up as it should be built up. I shall not discuss with an audience this puerile suggestion that a nation of seventy million freemen is in danger of losing its liberties from the existence of an army of one hundred thousand men, three fourths of whom will be employed in foreign islands, in certain coast fortresses, and on Indian reservations. No man of good sense and stout heart can such a proposition seriously. If we are such weaklings as the proposition implies, then we are unworthy of freedom in any event. To no body of men in the United States is the country so much indebted as to the splendid officers and enlisted men of the regular army and navy. There is no body from which the country has less to fear, and none of which it should be prouder, none which it should be more anxious to up-build.

Our army needs complete reorganization, —not merely enlarging, —and the reorganization can only come as a result of legislation. A proper general staff should be established, and the positions of ordnance, commissary, and quartermaster officers should be filled by detail from the line. Above all, the army must be given the chance to exercise in large bodies. Never again should we see, as we saw in the Spanish war, major-generals in command of divisions who had never before commanded three companies together in the field. Yet, incredible to relate, Congress has shown a queer inability to learn some of the lessons of war. There were large bodies of men in both branches who opposed the declaration of war, who opposed the ratification of peace, who opposed the up-building of the army, and who even opposed the purchase of the armor at a reasonable price for the battle-ships and cruisers, thereby putting an absolute stop to the building of any new fighting ships for the navy. If, during the years to come, any disaster should befall our arms, afloat or ashore, and thereby should shame the United States, remember the blame will lie upon the men whose names appear on the roll-calls of Congress on the wrong side of these great questions. On them will lie the burden of the loss of our soldiers and sailors, of any dishonor to the flag; and upon you and the people of this country will lie the blame if you do not repudiate, in no unmistakable way, what these men have done. The blame will not rest upon the untrained commander of the untried troops, upon the civil officers of a department the organization of which has been left utterly inadequate, or upon the admiral with an insufficient number of ships; but upon the public men who have so lamentably failed in forethought as to refuse to remedy these evils long in advance, and upon the nation that stands behind those public men.

So, at the present hour, no small share of the responsibility for the bloodshed in the Philippines, the blood of our brothers, and the blood of their wild and ignorant foes, lies at the thresholds of those who so long delayed the adoption of the treaty of peace, and of those who by their worse than foolish words deliberately invited a savage people to plunge into a war fraught with sure disaster for them—a war, too, in which our own brave men who follow the flag must pay with their blood for the silly, mock humanitarianism of the prattlers who sit at home in peace.

The army and the navy are the sword and the shield which this nation must carry if she is to do her duty among the nations of the earth—if she is not to stand merely as the China of the western hemisphere. Our proper conduct towards the tropic islands we have wrested from Spain is merely the form of which our duty has taken at the moment. Of course, we are bound to handle the affairs of our own household well. We must see that there is civic honesty, civic cleanliness, civic good sense in our home administration of the city, State, and nation. We must strive for honesty in office, for honesty towards the creditors of the nation and of the individual; for the widest freedom of the individual initiative where possible, and for the wisest control of individual initiative where it is hostile to the welfare of the many. But because we set our own household in order, we are not thereby excused from playing our part in the great affairs of the world. A man's first duty is to his own home, but he is not thereby excused from doing his duty to the State; for if he fails in this second duty it is under the penalty of ceasing to be a free-man. In the same way, while a nations first duty in within its own borders, it is not thereby absolved from facing its duties in the world as a whole; and if it refuses to do so, it merely forfeits its right to struggle for a place among the peoples that shape the destiny of mankind.

In the West Indies and the Philippines alike was are confronted by most difficult problems. It is cowardly to shrink from solving them in the proper way; for solved they must be, if not by us, then by some stronger and more manful race. If we are too weak, too selfish, or too foolish to solve them, some bolder and abler people must undertake the solution. Personally, I am far too firm a believer in the greatness of my country and the power of my countrymen to admit for one moment that we shall ever be driven to the ignoble alternative.

The problems are different for the different islands. Porto Rico is not large enough to stand alone. We must govern it wisely and well, primarily in the interest of its own people. Cuba is, in my judgment, entitled ultimately to settle for itself whether it shall be an independent state or an integral portion of the mightiest of republics. But until order and stable liberty are secured, we must remain in the island to insure them, and infinite tact, judgment, moderation, and courage must be shown by our military and civil representatives in keeping the island pacified, in relentlessly stamping out brigandage, in protecting all alike, and yet in showing proper recognition to the men who have fought for Cuban liberty. The Philippines offer a yet graver problem. Their population includes half-caste and native Christians, warlike Muslims, and wild pagans. Many of their people are utterly unfit for self-government and show no signs of becoming fit. Others may in time become fit but at the present can only take part in self-government under a wise supervision, at once firm and beneficent. We have driven Spanish tyranny from the islands. If we now let it be replaced by savage anarchy, our work has been for harm and not for good. I have scant patience with those who fear to undertake the task of governing the Philippines, and who openly avow that they do fear to undertake it, or that they shrink from it because of the expense and trouble; but I have even scanter patience with those who make a pretense of humanitarianism to hide and cover their timidity, and who can't about 'liberty' and the 'consent of the governed,' in order to excuse themselves for their unwillingness to play the part of men. Their doctrines, if carried out, would make it incumbent upon us to leave the Apaches of Arizona to work out their own salvation, and to decline to interfere in a single Indian reservation. Their doctrines condemn your forefathers and mine for ever having settled in these United States.

England's rule in India and Egypt has been of great benefit to England, for it has trained up generations of men accustomed to look at the larger and loftier side of public life. It has been of even greater benefit to India and Egypt. And finally, and most of all, it has advanced the cause of civilization. So, if we do our duty aright in the Philippines, we will add to that national renown which is the highest and finest part of national life, will greatly benefit the people of the Philippine Islands, and, above all, we will play our part well in the great work of uplifting mankind. But to do this work, keep ever in mind that we must show in a very high degree the qualities of courage, of honesty, and of good judgment. Resistance must be stamped out. The first and all-important work to be done is to establish the supremacy of our flag. We must put down armed resistance before we can accomplish anything else, and there should be no parleying, no faltering, in dealing with our foe. As for those in our own country who encourage the foe, we can afford contemptuously to disregard them; but it must be remembered that their utterances are not saved from being treasonable merely by the fact that they are despicable.

When once we have put down armed resistance, when once our rule is acknowledged, then an even more difficult task will begin, for then we must see to it that the islands are administered with absolute honesty and with good judgment. If we let the public service of the islands be turned into prey of the spoils of politician, we shall have begun to tread the path which Spain trod to her own destruction. We must send out there only good and able men, chosen for their fitness, and not because of their partisan service, and these men must not only administer impartial justice to the natives and serve their own government with honesty and fidelity, but show the utmost tact and firmness, remembering that, with such people as those with whom we are to deal, weakness is the greatest of crimes, and next to weakness comes lack of consideration for their principles and prejudices.

I preach to you, then, my countrymen, that our country calls not for the life of ease but for the life of strenuous endeavor. The twentieth century looms before us big with the fate of many nations. If we stand idly by, if we seek merely swollen, slothful ease and ignoble peace, if we shrink from the hard contests where men must win at the hazard of their lives and at the risk of all they hold dear, then the bolder and stronger peoples will pass us by, and will win for themselves the domination of the world. Let us therefore boldly face the life of strife, resolute to do our duty well and manfully; resolute to be both honest and brave, to serve high ideals, yet to use practical methods. Above all, let us shrink from no strife, through hard and dangerous endeavor, that we shall ultimately win the goal of true national greatness."

His speech projected the confidence of a man who had faith in his fellow citizens. It was a faith in people regardless of their station in life. Roosevelt was projecting imagery that extolled individual effort. He effectively rallied the people toward the key to prosperity and happiness—tenets of the American dream. He made the case that improved lives lead to a stronger country. It was, in his opinion, an essential ingredient to making America great.

He went on to argue that because life in America was difficult people, regardless of gender, could find purpose if they put in the effort and not capitulate to laziness, anger, or resentment. It was one of the speeches that put him on the map and opened the imagination of the working class toward a political outsider.

The irony of American politics is that the electorate is always in search of the outsider to do the inside man's job. Then, as now, people have come to despise the insider and give the outsider the benefit of the doubt.

When it came time for the Roosevelt's reelection, Platt was not in favor of it. He had already seen the way Roosevelt did things. Against Platt's wishes in 1900, the politically savvy Roosevelt announced his intention to run for a second term as governor. In a game of chess, he declared to Platt that he was not interested in the party's nomination as vice president. That was just strategic positioning by Roosevelt. He had already made up his mind that he would take the VP nomination if Platt did not support his run for governor. He really had little choice. If he didn't get the nomination for governor and turned down the nomination for VP, he would be forgotten among the electorate.

In 1900, William McKinley was reelected and began his second term in March of 1901. Big business felt safe with him in the White House. McKinley's Vice President, Garret Hobart, had died in office, and there was a vacancy to be filled. "Boss" Platt saw an opportunity to rip Roosevelt from Albany and replace him with someone more pliable. At the same time, putting him on the VP ticket before the election was the perfect solution.

If McKinley lost the election, then Roosevelt could fade into the background forever. If McKinley won, then Roosevelt would be in a dead desk job where he would not be any trouble.

Even though Roosevelt understood that the vice presidency was one that was financially inferior, he also feared it to be intellectually and politically inferior as well. It was, in his words, a "do-nothing, dead-end job." It was not all easy sailing either. Republican Senator Mark Hanna from Ohio did everything he could to prevent Roosevelt from being nominated at the convention in Philadelphia that year but ultimately failed.

The delegates in Philadelphia could not recognize Hanna's foresight—the reason behind his anger and insistence in opposing Roosevelt's selection as the nominee for vice president. His reasoning was simply "that there's only one life between that madman and the presidency." Everyone, including McKinley, wanted Roosevelt on the ticket so that he could sit back in Ohio and let the young and vibrant Roosevelt hit the campaign trail. He preferred that Roosevelt take on Williams Jennings Bryant, who was someone everyone viewed as a Socialist.

On the other side of the equation, Platt wanted to get rid of Roosevelt. They all realized that the best place to put him where he could do the least damage was in the vice president's office.

Roosevelt concentrated his campaign in the West. He focused on entry into the Philippines, which was a hot topic at the time. He also set his sights on monopolies that were forming and the new strategy of forming corporate trusts as well as the state of the economy for the working class. It was a Populist campaign on Roosevelt's part. He did not care about Bryan in the least. In fact, some of their views were the same. Roosevelt had done so well that the election results were better than even McKinley's own campaigning during his first run for president. As a slight to McKinley, Roosevelt gave credit for the win to himself and Bryan.

As vice president, Roosevelt started to believe that he could do the job better than McKinley and even said so to his close associate several times. During McKinley's term, unemployment and poverty were through the roof. The robber barons were making their wealth, but the poor were losing their jobs. The effects of mechanization were beginning to take their toll. The frustration among the populace was so high that Leon Czolgosz, an out-of-work laborer, got in front of him and at point-blank distance assassinated him. President McKinley was at the Pan-American Exhibition in Buffalo when Czolgosz shot him twice. Leon Czolgosz was executed on October 29, 1901, approximately forty-six days after he shot William McKinley and approximately thirty-eight days after McKinley passed away on September 14, 1901.

With McKinley gone, Theodore Roosevelt became the twenty-sixth president of the United States. Aside from McKinley, there were several casualties from those two bullets. Among them was Junius Pierpont Morgan. As soon as Roosevelt set foot in the White House, he began enforcing the Sherman Act and going after the large trusts, the brainchild of JP Morgan.

By the end of February 1902, Roosevelt's Justice Department filed a lawsuit against the Northern Securities Company. It was going after JP Morgan's corporation under orders from President Theodore Roosevelt. They were attacking the company based on violating the Sherman Antitrust Act, which had been created twelve years earlier in 1890. The case, known as Northern Securities Co. v. The United States, 193, US 197, was one of the first antitrust cases to have ever taken place. Over the next seven years, other trusts would fall victim to antitrust policies. U.S. government cases against trusts would cause their dismantling. One such case was when the railroad empire of Edward Henry Harriman, which included both the Southern Pacific and the Union Pacific Railroad, was broken.

Pierpont was incensed over the matter of the Northern Securities Company. He did not like politicians or anyone for that matter to tell him how to run his business. Unfortunately for Pierpont, however, the government won. In 1904, the Northern Securities Company was dissolved, and the three railroads that had merged to form the company were on their own again.

Senator Hanna's premonition had come to pass. President Theodore Roosevelt had taken a wrecking ball to the status quo, and no one could do anything about it. They placed him in the most innocuous position in all of Washington, but fate had other plans.

Chapter 6 - Cowboys

It's hard to imagine a New Yorker in a 3-piece suit and spectacles standing in the middle of the Badlands out West. Even the locals back then had a problem with it when he first arrived. His eyeglasses, among other things, made him conspicuous and untrustworthy at first.

After leaving the responsibilities of his first elected office, Teddy needed to be one again with nature. He was, after all, someone who found peace and comfort in the outdoors. He traveled across the country from New York to the Dakota Territory and on to Little Missouri by the Pacific Railroad. He liked the way the land rolled and the air cleared his chest. He felt at home in the Far West. It was the fall of 1883 when he arrived in the single-shack station that stood together with an equally run-down hotel across from it in the middle of nowhere.

It was approaching the turn of the twentieth century, and the Wild West was not so wild any more. The East, demarcated by the Mississippi River, was industrializing rapidly. The West, however silent, was not the once-virgin, beast-filled land that it had been for millennia. Large swaths of land were carved into ranches and now belonged to frontiersmen and their hands. Here, far from the smog and din of industrialization, is where Roosevelt laid down his hat and purchased two farms, Chimney Butte and the Elkhorn.

The first ranch, Chimney Butte, was purchased from the Ferris brothers and Bill Merrifield. They also went on to look after the ranch in Roosevelt's absence once he returned to the East Coast. The land he purchased consisted of land and a shack with a chicken coop and a stable. The men became friends fairly easily and rather quickly.

After a short interval from the time he arrived, the transaction to purchase the land was concluded. The men went on to collaborate on an additional venture to form a cattle ranch. This started a new phase of Roosevelt's life as a cowboy.

Life in the wide-open spaces changes the way a man looks at life and the things that matter the most. It is the polar opposite of being stuck in cramped streets of bustling cities. It is the land of saddle and rifle, where freedom takes on an added depth of meaning.

Even the nature of what is considered work is different here. It involved treading on grass and working with hands under a bright sun of the summer months. Wrangling cattle was the hallmark of the cowboy, and it had so fascinated Roosevelt that he wanted to try his hand at it. It was the convergence of two of his many sides—nature and the desire to challenge himself.

Recall that by this point Roosevelt was already an able horseman. He had broken his arm on a hunt sometime earlier in his life, but the incident never deterred him. Hunting in New England and working with cattle in the Badlands are two very different things. Both are challenging in their own way, but being out in the open herding cattle requires rough hands and stamina. Days were sweltering in the summer when the herd went out, and nights in the fall were freezing when the herd was brought back. The environment stretched and tested Roosevelt, who was willing to push the limits of his once frail constitution.

This was still the days of free grazing and ranch owners, and their hands would roam the vast plains and hillsides tending to the cattle before leading them home. As much as he found it a challenge to get among the locals, he was rapidly accepted and became part of the wranglers, who eventually worked for him. He was one of those men who liked to make friends but would keep to himself if he found the need to.

In contrast to his weak childhood, his exposure to boxing elevated him in many ways. It made him agile on his feet and quick in his mind, which is fairly different from being well read. It also made him a good fighter.

On one occasion when he was out herding cows, he got lost in unfamiliar terrain. The rain was pouring down in sheets, and he made a wrong turn somewhere and was separated from the herd. He found himself in a small town in the middle of nowhere. Teddy didn't want to go in, but it was either inside next to a fire or outside under the pouring rain. He reluctantly chose the former. As he made his way up the stairs, he heard what seemed like gunshots and yelling.

Undeterred and with curiosity piqued, he made his way into the saloon and found it populated with several people at various tables. Everyone but the man causing the commotion was silent. The man with the gun was obviously a bully and possibly inebriated. As soon as Roosevelt made it past the swinging doors, the man caught sight of him and instantly labeled him "four eyes." There is something about half-wits who like to label others' appearance. His name-calling did not perturb Roosevelt, who kept on walking to an empty seat by the warm hearth.

He called out again, "Four eyes!" Each repetition of the name-calling came with a louder and more agitated voice. It bothered him that this out-of-towner (obvious due to the glasses) was not paying any attention to his boisterous activity.

The man walked up to where Roosevelt was sitting and stood over him with obvious glee at an apparent battle advantage. Roosevelt continued to stay silent and just focused on getting warm. The man kept going on and on and waving his pistol. No one in the saloon dared say anything or intervene in any way. Roosevelt studied the situation and didn't do anything until he calculated that things had gone far enough and long enough. Instead of saying a word, he shot to his feet punched the man in his jaw with a left hook, followed in quick succession by a right jab, and then a third direct punch above the lip, below the nose. He stopped at three shots—all of which came at such lightning speed that no one in the saloon, much less the drunk, saw it coming. In a flash, the man was down and out.

It took only a short time for Roosevelt's reputation to spread across the arid Badlands and the lush valleys close by. From ranch hand to cook, from sheriff to mayor, everyone came to know him. When the time came for him to run for president, the town, country, and state went for him overwhelmingly.

During his time out West, aside from tending to his ranch, Roosevelt spent time hunting. He started small, with geese, ducks, deer, mountain sheep, elk, and grizzly bear. It was still plausible to encounter buffalo but only rarely. Most of the large herds had long since disappeared. One would find the prairies littered with buffalo carcasses, but there were no live buffalo as far as the eyes could see. He had trouble finding buffalo, but finding grizzly bears was a cinch.

In time, Roosevelt advanced his hunting. Not only did he travel farther, but he also learned to track larger game. He switched to hunting lions, elephants, rhinoceros, and even African lions. In his time in Idaho, he experienced a couple of harrowing encounters. Once, in Africa, he barely escaped an injured elephant. His closest shave with mortality, however, happened when he came upon a grizzly with the tenacity to match Roosevelt's. It happened on his second trip out West. His guide, who was intoxicated, could not accompany Roosevelt on the hunt, leaving Roosevelt alone in the wild.

Peering into a ravine from a rocky ridge above, Roosevelt found his furry nemesis. It was huddled as a dark object in the thick underbrush. Roosevelt took a moment to focus and then cocked his rifle and took aim. The bear had no hint of the events that were about to unfold. Roosevelt's first shot penetrated his target with deadly accuracy. To his surprise, instead of falling over, the bear lunged deeper into the thicket and out of sight. Roosevelt hurried down to the heavy underbrush where the grizzly disappeared. He could hear the bear grunting. The shot had found its mark but had not killed the stubborn target.

Roosevelt proceeded toward the sound. As he made his way into the shadows, he heard the pounding feet of a charging bear. He knew the bear was on the move and headed toward him. No sooner had that thought crossed his mind than the bear appeared directly in front of Roosevelt, towering above him and lunging forward. Roosevelt fired his second and third shots in rapid succession. Both hit their mark, and he was down to the last of his shells.

It seemed like direct shots and fatal ones at that, but the bear only paused for a split second before returning to his mission of engaging the shooter. In the final second, as the bear leaped toward Roosevelt, Roosevelt fired his last shot and jumped out of the path, both simultaneously. The shot that was aimed for his head struck the bear in his gaping mouth. He staggered and then fell to the ground. Each shot had been fatal but took time to be effective. The bear turned his head toward Roosevelt as geysers of scarlet gushed from several wounds, the worst one now being in his chest. The bear dropped to his side and rolled. The knowledge that he was vanquished finally set in, and he acquiesced. Roosevelt had won the day, as always, but it was close.

There has been some ink spilled in the pursuit of the argument over the Roosevelt's seeming duality. On the one hand, he seems to be someone who loves nature, yet on the other hand he seems to love killing the wild in nature. At first glance, the two are hard to reconcile, but peering into his mind by evidence of his actions, it is plain to see that his brand of hunting fit perfectly with his character as a naturalist.

The path between the two sides of his action is a narrow and thin one, often misunderstood. Just as it was misunderstood when he seemed to support the common folk, yet told them to work for their lot in life. Again, there is no inconsistency.

Roosevelt was able to straddle both sides of the equation because he was able to decipher the meaning of life at a much deeper level where there is no right or wrong at the surface, only intention. Roosevelt understood that man didn't work with nature. Man is a part of nature. He understood that it is not our responsibility to protect it. It is imperative that we do not harm it. Roosevelt's understanding of being part of nature and not harming it allowed him to be in a position where hunting was the test of two wills between man and beast. It was not between predator and prey. The incident between the grizzly and Roosevelt illustrated this perfectly. Both were at risk of mortal injury and had to put their wits against the other.

Chapter 7 - Presidency

Roosevelt's first time in the Oval Office was under McKinley's presidency. Three years later, he ran for and won the election of 1904. He had already been president for three years when he ran for office. It has always been part of American politics that the question of legitimacy seems to hang over the head of a vice president who takes over from a sitting president. That lasts until he wins an election under his own steam. It was true for Ford when he took over from Nixon, Johnson when he took over from Lincoln, and LBJ when he took over from JFK.

However, that wasn't so in Roosevelt's case. Public perception was not as skewed during his ascension because he had gained tremendous exposure during the campaign. Essentially, the lion's share of the campaign that put McKinley in the White House that season was carried out by Roosevelt.

Upon ascending to the presidency soon after McKinley's death, Roosevelt set his sights on the next election. He, too, wanted the presidency to be his own and not under the shadow of his predecessor. Aside from custom and convention, he needed to be able to garner the respect of the Republican members of Congress. After all, the biggest reason why he sat in that office, or had wanted to, was so that he could make just laws. He thought about the reason he left law school—to make good laws. He wanted to legislate equitably and for the betterment of all man, not just a select few. If he was to make this happen, he needed the legislative branch on his side. He also needed their support if he wanted to be nominated during the next election. All roads for Roosevelt led through members of Congress and building a good relationship with them.

With that strategic objective, he set a plan in motion. His first act was to work out an understanding with Senator Aldric of Rhode Island. He wanted to have a free hand in foreign affairs, and so he made a deal with the senator. Roosevelt would put his progressive ideas on the back burner in return for more say in foreign affairs. Aldric believed that to be a fair deal. That set up the friendship between the two men. Aldrich was one of four powerful men in the Republican Party structure, and he wielded tremendous power in the Senate.

Roosevelt stuck to his word but did not hesitate to use the White House as a bully pulpit from which to get his way on several other things, such as using the military in the coal miner's strike and the breakup of Northern Securities. He did this until the year before the election. In 1903, he toned down his progressive rhetoric and toed the party line. He even managed to swing Mark Hanna over to his side. It's a good thing that he managed that relationship well. By 1904, the year of the election, Mark Hanna was Chairman of the Republican National Committee and could have sunk Roosevelt's aspirations. Roosevelt needed the man who had argued against his last candidacy to give his blessing for the presidency. Once he had Hanna's blessing, he had to then take his case to the electorate.

His campaign was not as difficult this time around. He had the loudest megaphone on the planet. He started with strings of press conferences and tours of the country.

He did not hesitate to use the power of the Executive Order and issued one to set up a pension plan for all veterans.

Even though he made great effort to make amends with Senator Hanna, there was still some friction between them. Upon Hanna's sudden passing, whatever hurdles that existed between Roosevelt and the nomination for 1904 evaporated. He received unanimous support on the first ballot of the convention. Roosevelt chose Indiana Senator Charles W. Fairbanks as his running mate.

On the other side, the Democrats picked Alton Parker and Henry Davis to represent them on the ballot.

It was a fierce fight. The Democrats were fairly confident they would win the battle against this progressive "boy" (a reference to Roosevelt's young age and youthful exuberance).

They labeled Roosevelt as "spasmodic, erratic, sensational, spectacular, and arbitrary." All of which were true on the surface. He was indeed all that, but those were just his methods, not his accomplishments. On the accomplishment side of the ledger, he had done and was seen to have done a great deal for the country and its people.

The Democrats were pitching themselves as the more mature voice—the adult in the room. It was apparent in the strategy and optics. The candidate for VP was over eighty—twice the age of Roosevelt.

Roosevelt's strategy to win took a page out of McKinley's book. Roosevelt hung back, looking presidential and put his running mate in the foreground to appear at campaign events. Roosevelt himself moved heaven and earth at the White House and portrayed an image of energy and hard work—the essence of "The Strenuous Life."

That year Roosevelt spent his summer in Oyster Bay, directing and choreographing the Republican strategy. He was such a powerful orator and showman that he raised record-breaking amounts of campaign contributions from such people as Henry Clay Frick (Carnegie's onetime deputy), JP Morgan (his later nemesis), and Edward Harriman (a railroad tycoon). The three men were contributing as much as they could not because they agreed with his politics but because they hoped to put him in their pocket. They had all correctly sensed that he was a threat to their businesses. From public records, it seemed that they contributed more than $2,000,000. Adjusted for inflation, that's equivalent to $60,000,000 today. It doesn't seem that much compared with the gargantuan amounts that are shuffled around to campaigns today, but it was still considerable.

The Democrats were eventually overwhelmed by the sheer force of Roosevelt's personality and deft strategies. They lost the election by almost 200 electoral votes: 336 to 140.

Roosevelt won every Northern state and Missouri. His popularity was undeniable, stemming from his obvious brand of popular politics. The scale of his victory and the enthusiasm he had stirred up was unseen at the time in presidential politics.

On inaugural morning of March 5, 1905, he delivered an inspiring speech that has stood atop a mountain of speeches by other men since.

"My fellow-citizens, no people on earth have more cause to be thankful than ours, and this is said reverently, in no spirit of boastfulness in our own strength, but with gratitude to the Giver of Good who has blessed us with the conditions which have enabled us to achieve so large a measure of well-being and of happiness. To us as a people it has been granted to lay the foundations of our national life in a new continent. We are the heirs of the ages, and yet we have had to pay few of the penalties which in old countries are exacted by the dead hand of a bygone civilization. We have not been obliged to fight for our existence against any alien race; and yet our life has called for the vigor and effort without which the manlier and hardier virtues wither away. Under such conditions it would be our own fault if we failed; and the success which we have had in the past, the success which we confidently believe the future will bring, should cause in us no feeling of vainglory, but rather a deep and abiding realization of all which life has offered us; a full acknowledgment of the responsibility which is ours; and a fixed determination to show that under a free government a mighty people can thrive best, alike as regards the things of the body and the things of the soul.

Much has been given us, and much will rightfully be expected from us. We have duties to others and duties to ourselves; and we can shirk neither. We have become a great nation, forced by the fact of its greatness into relations with the other nations of the earth, and we must behave as beseems a people with such responsibilities. Toward all other nations, large and small, our attitude must be one of cordial and sincere friendship. We must show not only in our words, but in our deeds, that we are earnestly desirous of securing their good will by acting toward them in a spirit of just and generous recognition of all their rights. But justice and generosity in a nation, as in an individual, count most when shown not by the weak but by the strong. While ever careful to refrain from wrongdoing others, we must be no less insistent that we are not wronged ourselves. We wish peace, but we wish the peace of justice, the peace of righteousness. We wish it because we think it is right and not because we are afraid. No weak nation that acts manfully and justly should ever have cause to fear us, and no strong power should ever be able to single us out as a subject for insolent aggression.

Our relations with the other powers of the world are important; but still more important are our relations among ourselves. Such growth in wealth, in population, and in power as this nation has seen during the century and a quarter of its national life is inevitably accompanied by a like growth in the problems which are ever before every nation that rises to greatness. Power invariably means both responsibility and danger. Our forefathers faced certain perils which we have outgrown. We now face other perils, the very existence of which it was impossible that they should foresee. Modern life is both complex and intense, and the tremendous changes wrought by the extraordinary industrial development of the last half century are felt in every fiber of our social and political being. Never before have men tried so vast and formidable an experiment as that of administering the affairs of a continent under the forms of a Democratic republic. The conditions which have told for our marvelous material well-being, which have developed to a very high degree our energy, self-reliance, and individual initiative, have also brought the care and anxiety inseparable from the accumulation of great wealth in industrial centers. Upon the success of our experiment much depends, not only as regards our own welfare, but as regards the welfare of mankind. If we fail, the cause of free self-government throughout the world will rock to its foundations, and therefore our responsibility is heavy, to ourselves, to the world as it is to-day, and to the generations yet unborn. There is no good reason why we should fear the future, but there is every reason why we should face it seriously, neither hiding from ourselves the gravity of the problems before us nor fearing to approach these problems with the unbending, unflinching purpose to solve them aright.

Yet, after all, though the problems are new, though the tasks set before us differ from the tasks set before our fathers who founded and preserved this Republic, the spirit in which these tasks must be undertaken and these problems faced, if our duty is to be well done, remains essentially unchanged. We know that self-government is difficult. We know that no people needs such high traits of character as that people which seeks to govern its affairs aright through the freely expressed will of the freemen who compose it. But we have faith that we shall not prove false to the memories of the men of the mighty past. They did their work, they left us the splendid heritage we now enjoy. We in our turn have an assured confidence that we shall be able to leave this heritage unwasted and enlarged to our children and our children's children. To do so we must show, not merely in great crises, but in the everyday affairs of life, the qualities of practical intelligence, of courage, of hardihood, and endurance, and above all the power of devotion to a lofty ideal, which made great the men who founded this Republic in the days of Washington, which made great the men who preserved this Republic in the days of Abraham Lincoln."

With legitimacy in his hand and almost the full two terms in his pocket, Roosevelt vowed that he would not run again. That was both a noble intent and a political ploy. The strategy for all final-term presidents is that they can do the things they think are right and stay away from doing what was popular. Roosevelt had what was designed to get him reelected, not what was for him to make a difference. When the rest of the party knows he has no intention of running again, they have no leverage on him.

By the time 1908 rolled around, he had decided to keep his promise and leave. He passed the mantle to Howard Taft, who went on to win the nomination and the presidency. Before leaving, however, he took Taft under his wing and showed him the ropes. He wanted to make sure his legacy and what he had started during his almost two terms would continue into the next.

Taft had been the Secretary of War under Roosevelt and governor of the Philippines. In taking on the presidency, Taft vowed to continue the policies and even maintain the cabinet secretaries who had served under Roosevelt. This was implausible, however, as Taft soon found that to be effective, he needed to have room to maneuver. He started shedding the old and orchestrated a new batch of officials to do what he saw was necessary. He even stopped consulting with Roosevelt on appointments.

Roosevelt needed a break. It had been a busy decade. He chose Africa as his destination and took his son with him. They spent an extended vacation amassing more than three thousand wildlife trophies, ranging from elephants to lions.

With the safari done, he traveled to Egypt, where he rendezvoused with Edith and proceeded north to tour Europe. By the time they returned to Oyster Bay, it was the summer of 1910. It had been almost two years since the last election. The

Roosevelts disembarked in New York to a jubilant crowd of well-wishers. It was a hero's welcome.

He returned to an America that was not as healthy as when he had left. Much had changed. Some good but many not so much. He suspected that Taft was in over his head, but Roosevelt decided to give it a little time and place his ears to the ground before he proffered any judgment.

As much benefit of the doubt that he tried to muster, the more negative feedback he got from others still in Washington. The prognosis was dire. The economy was headed for bad times, and the writing was on the wall. Taft had gotten into the habit of reversing some of Roosevelt's politics, and that was rubbing Roosevelt the wrong way.

Roosevelt had been a progressive all his life, and his politics had infected the public consciousness. Progressivism had taken root in the country, and it ran counter to Taft's efforts. The more Taft tried to brand his politics on the country, the more the country recoiled. Calls for the return of Roosevelt's policies were coming to a boil.

The progressive wing of the party began to pressure Roosevelt to return to politics and challenge Taft for the nomination. Roosevelt was hesitant at first, but after much thought and constant pressure, he decided to do so. The powers that were present in the party, however, were not willing to alter the course of history and return to a president, popular as he may have been, who did not listen to the establishment.

Chapter 8 - Nationalism

When the Convention was held in Chicago that year, there was an effective split between the progressives who supported Roosevelt's return and the establishment that supported Taft.

By the time of the convention, Roosevelt had done his homework and his groundwork. He came prepared to battle the establishment and was in the lead with the delegate count.

If the race had been fair, Roosevelt would have won the nomination. Since Taft and the establishment controlled the floor, they had managed to tinker with the composition of the delegates and excluded Roosevelt's supporters from entering. Upon seeing this, Roosevelt pulled his name out of the running. Taft won on the first ballot.

Because of the crooked play, there was a mass exodus of members from the Republican Party.

Roosevelt and his strongest supporters split and went on to create the Progressive Party.

They held their own convention and unanimously nominated Roosevelt as their candidate for president. They also chose Hiram Johnson as Roosevelt's running mate. This was a time of chaos. The party of Lincoln had been split at the seams that joined progressive to conservative. The new Progressive Party had extracted whatever semblance of progressivism that remained in the Republican Party and left the shell of establishment conservatives.

During the convention, Roosevelt was visibly animated. It was both a liberating feeling to no longer be curtailed by the establishment side of the party but also a drag on him to see the chasm widen between the ruling class of the establishment and the true masters of government—the people.

His speech is worth reading in its entirety. It forms the basis of the politics that then infused the Democratic Party and the galvanization of the conservative side of the Republican Party.

He ended that long speech by coloring the times with the color of doom. "We stand at Armageddon, and we battle for the Lord" were the last words of the speech that met with thunderous applause from an electrified crowd.

It was here at this convention and during this address that he coined "as strong as Bull Moose." It was an obvious reference to his hunting days. From that point, the party came to be known as the Bull Moose Party.

It was here that what had been long brewing was aired in public—New Nationalism.

Roosevelt had buoyed the idea of economic opportunity for all and political justice as a right. He sought minimum wage for women and limiting the workday to just eight hours. He surfaced the need for a social security plan and a national health program.

It was here, too, that he called for a federally governed securities commission and the direct election of U.S. senators, which had been elected by the states' individual assemblies. His platform wanted the government to be more accountable to the people.

The race that was building was certainly getting interesting. There was the Grand Old Party on one hand, the once conservative Democratic Party on the other hand, and the emerging juxtaposition of the two—the new Progressive or Bull Moose Party.

The Republicans had Taft, the Progressives had Roosevelt, and the Democrats had New Jersey Governor Woodrow Wilson.

The real battle of the campaign took place between Roosevelt and Wilson. Taft was not moving the meter by much, but most people wanted to hear what programs the two other parties had in store. Wilson was standing on something he called the "New Freedom," while Roosevelt was standing on new progressivism. In policy, they may have appeared different, but in substance, they shared the same soul except for one major difference. Roosevelt was a federalist in nature. He believed that the federal structure would be able to spread to cover all the people equally. His nature that tended toward equity and equanimity naturally made him a federalist. On the other hand, Wilson didn't want to centralize control in Washington. He was very much a proponent of state freedoms and rights. While their policies had the same soul, they differed in how to enact and enforce it.

One of the points of contention between the two parties rested on trusts and monopolies. Remember that Roosevelt was known as the trustbuster, and that he saw trusts and monopolies as a problem. Wilson didn't oppose that idea; in fact, he wanted to push it further. While Roosevelt understood that some monopolies were in the best interest of the country, Wilson believed that no monopoly should exist.

Wilson also argued for protectionist policies in the form of tariffs to protect burgeoning industries. It was a long and hard-fought campaign. Roosevelt had put in every last measure of effort and led a gallant fight for the honor of being president. He fought so hard that in one of his last stump speeches he thundered on despite being shot in the chest.

When the last vote was counted, Wilson had captured about 42% of the vote, while Roosevelt got 27%. It was obvious that Taft's 23% had split the vote and handed the presidency to Wilson. The vote tally did not tell the whole story. The electoral votes were starker in comparison. Wilson scooped up 435 electoral votes, handing only 88 to Roosevelt. Taft was left with a paltry 8 electoral votes.

Roosevelt had won in only six states—Pennsylvania, Michigan, Minnesota, South Dakota, Washington, and California. It may have handed Roosevelt a loss, but it placed his progressive mark on the generations to come. The conservative wing of the Republican Party that had fought to survive by delegitimizing the delegates and swaying the vote away from Roosevelt had not read the writing on the wall. While Roosevelt did not become president, his policies went on to become the basis of the

Democratic Party and enacted by Wilson during his time in office.

Theodore Roosevelt's political philosophy toward the latter part of his presidency and during his return to national politics evolved around federal intervention in social justice and economic welfare of the masses.

His ideas and motivations are encapsulated in a speech delivered during the Progressive Party's convention in Chicago. In that speech, he straddled the concerns of the Republican Party's progressive wing and the Democratic Party's conservative wing.

"To you, men and women who have come here to this great city of this great State formally to launch a new party, a party of the people of the whole Union, the National Progressive Party, I extend my hearty greeting. You are taking a bold and a greatly needed step for the service of our beloved country. The old parties are husks, with no real soul within either, divided on artificial lines, boss-ridden and privilege-controlled, each a jumble of incongruous elements, and neither daring to speak out wisely and fearlessly what should be said on the vital issues of the day. This new movement is a movement of truth, sincerity, and wisdom, a movement which proposes to put at the service of all our people the collective power of the people, through their Governmental agencies, alike in the Nation and in the several States. We propose boldly to face the real and great questions of the day, and not skillfully to evade them as do the old parties. We propose to raise aloft a standard to which all honest men can repair, and under which all can fight, no matter what their past political differences, if they are content to face the future and no longer to dwell among the dead issues of the past. We propose to put forth a platform which shall not be a platform of the ordinary and insincere kind, but shall be a contract with the people; and, if the people accept this contract by putting us in power, we shall hold ourselves under honorable obligation to fulfill every promise it contains as loyally as if it were actually enforceable under the penalties of the law."

His frustration with what had happened at the Republican National Convention was palpable. For a man whose moral center was as prominent as Roosevelt's, cheating was unacceptable. It was a violation of the natural order of things, and it was a sign of times to come. The conservative Republicans in the Party of Lincoln were in the minority, and the progressives were in the majority. He felt that cheating undermined the soul of democracy and skewed the results of an election—the heart of the democratic process.

There were larger frustrations within him and among his supporters about the direction the party would take and drag the country along with them. Their policies, whatever they were, were the policies of the minority since Taft's actions at the convention delegitimized the Republican nomination and stained the following election. It was easy to see in the results that if Roosevelt had been allowed to seat his delegates and won the nomination, he would have gone on to win the election.

As he continued the speech, he began revealing the various problems that plagued the country and the solutions that he felt should be instituted without delay. He pointedly labeled the Republican Party as corrupt in this part of the speech.

"The prime need today is to face the fact that we are now in the midst of a great economic evolution. There is urgent necessity of applying both common sense and the highest ethical standard to this movement for better economic conditions among the mass of our people if we are to make it one of healthy evolution and not one of revolution. It is, from the standpoint of our country, wicked as well as foolish longer to refuse to face the real issues of the day. Only by so facing them can we go forward; and to do this we must break up the old party organizations and obliterate the old cleavage lines on the dead issues inherited from fifty years ago. Our fight is a fundamental fight against both of the old corrupt party machines, for both are under the dominion of the plunder league of the professional politicians who are controlled and sustained by the great beneficiaries of privilege and reaction. How close is the alliance between the two machines is shown by the attitude of that portion of those Northeastern newspapers, including the majority of the great dailies in all the Northeastern cities—Boston, Buffalo, Springfield, Hartford, Philadelphia, and, above all, New York—which are controlled by or representative of the interests which, in popular phrase, are conveniently grouped together as the Wall Street interests. The large majority of these papers supported Judge Parker for the Presidency in 1904; almost unanimously they supported Mr. Taft for the Republican nomination this year; the large majority are now supporting Professor Wilson for the election. Some of them still prefer Mr. Taft to Mr. Wilson, but all make either Mr. Taft or Mr. Wilson their first choice; and one of the ludicrous features of the campaign is that those papers supporting Professor Wilson show the most jealous partisanship for Mr. Taft whenever they think his interests are jeopardized by the Progressive movement—that, for instance, any Electors will obey the will of the majority of the Republican voters at the primaries, and vote for me instead of obeying the will of the Masters. Barnes-Penrose-Guggenheim combination by voting for Mr. Taft. No better proof can be given than this of the fact that the fundamental concern of the privileged interests is to beat the new party. Some of them would rather beat it with Mr. Wilson; others would rather beat it with Mr. Taft; but the difference between Mr. Wilson and Mr. Taft they consider as trivial, as a mere matter of personal preference. Their real fight is for either, as against the Progressives. They represent the allied Reactionaries of the country, and they are against the new party because to their unerring vision it is evident that the real danger to privilege comes from the new party, and from the new party alone. The men who presided over the Baltimore and the Chicago Conventions, and the great bosses who controlled the two Conventions, Mr. Root and Mr. Parker, Mr. Barnes and Mr. Murphy, Mr. Penrose and Mr. Taggart, Mr. Guggenheim and Mr. Sullivan, differ from one another of course on certain points. But these are the differences which one corporation lawyer has with another corporation lawyer when acting for different corporations. They come together at once as against a common enemy when the dominion of both is threatened by the supremacy of the people of the United States, now aroused to the need of a national alignment on the vital economic issues of this generation.

Neither the Republican nor the Democratic platform contains the slightest promise of approaching the great problems of today either with understanding or good faith; and yet never was there a greater need in this Nation than now of understanding, and of action taken in good faith, on the part of the men and the organizations shaping our governmental policy. Moreover, our needs are such that there should be coherent action among those responsible for the conduct of National affairs and those responsible for the conduct of State affairs; because our aim should be the same in both State and Nation; that is, to use the Government as an efficient agency for the practical betterment of social and economic conditions throughout this land. There are other important things to be done, but this is the most important thing. It is preposterous to leave a movement in the hands of men who have broken their promises as have the present heads of the Republican organization (not of the Republican voters, for they in no shape represent the rank and file of Republican voters). These men by their deeds give the lie to their words. There is no health in them, and they cannot be trusted. But the Democratic party is just as little to be trusted. The Underwood-Fitzgerald combination in the House of Representatives has shown that it cannot safely be trusted to maintain the interests of this country abroad or to represent the interests of the plain people at home. The control of the various State bosses in the State organizations has been strengthened by the action at Baltimore; and scant indeed would be the use of exchanging the whips of Messrs. Barnes, Penrose, and Guggenheim for the scorpions of Messrs. Murphy, Taggart, and Sullivan. Finally, the Democratic platform not only shows an utter failure to understand either present conditions or the means of making these conditions better, but also a reckless willingness to try to attract various sections of the electorate by making mutually incompatible promises which there is not the slightest intention of redeeming, and which, if redeemed, would result in sheer ruin. Far-seeing patriots should turn scornfully from men who seek power on a platform which with exquisite nicety combines silly inability to understand the National needs and dishonest insincerity in promising conflicting and impossible remedies.

If this country is really to go forward along the path of social and economic justice, there must be a new party of Nationwide and non-sectional principles, a party where the titular National chiefs and the real State leaders shall be in genuine accord, a party in whose counsels the people shall be supreme, a party that shall represent in the Nation and the several States alike the same cause, the cause of human rights and of governmental efficiency. At present both the old parties are controlled by professional politicians in the interests of the privileged classes, and apparently each has set up as its ideal of business and political development a government by financial despotism tempered by make-believe political assassination. Democrat and Republican alike, they represent government of the needy many by professional politicians in the interests of the rich few. This is class government, and class government of a peculiarly unwholesome kind."

The right to rule belonged to the people, not the blue bloods. From the time he left law school and wanted to find his path to governing, he already felt that the governing class was the people. This was his truth. It was his guiding principle. This was not what the conservative elements in the Republican Party agreed with. His path from the government of New York to the White House had been one created by the will of his mind. Once unshackled from the Republican Party, he was free to let the inspiration for progressive changes to take root. He methodically laid out the steps to elevate progressivism to the national level.

"It seems to me, therefore, that the time is ripe, and overripe, for a genuine Progressive movement, Nationwide and justice-loving, sprung from and responsible to the people themselves, and sundered by a great gulf from both of the old party organizations, while representing all that is best in the hopes, beliefs, and aspirations of the plain people who make up the immense majority of the rank and file of both the old parties.

The first essential in the Progressive program is the right of the people to rule. But a few months ago, our opponents were assuring us with insincere clamor that it was absurd for us to talk about desiring that the people should rule, because, as a matter of fact, the people actually do rule. Since that time the actions of the Chicago Convention, and to an only less degree of the Baltimore Convention, have shown in striking fashion how little the people do rule under our present conditions. We should provide by National law for Presidential primaries. We should provide for the election of United States Senators by popular vote. We should provide for a short ballot; nothing makes it harder for the people to control their public servants than to force them to vote for so many officials that they cannot really keep track of any one of them, so that each becomes indistinguishable in the crowd around him. There must be stringent and efficient corrupt practices acts, applying to the primaries as well as the elections; and there should be publicity of campaign contributions during the campaign. We should provide throughout this Union for giving the people in every State the real right to rule themselves, and really and not nominally to control their public servants and their agencies for doing the public business; all incident of this being giving the people the right themselves to do this public business if they find it impossible to get what they desire through the existing agencies. I do not attempt to dogmatize as to the machinery by which this end should be achieved. In each community it must be shaped so as to correspond not merely with the needs but with the customs and ways of thought of that community, and no community has a right to dictate to any other in this matter. But wherever representative government has in actual fact become non-representative there the people should secure to themselves the initiative, the referendum, and the recall, doing it in such fashion as to make it evident that they do not intend to use these instrumentality wantonly or frequently, but to hold them ready for use in order to correct the misdeeds or failures of the public servants when it has become evident that these misdeeds and failures cannot be corrected in ordinary and normal fashion. The administrative officer should be given full power for otherwise he cannot do well the people's work; and the people should be given full power over him."

He was also responsible enough to clarify that he had no intention to altering the system of representative government. He was not planning a revamp of government. He was planning a restatement of values.

"I do not mean that we shall abandon representative government; on the contrary, I mean that we shall devise methods by which our Government shall become really representative. To use such measures as the initiative, referendum, and recall indiscriminately and promiscuously on all kinds of occasions would undoubtedly cause disaster; but events have shown that at present our institutions are not representative—at any rate in many States, and sometimes in the Nation—and that we cannot wisely afford to let this condition of things remain longer uncorrected. We have permitted the growing up of a breed of politicians who, sometimes for improper political purposes, sometimes as a means of serving the great special interests of privilege which stand behind them, twist so-called representative institutions into a means of thwarting instead of expressing the deliberate and well-thought-out judgment of the people as a whole. This cannot be permitted. We choose our representatives for two purposes. In the first place, we choose them with the desire that, as experts, they shall study certain matters with which we, the people as a whole, cannot be intimately acquainted, and that in regards to these matters, they shall formulate a policy for our betterment. Even as regards such a policy, and the actions taken thereunder, we ourselves should have the right ultimately to vote our disapproval of it, if we feel such disapproval. But, in the next place, our representatives are chosen to carry out certain policies as to which we have definitely made up our minds, and here we expect them to represent us by doing what we have decided ought to be done. All I desire to do by securing more direct control of the governmental agents and agencies of the people is to give the people the chance to make their representatives really represent them whenever the Government becomes misrepresentative instead of representative.

I have not come to this way of thinking from closet study, or as a mere matter of theory; I have been forced to it by a long experience with the actual conditions of our political life. A few years ago, for instance, there was very little demand in this country for Presidential primaries. There would have been no demand now if the politicians had really endeavored to carry out the will of the people as regards nominations for President. But, largely under the influence of special privilege in the business world, there have arisen castes of politicians who not only do not represent the people, but who make their bread and butter by thwarting the wishes of the people. This is true of the bosses of both political parties in my own State of New York, and it is just as true of the bosses of one or the other political party in a great many States of the Union. The power of the people must be made supreme within the several party organizations.

In the contest which culminated six weeks ago in this city I speedily found that my chance was at a minimum in any State where I could not get an expression of the people themselves in the primaries. I found that if I could appeal to the rank and file of the Republican voters, I could generally win, whereas, if I had to appeal to the political caste—which includes the noisiest defenders of the old system—I generally lost. Moreover, I found, as a matter of fact, not as a matter of theory, that these politicians habitually and unhesitatingly resort to every species of mean swindling and cheating in order to carry their point. It is because of the general recognition of this fact that the words politics and politicians have grown to have a sinister meaning throughout this country. The bosses and their agents in the National Republican Convention at Chicago treated political theft as a legitimate political weapon. It is instructive to compare the votes of States where there were open primaries and the votes of States where there were not. In Illinois, Pennsylvania and Ohio we had direct primaries, and the Taft machine was beaten two to one. Between and bordering on these States were Michigan, Indiana, and Kentucky. In these States we could not get direct primaries, and the politicians elected two delegates to our one. In the first three States the contests were absolutely open, absolutely honest. The rank and file expressed their wishes, and there was no taint of fraud about what they did. In the other three States the contest was marked by every species of fraud and violence on the part of our opponents, and half the Taft delegates in the Chicago Convention from these States had tainted titles. The entire Wall Street press at this moment is vigorously engaged in denouncing the direct primary system and upholding the old convention system, or, as they call it, the 'old representative system.' They are so doing because they know that the bosses and the powers of special privilege have tenfold the chance under the convention system that they have when the rank and file of the people can express themselves at the primaries. The nomination of Mr. Taft at Chicago was a fraud upon the rank and file of the Republican Party; it was obtained only by defrauding the rank and file of the party of their right to express their choice; and such fraudulent action does not bind a single honest member of the party.

Well, what the National Committee and the fraudulent majority of the National Convention did at Chicago in misrepresenting the people has been done again and again in Congress, perhaps especially in the Senate and in the State legislatures. Again and again laws demanded by the people have been refused to the people because the representatives of the people misrepresented them. Now my proposal is merely that we shall give to the people the power, to be used not wantonly but only in exceptional cases, themselves to see to it that the governmental action taken in their name is really the action that they desire."

He did not leave out the element of justice that was needed to make his plans take flight. The courts were a central part of the system of government, and he wanted to refine their place in the New America.

"The American people, and not the courts, are to determine their own fundamental policies. The people should have power to deal with the effect of the acts of all their governmental agencies. This must be extended to include the effects of judicial acts as well as the acts of the executive and legislative representatives of the people. Where the judge merely does justice as between man and man, not dealing with Constitutional questions, then the interest of the public is only to see that he is a wise and upright judge. Means should be devised for making it easier than at present to get rid of an incompetent judge; means should be devised by the bar and the bench acting in conjunction with the various legislative bodies to make justice far more expeditious and more certain than at present. The stick-in-the-bark legalism, the legalism that subordinates equity to technicalities, should be recognized as a potent enemy of justice. But this is not the matter of most concern at the moment. Our prime concern is that in dealing with the fundamental law of the land, in assuming finally to interpret it, and therefore finally to make it, the acts of the courts should be subject to and not above the final control of the people as a whole. I deny that the American people have surrendered to any set of men, no matter what their position or their character, the final right to determine those fundamental questions upon which free self-government ultimately depends. The people themselves must be the ultimate makers of their own Constitution, and where their agents differ in their interpretations of the Constitution the people themselves should be given the chance, after full and deliberate judgment, authoritatively to settle what interpretation it is that their representatives shall thereafter adopt as binding.

Whenever in our Constitutional system of government there exist general prohibitions that, as interpreted by the courts, nullify, or may be used to nullify, specific laws passed, and admittedly passed, in the interest of social justice, we are for such immediate law, or amendment to the Constitution, if that be necessary, as will thereafter permit a reference to the people of the public effect of such decision under forms securing full deliberation, to the end that the specific act of the legislative branch of the Government thus judicially nullified, and such amendments thereof as come within its scope and purpose, may constitutionally be excepted by vote of the people from the general prohibitions, the same as if that particular act had been expressly excepted when the prohibition was adopted. This will necessitate the establishment of machinery for making much easier of amendment both the National and the several State Constitutions, especially with the view of prompt action on certain judicial decisions—action as specific and limited as that taken by the passage of the Eleventh Amendment to the National Constitution. We are not in this decrying the courts. That was reserved for the Chicago Convention in its plank respecting impeachment. Impeachment implies the proof of dishonesty. We do not question the general honesty of the courts. But in applying to present-day social conditions the general prohibitions that were intended originally as safeguards to the citizen against the arbitrary power of Government in the hands of caste and privilege, these prohibitions have been turned by the courts from safeguards against political and social privilege into barriers against political and social justice and advancement. Our purpose is not to impugn the courts, but to emancipate them from a position where they stand in the way of social justice; and to emancipate the people, in an orderly way, front the iniquity of enforced submission to a doctrine which would turn Constitutional provisions which were intended to favor social justice and advancement into prohibitions against such justice and advancement.

We in America have peculiar need thus to make the acts of the courts subject to the people, because, owing to causes which I need not now discuss, the courts have here grown to occupy a position unknown in any other country, a position of superiority over both the legislature and the executive. Just at this time, when we have begun in this country to move toward social and industrial betterment and true industrial democracy, this attitude on the part of the courts is of grave portent, because privilege has entrenched itself in many courts, just as it formerly entrenched itself in many legislative bodies and in many executive offices. Even in England, where the Constitution is based upon the theory of the supremacy of the legislative body over the courts, the cause of democracy has at times been hampered by court action. In a recent book by a notable English Liberal leader, Mr. L. T. Hobhouse, there occurs the following sentences dealing with this subject: 'Labor itself had experienced the full brunt of the attack. It had come, not from the politicians, but from the judges; but in this country we have to realize that within wide limits the judges are in effect legislators, and legislators with a certain persistent bent which can be held in check only by the constant vigilance and repeated efforts of the recognized organ for the making and repeal of law.'

It thus appears that even in England it is necessary to exercise vigilance in order to prevent reactionary thwarting of the popular will by courts that are subject to the power of the Legislature. In the United States, where the courts are supreme over the Legislature, it is vital that the people should keep in their own hands the right of interpreting their own Constitution when their public servants differ as to the interpretation.

I am well aware that every upholder of privilege, every hired agent or beneficiary of the special interests, including many well-meaning parlor reformers, will denounce all this as 'Socialism' or 'anarchy'—the same terms they used in the past in denouncing the movements to control the railways and to control public utilities. As a matter of fact, the propositions I make constitute neither anarchy nor Socialism, but, on the contrary, a corrective to Socialism and an antidote to anarchy.

I especially challenge the attention of the people to the need of dealing in far-reaching fashion with our human resources, and therefore our labor power. In a century and a quarter as a nation the American people have subdued and settled the vast reaches of a continent; ahead lies the greater task of building upon this foundation, by themselves, for themselves, and with themselves, an American common wealth which in its social and economic structure shall be four square with democracy. With England striving to make good the human wreckage to which a scrapheap scheme of industrialism has relegated her, with Germany putting the painstaking resources of an Empire at the work of developing her crafts and industrial sciences, with the Far East placing in the hands of its millions the tools invented and fashioned by Western civilization, it behooves Americans to keep abreast of the great industrial changes and to show that the people themselves, through popular self-government, call meet an age of crisis with wisdom and strength.

In the last twenty years an increasing percentage of our people have come to depend on industry for their livelihood, so that today the wage-workers in industry rank in importance side by side with the tillers of the soil. As a people we cannot afford to let any group of citizens or any individual citizen live or labor under conditions which are injurious to the common welfare. Industry, therefore, must submit to such public regulation as will make it a means of life and health, not of death or inefficiency. We must protect the crushable elements at the base of our present industrial structure.

The first charge on the industrial statesmanship of the day is to prevent human waste. The dead weight of orphanage and depleted craftsmanship, of crippled workers and workers suffering from trade diseases, of casual labor, of insecure old age, and of household depletion due to industrial conditions are, like our depleted soils, our gashed mountain-sides and flooded river bottoms, so many strains upon the National structure, draining the reserve strength of all industries and showing beyond all peradventure the public element and public concern in industrial health.

Ultimately, we desire to use the Government to aid, as far as can safely be done, in helping the industrial tool-users to become in part tool-owners, just as our farmers now are. Ultimately the Government may have to join more efficiently than at present in strengthening the hands of the workingmen who already stand at a high level, industrially and socially, and who are able by joint action to serve themselves. But the most pressing and immediate need is to deal with the cases of those who are on the level, and who are not only in need themselves, but, because of their need, tend to jeopardize the welfare of those who are better off. We hold that under no industrial order, in no commonwealth, in no trade, and in no establishment should industry be carried on under conditions inimical to the social welfare. The abnormal, ruthless, spendthrift industry of establishment tends to drag down all to the level of the least considerate.

Here the sovereign responsibility of the people as a whole should be placed beyond all quibble and dispute.

The public needs have been well summarized as follows:

We hold that the public has a right to complete knowledge of the facts of work.

On the basis of these facts and with the recent discoveries of physicians and neurologists, engineers and economists, the public call formulate minimum occupational standards below which, demonstrably, work can be prosecuted only at a human deficit.

In the third place, we hold that all industrial conditions which fall below such standards should come within the scope of governmental action and control in the same way that subnormal sanitary conditions are subject to public regulation and for the same reason—because they threaten the general welfare.

To the first end, we hold that the constituted authorities should be empowered to require all employers to file with them for public purposes such wage scales and other data as the public element in industry demands. The movement for honest weights and measures has its counterpart in industry. All tallies, scales and check systems should be open to public inspection and inspection of committees of the workers concerned. All deaths, injuries, and diseases due to industrial operation should be reported to public authorities.

To the second end, we hold that minimum wage commissions should be established in the Nation and in each State to inquire into wages paid in various industries and to determine the standard which the public ought to sanction as a minimum; and we believe that, as a present installment of what we hope for in the future, there should be at once established in the Nation and its several States minimum standards for the wages of women, taking the present Massachusetts law as a basis from which to start and on which to improve. We pledge the Federal Government to an investigation of industries along the lines pursued by the Bureau of Alines with the view to establishing standards of sanitation and safety; we call for the standardization of mine and factory inspection by interstate agreement or the establishment of a Federal standard. We stand for the passage of legislation in the Nation and in all States providing standards of compensation for industrial accidents and death, and for diseases clearly due to the nature of conditions of industry, and we stand for the adoption by law of a fair standard of compensation for casualties resulting fatally which shall clearly fix the minimum compensation in all cases.

In the third place, certain industrial conditions fall clearly below the levels which the public today sanction.

We stand for a living wage. Wages are subnormal if they fail to provide a living for those who devote their time and energy to industrial occupations.

The monetary equivalent of a living wage varies according to local conditions, but must include enough to secure the elements of a normal standard of living—a standard high enough to make morality possible, to provide for education and recreation, to care for immature members of the family, to maintain the family during periods of sickness, and to permit of reasonable saving for old age.

Hours are excessive if they fail to afford the worker sufficient time to recuperate and return to his work thoroughly refreshed. We hold that the night labor of women and children is abnormal and should be prohibited; we hold that the employment of women over forty-eight hours per week is abnormal and should be prohibited. We hold that the seven-day working week is abnormal, and we hold that one day of rest in seven should be provided in law. We hold that the continuous industries, operating twenty-four hours out of twenty-four, are abnormal, and where, because of public necessity or of technical reasons (such as molten metal), the twenty-four hours must be divided into two shifts of twelve hours or three shifts of eight, they should by law be divided into three of eight.

Safety conditions are abnormal when, through unguarded machinery, poisons, electrical voltage, or otherwise, the workers are subjected to unnecessary hazards of life and limb; and all such occupations should come under governmental regulation and control.

Home life is abnormal when tenement manufacture is carried on in the household. It is a serious menace to health, education, and childhood, and should therefore be entirely prohibited. Temporary construction camps are abnormal homes and should be subjected to governmental sanitary regulation.

The premature employment of children is abnormal and should be prohibited; so also the employment of women in manufacturing, commerce, or other trades where work compels standing constantly; and also any employment of women in such trades for a period of at least eight weeks at time of childbirth.

Our aim should be to secure conditions which will tend everywhere towards regular industry, and will do away with the necessity for rush periods, followed by out-of-work seasons, which put so severe a strain on wage-workers.

It is abnormal for any industry to throw back upon the community the human wreckage due to its wear and tear, and the hazards of sickness, accident, invalidism, involuntary unemployment, and old age should be provided for through insurance. This should be made a charge in whole or in part upon the industries the employer, the employee, and perhaps the people at large, to contribute severally in some degree. Wherever such standards are not met by given establishments, by given industries, are unprovided for by a legislature, or are balked by unenlightened courts, the workers are in jeopardy, the progressive employer is penalized, and the community pays a heavy cost in lessened efficiency and in misery. What Germany has done in the way of old age pensions or insurance should be studied by us, and the system adapted to our uses, with whatever modifications are rendered necessary by our different ways of life and habits of thought.

Workingwomen have the same need to combine for protection that workingmen have; the ballot is as necessary for one class as for the other; we do not believe that with the two sexes there is identity of function; but we do believe that there should be equality of right; and therefore we favor woman suffrage. In those conservative States where there is genuine doubt how the women stand on this matter, I suggest that it be referred to a vote of the women, so that they may themselves make the decision. Surely if women could vote, they would strengthen the hands of those who are endeavoring to deal in efficient fashion with evils such as the white slave traffic; evils which can in part be dealt with Nationally, but which in large part can be reached only by determined local action, such as insisting on the widespread publication of the names of the owners, the landlords, of houses used for immoral purposes.

No people are more vitally interested than workingmen and workingwomen in questions affecting the public health. The pure food law must be strengthened and efficiently enforced. In the National Government one department should be entrusted with all the agencies relating to the public health, from the enforcement of the pure food law to the administration of quarantine. This department, through its special health service, would co-operate intelligently with the various State and municipal bodies established for the same end. There would be no discrimination against or for any one set of therapeutic methods, against or for any one school of medicine or system of healing; the aim would be merely to secure under one administrative body efficient sanitary regulation in the interest of the people as a whole.

There is no body of our people whose interests are more inextricably interwoven with the interests of all the people than is the case with the farmers. The Country Life Commission should be revived with greatly increased powers; its abandonment was a severe blow to the interests of our people.

The welfare of the farmer is a basic need of this Nation. It is the men from the farm who in the past have taken the lead in every great movement within this Nation, whether in time of war or in time of peace. It is well to have our cities prosper, but it is not well if they prosper at the expense of the country. I am glad to say that in many sections of our country there has been an extraordinary revival of recent years in intelligent interest in and work for those who live in the open country. In this movement the lead must be taken by the farmers themselves; but our people as a whole, through their governmental agencies, should back the farmers. Everything possible should be done to better the economic condition of the farmer, and also to increase the social value of the life of the farmer, the farmer's wife, and their children. The burdens of labor and loneliness bear heavily on the women in the country; their welfare should be the especial concern of all of us. Everything possible should be done to make life in the country profitable so as to be attractive from the economic standpoint and also to give an outlet among farming people for those forms of activity which now tend to make life in the cities especially desirable for ambitious men and women. There should be just the same chance to live as full, as well-rounded, and as highly useful lives in the country as in the city.

The Government must co-operate with the farmer to make the farm more productive. There must be no skinning of the soil. The farm should be left to the farmer's soil in better, and not worse, condition because of its cultivation. Moreover, every invention and improvement, every discovery and economy, should be at the service of the farmer in the work of production; and, in addition, he should be helped to co-operate in business fashion with his fellows, so that the money paid by the consumer for the product of the soil shall to as large a degree as possible go into the pockets of the man who raised that product from the soil. So long as the farmer leaves co-operative activities with their profit-sharing to the city man of business, so long will the foundations of wealth be undermined and the comforts of enlightenment be impossible in the country communities. In every respect this

Nation has to learn the lessons of efficiency in production and distribution, and of avoidance of waste and destruction; we must develop and improve instead of exhausting our resources. It is entirely possible by improvements in production, in the avoidance of waste, and in business methods on the part of the farmer to give him all increased income from his farm while at the same time reducing to the consumer the price of the articles raised on the farm. Important although education is everywhere, it has a special importance in the country. The country school must fit the country life; in the country, as elsewhere, education must be hitched up with life. The country church and the country Young Men's and Young Women's Christian Associations have great parts to play. The farmers must own and work their own land; steps must be taken at once to put a stop to the tendency towards absentee landlordism and tenant farming; this is one of the most imperative duties confronting the Nation. The question of rural banking and rural credits is also of immediate importance.

The present conditions of business cannot be accepted as satisfactory. There are too many who do not prosper enough, and of the few who prosper greatly there are certainly some whose prosperity does not mean well for the country. Rational Progressives, no matter how radical, are well aware that nothing the Government can do will make some men prosper, and we heartily approve the prosperity, no matter how great, of any man, if it comes as an incident to rendering service to the community; but we wish to shape conditions so that a greater number of the small men who are decent, industrious and energetic shall be able to succeed, and so that the big man who is dishonest shall not be allowed to succeed at all.

Our aim is to control business, not to strangle it—and, above all, not to continue a policy of make-believe strangle toward big concerns that do evil, and constant menace toward both big and little concerns that do well. Our aim is to promote prosperity, and then see to its proper division. We do not believe that any good comes to any one by a policy which means destruction of prosperity; for in such cases it is not possible to divide it because of the very obvious fact that there is nothing to divide. We wish to control big business so as to secure among other things good wages for the wage-workers and reasonable prices for the consumers. Wherever in any business the prosperity of the business man is obtained by lowering the wages of his workmen and charging an excessive price to the consumers we wish to interfere and stop such practices. We will not submit to that kind of prosperity any more than we will submit to prosperity obtained by swindling investors or getting unfair advantages over business rivals. But it is obvious that unless the business is prosperous the wage-workers employed therein will be badly paid and the consumers badly served. Therefore, not merely as a matter of justice to the business man, but from the standpoint of the self-interest of the wage-worker and the consumer we desire that business shall prosper; but it should be so supervised as to make prosperity also take the shape of good wages to the wage-worker and reasonable prices to the consumer, while investors and business rivals are insured just treatment, and the farmer, the man who tills the toil, is protected as seriously as the wage worker himself.

Unfortunately, those dealing with the subject have tended to divide into two camps, each as unwise as the other. One camp has fixed its eyes only on the need of prosperity, loudly announcing that our attention must be confined to securing it in bulk, and that the division must be left to take care of itself. This is merely the plan, already tested and found wanting, of giving prosperity to the big men on top, and trusting to their mercy to let something leak through to the mass of their countrymen below—which, in effect, means that there shall be no attempt to regulate the ferocious scramble in which greed and cunning reap the largest rewards. The other set has fixed its eyes purely on the injustices of distribution, omitting all consideration of the need of having something to distribute, and advocates action which, it is true, would abolish most of the inequalities of the distribution of prosperity, but only by the unfortunately simple process of abolishing the prosperity itself. This means merely that conditions are to be evened, not up, but down, so that all shall stand on a common level, where nobody has any prosperity at all. The task of the wise radical must be to refuse to be misled by either set of false advisers; he must both favor and promote the agencies that make for prosperity, and at the same time see to it that these agencies are so used as to be primarily of service to the average man.

Again and again while I was President, from 1902 to 1908, I pointed out that under the Anti-Trust Law alone it was neither possible to put a stop to business abuses nor possible to secure the highest efficiency in the service rendered by business to the general public. The Anti-Trust Law must be kept on our statute-books, and, as hereafter shown, must be rendered more effective in the cases where it is applied. But to treat the Anti-Trust Law as an adequate, or as by itself a wise, measure of relief and betterment is a sign not of progress, but of toryism and reaction. It has been of benefit so far as it has implied the recognition of a real and great evil, and the at least sporadic application of the principle that all men alike must obey the law. But as a sole remedy, universally applicable, it has in actual practice completely broken down; as now applied it works more mischief than benefit. It represents the waste of effort—always damaging to a community—which arises from the attempt to meet new conditions by the application of outworn remedies instead of fearlessly and in common-sense fashion facing the new conditions and devising the new remedies which alone can work effectively for good. The Anti-Trust Law, if interpreted as the Baltimore platform demands it shall be interpreted, would apply to every agency by which not merely industrial but agricultural business is carried on in this country; under such an interpretation it ought in theory to be applied universally, in which case practically all industries would stop; as a matter of fact, it is utterly out of the question to enforce it universally; and, when enforced sporadically, it causes continual unrest, puts the country at a disadvantage with its trade competitors in international commerce, hopelessly puzzles honest business men and honest farmers as to what their rights are, and yet, as has just been shown in the cases of the Standard Oil and the Tobacco Trust, it is no real check on the great trusts at which it was in theory aimed, and indeed operates to their benefit. Moreover, if we are to compete with other nations in the markets of the world as well as to develop our own material civilization at home, we must utilize those forms of industrial organization that are indispensable to the highest industrial productivity and efficiency.

An important volume entitled 'Concentration and Control' has just been issued by President Charles R. Van Hise, of the University of Wisconsin. The University of Wisconsin has been more influential than any other agency in making Wisconsin what it has become, a laboratory for wise social and industrial experiment in the betterment of conditions. President Van Hise is one of those thoroughgoing but sane and intelligent radicals from whom much of leadership is to be expected in such a matter. The sub-title of his book shows that his endeavor is to turn the attention of his countrymen toward practically solving the trust problem of the United States. In his preface he states that his aim is to suggest a way to gain the economic advantages of the concentration of industry and at the same time to guard the interests of the public, and to assist in the rule of enlightenment, reason, fair play, mutual consideration, and toleration. In sum, he shows that unrestrained competition as an economic principle has become too destructive to be permitted to exist, and that the small men must be allowed to co-operate under penalty of succumbing before their big competitors; and yet such co-operation, vitally necessary to the small man, is criminal under the present law. He says:

'With the alternative before the business men of co-operation or failure, we may be sure that they will co-operate. Since the law is violated by practically every group of men engaged in trade from one end of the country to the other, they do not feel that in combining they are doing a moral wrong. The selection of the individual or corporation for prosecution depends upon the arbitrary choice of the Attorney-General, perhaps somewhat influenced by the odium which attaches to some of the violators of the law. They all take their chance, hoping that the blow will fall elsewhere. With general violation and sporadic enforcement of an impracticable law, we cannot hope that our people will gain respect for it.

'In conclusion, there is presented as the solution of the difficulties of the present industrial situation, concentration, co-operation, and control. Through concentration we may have the economic advantages coming from magnitude of operations. Through co-operation we may limit the wastes of the competitive system. Through control by commission, we may secure freedom for fair competition, elimination of unfair practices, conservation of our natural resources, fair wages, good social conditions, and reasonable prices.

'Concentration and co-operation in industry in order to secure efficiency are a world-wide movement. The United States cannot resist it. If we isolate ourselves and insist upon the subdivision of industry below the highest economic efficiency, and do not allow co-operation, we shall be defeated in the world's markets. We cannot adopt an economic system less efficient than our great competitors, Germany, England, France, and Austria. Either we must modify our present obsolete laws regarding concentration and co-operation so as to conform with the world movement, or else fall behind in the race for the world's markets. Concentration and co-operation are conditions imperatively essential for industrial advance; but if we allow concentration and co-operation there must be control in order to protect the people, and adequate control is only possible through the administrative commission. Hence concentration, co-operation, and control are the key words for a scientific solution of the mighty industrial problem which now confronts this Nation.'

In his main thesis President Van Hise is unquestionably right. The Democratic platform offers nothing in the way of remedy for present industrial conditions except, first, the enforcement of the Anti-Trust Law in a fashion which, if words mean anything, means bringing business to a standstill; and, second, the insistence upon an archaic construction of the States' rights doctrine in thus dealing with inter-State commerce—an insistence which, in the first place, is the most flagrant possible violation of the Constitution to which the members of the Baltimore Convention assert their devotion, and which, in the next place, nullifies and makes an empty pretense of their first statement. The proposals of the platform are so conflicting and so absurd that it is hard to imagine how any attempt could be made in good faith to carry them out; but, if such attempt were sincerely made, it could only produce industrial chaos. Were such an attempt made, every man who acts honestly would have something to fear, and yet no great adroit criminal able to command the advice of the best corporation lawyers would have much to fear.

What is needed is action directly the reverse of that thus confusedly indicated. We Progressives stand for the rights of the people. When these rights can best be secured by insistence upon States' rights, then we are for States' rights; when they call best be secured by insistence upon National rights, then we are for National rights. Inter-State commerce call be effectively controlled only by the Nation. The States cannot control it under the Constitution, and to amend the Constitution by giving them control of it would amount to a dissolution of the Government. The worst of the big trusts have always endeavored to keep alive the feeling in favor of having the States themselves, and not the Nation, attempt to do this work, because they know that in the long-run such effort would be ineffective. There is no surer way to prevent all successful effort to deal with the trusts than to insist that they be dealt with by the States rather than by the Nation, or to create a conflict between the States and the Nation on the subject. The well-meaning ignorant man who advances such a proposition does as much damage as if he were hired by the trusts themselves, for he is playing the game of every big crooked corporation in the country. The only effective way in which to regulate the trusts is through the exercise of the collective power of our people as a whole through the Governmental agencies established by the Constitution for this very purpose. Grave injustice is done by the Congress when it fails to give the National Government complete power in this matter; and still graver injustice by the federal courts when they endeavor in any way to pare down the right of the people collectively to act in this matter as they deem wise; such conduct does itself tend to cause the creation of a twilight zone in which neither the Nation nor the States have power. Fortunately, the Federal courts have more and more of recent years tended to adopt the true doctrine, which is that all these matters are to be settled by the people themselves, and that the conscience of the people, and not the preferences of any servants of the people, is to be the standard in deciding what action shall be taken by the people. As Lincoln phrased it: 'The [question] of National power and State rights as a principle is no other than the principle of generality and locality. Whatever concerns the whole should be confided to the whole—to the

General Government; while whatever concerns only the State should be left exclusively to the State.'

It is utterly hopeless to attempt to control the trusts merely by the Anti-Trust Law, or by any law the same in principle, no matter what the modifications may be in detail. In the first place, these great corporations cannot possibly be controlled merely by a succession of lawsuits. The administrative branch of the Government must exercise such control. The preposterous failure of the Commerce Court has shown that only damage comes from the effort to substitute judicial for administrative control of great corporations. In the next place, a loosely drawn law which promises to do everything would reduce business to complete ruin if it were not also so drawn as to accomplish almost nothing.

As construed by the Democratic platform, the Anti-Trust Law would, if it could be enforced, abolish all business of any size or any efficiency. The promise thus to apply and construe the law would undoubtedly be broken, but the mere fitful effort thus to apply it would do no good whatever, would accomplish widespread harm, and would bring all trust legislation into contempt. Contrast what has actually been accomplished under the Inter-State Commerce Law with what has actually been accomplished under the Anti-Trust Law. The first has, on the whole, worked in a highly efficient manner and achieved real and great results; and it promises to achieve even greater results (although I firmly believe that if the power of the Commissioners grows greater, it will be necessary to make them and their superior, the President, even more completely responsible to the people for their acts). The second has occasionally done good, has usually accomplished nothing, has generally left the worst conditions wholly unchanged, and has been responsible for a considerable amount of downright and positive evil.

What is needed is the application to all industrial concerns and all co-operating interests engaged in inter-State commerce in which there is either monopoly or control of the market of the principles on which we have gone in regulating transportation concerns engaged in such commerce. The Anti-Trust Law should be kept on the statute-books and strengthened so as to make it genuinely and thoroughly effective against every big concern tending to monopoly or guilty of anti-social practices. At the same time, a National industrial commission should be created which should have complete power to regulate and control all the great industrial concerns engaged in inter-State business—which practically means all of them in this country. This commission should exercise over these industrial concerns like powers to those exercised over the railways by the Inter-State Commerce Commission, and over the National banks by the Comptroller of the Currency, and additional powers if found necessary. The establishment of such a commission would enable us to punish the individual rather than merely the corporation, just as we now do with banks, where the aim of the Government is not to close the bank, but to bring to justice personally any bank official who has gone wrong. This commission should deal with all the abuses of the trusts—all the abuses such as those developed by the Government suit against the Standard Oil and Tobacco Trusts—as the Inter-State Commerce Commission now deals with rebates. It should have complete power to make the capitalization absolutely honest and put a stop to all stock watering. Such supervision over the issuance of corporate securities would put a stop to exploitation of the people by dishonest capitalists desiring to declare dividends on watered securities, and would open this kind of industrial property to ownership by the people at large. It should have free access to the books of each corporation and power to find out exactly how it treats its employees, its rivals, and the general public. It should have power to compel the unsparing publicity of all the acts of any corporation which goes wrong. The regulation should be primarily under the administrative branch of the Government, and not by lawsuit. It should prohibit and effectually punish monopoly achieved through wrong, and also actual wrongs done by industrial corporations which are not monopolies, such as the artificial raising of prices, the artificial restriction on productivity, the elimination of competition by unfair or predatory practices, and the like; leaving industrial organizations free within the limits of fair and honest dealing to promote through the inherent efficiency of organization the power of the United States as a competitive nation among nations, and the greater abundance at home that will come to our people from that power wisely exercised. Any corporation voluntarily coming under the commission should not be prosecuted under the Anti-Trust Law as long as it obeys in good faith the orders of the commission. The commission would be able to interpret in advance, to any honest man asking the interpretation, what he may do and what he may not do in carrying on a legitimate business. Any corporation not corning under the commission should be exposed to prosecution under the Anti-Trust Law, and any corporation violating the orders of the commission should also at once become exposed to such prosecution; and when such a prosecution is successful, it should be the duty of the commission to see that the decree of the Court is put into effect completely and in good faith, so that the combination is absolutely broken up, and is not allowed to come together again, nor the constituent parts thereof permitted to do business save under the conditions laid down by the commission. This last provision would prevent the repetition of such gross scandals as those attendants upon the present Administration's prosecution of the Standard Oil and the Tobacco Trusts. The Supreme Court of the United States in condemning these two trusts to dissolution used language of unsparing severity concerning their actions. But the decree was carried out in such a manner as to turn into a farce this bitter condemnation of the criminals by the highest court in the country, not one particle of benefit to the community at large was gained; on the contrary, the prices went up to consumers, independent competitors were placed in greater jeopardy than ever before, and the possessions of the wrong-doers greatly appreciated in value. There never was a more flagrant travesty of justice, never an instance in which wealthy wrong-doers benefited more conspicuously by a law which was supposed to be aimed at them, and which undoubtedly would have brought about severe punishment of less wealthy wrong-doers.

The Progressive proposal is definite. It is practicable. We promise nothing that we cannot carry out. We promise nothing which will jeopardize honest business. We promise adequate control of all big business and the stern suppression of the evils connected with big business, and this promise we can absolutely keep. Our proposal is to help honest business activity, however extensive, and to see that it is rewarded with fair returns so that there may be no oppression either of business men or of the common people. We propose to make it worthwhile for our business men to develop the most efficient business agencies for use in international trade; for it is to the interest of our whole people that we should do well in international business. But we propose to make those business agencies do complete justice to our own people. Every dishonest business man will unquestionably prefer either the program of the Republican Convention or the program of the

Democratic Convention to our proposal, because neither of these programs means or can mean what it purports to mean. But every honest business man, big or little, should support the Progressive program, and it is the one and only program which offers real hope to all our people; for it is the one program under which the Government can be used with real efficiency to see justice done by the big corporation alike to the wage-earners it employs, to the small rivals with whom it competes, to the investors who purchase its securities, and to the consumers who purchase its products or to the general public which it ought to serve, as well as to the business man himself.

We favor co-operation in business, and ask only that it be carried on in a spirit of honesty and fairness. We are against crooked business, big or little. We are in favor of honest business, big or little. We propose to penalize conduct and not size. But all very big business, even though honestly conducted, is fraught with such potentiality of menace that there should be thoroughgoing governmental control over it, so that its efficiency in promoting prosperity at home and increasing the power of the Nation in international commerce may be maintained, and at the same time fair play insured to the wage-workers, the small business competitors, the investors, and the general public. Wherever it is practicable we propose to preserve competition; but where under modern conditions competition has been eliminated and cannot be successfully restored, then the Government must step in and itself supply the needed control on behalf of the people as a whole.

It is imperative to the welfare of our people that we enlarge and extend our foreign commerce. We are per-eminently fitted to do this because as a people we have developed high skill in the art of manufacturing; our business-men are strong executives, strong organizers. In every way possible our Federal Government should co-operate in this important matter. Any one who has had opportunity to study and observe first-hand Germany's course in this respect must realize that their policy of co-operation between Government and business has in comparatively few years made them a leading competitor for the commerce of the world. It should be remembered that they are doing this on a national scale and with large units of business, while the Democrats would have us believe that we should do it with small units of business, which would be controlled not by the National Government but by forty-nine conflicting State sovereignty. Such a policy is utterly out of keeping with the progress of the times and gives our great commercial rivals in Europe—hungry for international markets— golden opportunities of which they are rapidly taking advantage.

I very much wish that legitimate business would no longer permit itself to be frightened by the outcries of illegitimate business into believing that they have any community of interest. Legitimate business ought to understand that its interests are jeopardized when they are confounded with those of illegitimate business; and the latter, whenever threatened with just control, always tries to persuade the former that it also is endangered. As a matter of fact, if legitimate business can only be persuaded to look cool-headedly into our proposition, it is bound to support us.

There are a number of lesser, but still important, ways of improving our business situation. It is not necessary to enumerate all of them; but I desire to allude to two, which can be adopted forthwith. Our patent laws should be remodeled; patents can secure ample royalties to investors without our permitting them to be tools of monopoly or shut out from general use; and a parcels post, on the zone principle, should be established.

I believe in a protective tariff, but I believe in it as a principle, approached from the standpoint of the interests of the whole people, and not as a bundle of preferences to be given to favored individuals. In my opinion, the American people favor the principle of a protective tariff, but they desire such a tariff to be established primarily in the interests of the wage-worker and the consumer. The chief opposition to our tariff at the present moment comes from the general conviction that certain interests have been improperly favored by over-protection. I agree with this view. The commercial and industrial experience of this country has demonstrated the wisdom of the protective policy, but it has also demonstrated that in the application of that policy certain clearly recognized abuses have developed. It is not merely the tariff that should be revised, but the method of tariff-making and of tariff administration. Wherever nowadays an industry is to be protected it should be on the theory that such protection will serve to keep up the wages and the standard of living of the wage-worker in that industry with full regard for the interest of the consumer. To accomplish this the tariff to be levied should as nearly as is scientifically possible approximate the differential between the cost of production at home and abroad. This differential is chiefly, if not wholly, in labor cost. No duty should be permitted to stand as regards any industry unless the workers receive their full share of the benefits of that duty. In other words, there is no warrant for protection unless a legitimate share of the benefits gets into the pay envelope of the wage-worker.

The practice of undertaking a general revision of all the schedules at one time and of securing information as to conditions in the different industries and as to rates of duty desired chiefly from those engaged in the industries, who themselves benefit directly from the rates they propose, has been demonstrated to be not only iniquitous but futile. It has afforded opportunity for practically all of the abuses which have crept into our tariff-making and our tariff administration. The day of the log-rolling tariff must end. The progressive thought of the country has recognized this fact for several years, and the time has come when all genuine Progressives should insist upon a thorough and radical change in the method of tariff-making.

The first step should be the creation of a permanent commission of non-partisan experts whose business shall be to study scientifically all phases of tariff-making and of tariff effects. This commission should be large enough to cover all the different and widely varying branches of

American industry. It should have ample powers to enable it to secure exact and reliable information. It should have authority to examine closely all correlated subjects, such as the effect of any given duty on the consumers of the article on which the duty is levied; that is, it should directly consider the question as to what any duty costs the people in the price of living. It should examine into the wages and conditions of labor and life of the workingmen in any industry, so as to ensure our refusing protection to any industry unless the showing as regards the share labor receives therefrom is satisfactory. This commission would be wholly different from the present unsatisfactory Tariff Board, which was created under a provision of law which failed to give it the powers indispensable if it was to do the work it should do.

It will be well for us to study the experience of Germany in considering this question. The German Tariff Commission has proved conclusively the efficiency and wisdom of this method of handling tariff questions. The reports of a permanent, expert, and non-partisan tariff commission would at once strike a most powerful blow against the chief iniquity of the old log-rolling method of tariff-making. One of the principal difficulties with the old method has been that it was impossible for the public generally, and especially for those Members of Congress not directly connected with the committees handling a tariff bill, to secure anything like adequate and impartial information on the particular subjects under consideration. The reports of such a tariff commission would at once correct this evil and furnish to the general public full, complete, and disinterested information on every subject treated in a tariff bill. With such reports it would no longer be possible to construct a tariff bill in secret or to jam it through either house of Congress without the fullest and most illuminating discussion. The path of the tariff 'joker' would be rendered infinitely difficult.

As a further means of disrupting the old crooked, log-rolling method of tariff-making, all future revisions of the tariff should be made schedule by schedule as changing conditions may require.

Thus, a great obstacle will be thrown in the way of the trading of votes which has marked so scandalously the enactment of every tariff bill of recent years. The tariff commission should render reports at the call of Congress or of either branch of Congress and to the President. Under the Constitution, Congress is the tariff-making power. It should not be the purpose in creating a tariff commission to take anything away from this power of Congress, but rather to afford a wise means of giving to Congress the widest and most scientific assistance possible, and of furnishing it and the public with the fullest disinterested information. Only by this means can the tariff be taken out of politics. The creation of such a permanent tariff commission, and the adoption of the policy of schedule-by-schedule revision, will do more to accomplish this highly desired object than any other means yet devised.

The Democratic platform declares for a tariff for revenue only, asserting that a protective tariff is unconstitutional. To say that a protective tariff is unconstitutional, as the Democratic platform insists, is only excusable on a theory of the

Constitution which would make it unconstitutional to legislate in any shape or way for the betterment of social and industrial conditions. The abolition of the protective tariff or the substitution for it of a tariff for revenue only, as proposed by the Democratic platform, would plunge this country into the most widespread industrial depression we have yet seen, and this depression would continue for an indefinite period. There is no hope from the standpoint of our people from action such the Democrats propose. The one and only chance to secure stable and favorable business conditions in this country, while at the same time guaranteeing fair play to farmer, consumer, business man, and wage-worker, lies in the creation of such a commission as I herein advocate. Only by such a commission and only by such activities of the commission will it be possible for us to get a reasonably quick revision of the tariff schedule by schedule—a revision which shall be downwards and not upwards, and at the same time secure a square deal not merely to the manufacturer, but to the wage-worker and to the general consumer.

There can be no more important question than the high cost of living necessities. The main purpose of the Progressive movement is to place the American people in possession of their birthright, to secure for all the American people unobstructed access to the fountains of measureless prosperity which their Creator offers them. We in this country are blessed with great natural resources, and our men and women have a very high standard of intelligence and of industrial capacity. Surely such being the case, we cannot permanently support conditions under which each family finds it increasingly difficult to secure the necessaries of life and a fair share of its comforts through the earnings of its members. The cost of living in this country has risen during the last few years out of all proportion to the increase in the rate of most salaries and wages; the same situation confronts alike the majority of wage-workers, small business men, small professional men, the clerks, the doctors, clergymen. Now, grave though the problem is, there is one way to make it graver, and that is to deal with it insincerely, to advance false remedies, to promise the impossible. Our opponents, Republicans and Democrats alike, propose to deal with it in this way. The Republicans in their platform promise all inquiry into the facts. Most certainly there should be such inquiry. But the way the present Administration has failed to keep its promises in the past, and the rank dishonesty of action on the part of the Penrose-Barnes-Guggenheim National Convention, makes their every promise worthless. The Democratic platform affects to find the entire cause of the high cost of living in the tariff, and promises to remedy it by free trade, especially free trade in the necessaries of life. In the first place, this attitude ignores the patent fact that the problem is world-wide, that everywhere, in England and France, as in Germany and Japan, it appears with greater or less severity; that in England, for instance, it has become a very severe problem, although neither the tariff nor, save to a small degree, the trusts can there have any possible effect upon the situation. In the second place, the Democratic platform, if it is sincere, must mean that all duties will be taken off the products of the farmer. Yet most certainly we cannot afford to have the farmer struck down. The welfare of the tiller of the soil is as important as the welfare of the wage worker himself, and we must sedulously guard both. The farmer, the producer of the necessities of life, can himself live only if he raises these necessities for a profit. On the other hand, the consumer who must have that farmer's product in order to live, must be allowed to purchase it at the lowest cost that can give the farmer his profit, and everything possible must be done to eliminate any middleman whose function does not tend to increase the cheapness of distribution of the product; and, moreover, everything must be done to stop all speculating, all gambling with the bread-basket which has even the slightest deleterious effect upon the producer and consumer. There must be legislation which will bring about a closer business relationship between the farmer and the consumer. Recently experts in the Agricultural Department have figured that nearly fifty per cent of the price for agricultural products paid by the consumer goes into the pockets, not of the farmer, but of various middlemen; and it is probable that over half of what is thus paid to middlemen is needless, can be saved by wise business methods (introduced through both law and custom), and can therefore be returned to the farmer and the consumer. Through the proposed Inter-State Industrial Commission, we can effectively do away with any arbitrary control by combinations of the necessities of life. Furthermore, the Governments of the Nation and of the several States must combine in doing everything they can to make the farming business profitable, so that he shall get more out of the soil, and enjoy better business facilities for marketing what he thus gets. In this manner his return will be increased while the price to the consumer is diminished. The elimination of the middleman by agricultural exchanges and by the use of improved business methods generally, the development of good roads, the reclamation of arid lands and swamp lands, the improvement in the productivity of farms, the encouragement of all agencies which tend to bring people back to the soil and to make country life more interesting as well as more profitable—all these movements will help not only the farmer but the man who consumes the farmer's products.

There is urgent need of non-partisan expert examination into any tariff schedule which seems to increase the cost of living, and, unless the increase thus caused is more than countervailed by the benefit to the class of the community which actually receives the protection, it must of course mean that that particular duty must be reduced. The system of levying a tariff for the protection and encouragement of American industry so as to secure higher wages and better conditions of life for American laborers must never be perverted so as to operate for the impoverishment of those whom it was intended to benefit. But, in any event, the effect of the tariff on the cost of living is slight; any householder can satisfy himself of this fact by considering the increase in price of articles, like milk and eggs, where the influence of both the tariff and the trusts is negligible. No conditions have been shown which warrant us in believing that the abolition of the protective tariff as a whole would bring any substantial benefit to the consumer, while it would certainly cause unheard of immediate disaster to all wage-workers, all business men, and all farmers, and in all probability would permanently lower the standard of living here. In order to show the utter futility of the belief that the abolition of the tariff and the establishment of free trade would remedy the condition complained of, all that is necessary is to look at the course of industrial events in England and in Germany during the last thirty years, the former under free trade, the latter under a protective system. During these thirty years it is a matter of common knowledge that Germany has forged ahead relatively to England, and this not only as regards the employers, but as regards the wage-earners—in short, as regards all members of the industrial classes. Doubtless, many causes have combined to produce this result; it is not to be ascribed to the tariff alone, but, on the other hand it is evident that it could not have come about if a protective tariff were even a chief cause among many other causes of the high cost of living.

It is also asserted that the trusts are responsible for the high cost of living. I have no question that, as regards certain trusts, this is true. I also have no question that it will continue to be true just as long as the country confines itself to acting as the Baltimore platform demands that we act. This demand is, in effect, for the States and National Government to make the futile attempt to exercise forty-nine sovereign and conflicting authorities in the effort jointly to suppress the trusts, while at the same time the National Government refuses to exercise proper control over them. There will be no diminution in the cost of trust-made articles so long as our Government attempts the impossible task of restoring the flint-lock conditions of business sixty years ago by trusting only to a succession of lawsuits under the Anti-Trust Law—a method which it has been definitely shown usually results to the benefit of any big business concern which really ought to be dissolved, but which cause disturbance and distress to multitudes of smaller concerns. Trusts which increase production—unless they do it wastefully, as in certain forms of mining and lumbering—cannot permanently increase the cost of living; it is the trusts which limit production, or which without limiting production, take advantage of the lack of governmental control, and eliminate competition by combining to control the market, that cause all increase in the cost of living. There should be established at once, as I have elsewhere said, under the National Government an inter-State industrial commission, which should exercise full supervision over the big industrial concerns doing an inter-State business into which an element of monopoly enters. Where these concerns deal with the necessaries of life the commission should not shrink, if the necessity is proved, of going to the extent of exercising regulatory control over the conditions that create or determine monopoly prices.

By such action we shall certainly be able to remove the element of contributory causation on the part of the trusts and the tariff towards the high cost of living. There will remain many other elements. Wrong taxation, including failure to tax swollen inheritances and unused land and other natural resources held for speculative purposes, is one of these elements. The modern tendency to leave the country for the town is another element; and exhaustion of the soil and poor methods of raising and marketing the products of the soil make up another element, as I have already shown. Another element is that of waste and extravagance, individual and National. No laws which the wit of man call devise will avail to make the community prosperous if the average individual lives in such fashion that his expenditure always exceeds his income.

National extravagance—that is, the expenditure of money which is not warranted—we can ourselves control, and to some degree we can help in doing away with the extravagance caused by international rivalries.

These are all definite methods by which something can be accomplished in the direction of decreasing the cost of living. All taken together will not fully meet the situation. There are in it elements which as yet we do not understand. We can be certain that the remedy proposed by the Democratic party is a quack remedy. It is just as emphatically a quack remedy as was the quack remedy, the panacea, the universal cure-all which they proposed sixteen years ago. It is instructive to compare what they now say with what they said in 1896. Only sixteen years ago they were telling us that the decrease in prices was fatal to our people, that the fall in the production of gold, and, as a consequence, the fall in the prices of commodities, was responsible for our ills. Now they ascribe these ills to diametrically opposite causes, such as the rise in the price of commodities. It may well be that the immense output of gold during the last few years is partly responsible for certain phases of the present trouble—which is an instructive commentary on the wisdom of those men who sixteen years ago insisted that the remedy for everything was to be found in the mere additional output of coin, silver and gold alike. There is no more curious delusion than that the Democratic platform is a Progressive platform. The Democratic platform, representing the best thought of the acknowledged Democratic leaders at Baltimore, is purely retrogressive and reactionary. There is no progress in it. It represents an effort to go back; to put this Nation of a hundred million, existing under modern conditions, back to where it was as a Nation of twenty-five million in the days of the stage-coach and canal boat. Such an attitude is Toryism, not Progressivism.

In addition, then, to the remedies that we can begin forthwith, there should be a fearless, intelligent, and searching inquiry into the whole subject made by an absolutely non-partisan body of experts, with no prejudices to warp their minds, no object to serve, who shall recommend any necessary remedy, heedless of what interest may be helped or hurt thereby, and caring only for the interests of the people as a whole.

We believe that there exists an imperative need for prompt legislation for the improvement of our national currency system. The experience of repeated financial crises in the last forty years has proved that the present method of issuing, through private agencies, notes secured by Government bonds is both harmful and unscientific. This method was adopted as a means of financing the Government during the Civil War through furnishing a domestic market for Government bonds. It was largely successful in fulfilling that purpose; but that need is long past, and the system has outlived this feature of its usefulness. The issue of currency is fundamentally a governmental function. The system to be adopted should have as its basic principles soundness and elasticity. The currency should flow forth readily at the demand of commercial activity, and retire as promptly when the demand diminishes. It should be automatically sufficient for all of the legitimate needs of business in any section of the country. Only by such means can the country be freed from the danger of recurring panics. The control should be lodged with the Government, and should be safeguarded against manipulation by Wall Street or the large interests. It should be made impossible to use the machinery or perquisites of the currency system for any speculative purposes. The country must be safeguarded against the over-expansion or unjust contraction of either credit or circulating medium.

There can be no greater issue than that of Conservation in this country. Just as we must conserve our men, women, and children, so we must conserve the resources of the land on which they live. We must conserve the soil so that our children shall have a land that is more and not less fertile than that our fathers dwelt in. We must conserve the forests, not by disuse but by use, making them more valuable at the same time that we use them. We must conserve the mines. Moreover, we must insure so far as possible the use of certain types of great natural resources for the benefit of the people as a whole. The public should not alienate its fee in the water power which will be of incalculable consequence as a source of power in the immediate future. The Nation and the States within their several spheres should by immediate legislation keep the fee of the water power, leasing its use only for a reasonable length of time on terms that will secure the interests of the public. Just as the Nation has gone into the work of irrigation in the West, so it should go into the work of helping reclaim the swamp lands of the South. We should undertake the complete development and control of the Mississippi as a National work, just as we have undertaken the work of building the Panama Canal. We can use the plant, and we call use the human experience, left free by the completion of the Panama Canal in so developing the Mississippi as to make it a mighty highroad of commerce, and a source of fructification and not of death to the rich and fertile lands lying along its lower length.

In the West, the forests, the grazing lands, the reserves of every kind, should be so handled as to be in the interests of the actual settler, the actual home-maker. He should be encouraged to use them at once, but in such a way as to preserve and not exhaust them. We do not intend that our natural resources shall be exploited by the few against the interests of the many, nor do we intend to turn them over to any man who will wastefully use them by destruction, and leave to those who come after us a heritage damaged by just so much. The man in whose interests we are working is the small farmer and settler, the man who works with his own hands, who is working not only for himself but for his children, and who wishes to leave to them the fruits of his labor. His permanent welfare is the prime factor for consideration in developing the policy of Conservation; for our aim is to preserve our natural resources for the public as a whole, for the average man and the average woman who make up the body of the American people.

Alaska should be developed at once, but in the interest of the actual settler. In Alaska the Government has an opportunity of starting in what is almost a fresh field to work out various problems by actual experiment. The Government should at once construct, own, and operate the railways in Alaska. The Government should keep the fee of all the coal-fields and allow them to be operated by lessees with the condition in the lease that non-use shall operate as a forfeit. Telegraph lines should be operated as the railways are. Moreover, it would be well in Alaska to try a system of land taxation which will, so far as possible, remove all the burdens from those who actually use the land, whether for building or for agricultural purposes, and will operate against any man who holds the land for speculation, or derives an income from it based, not on his own exertions, but on the increase in value due to activities not his own. There is very real need that this Nation shall seriously prepare itself for the task of remedying social injustice and meeting social problems by well-considered governmental effort; and the best preparation for such wise action is to test by actual experiment under favorable conditions the device which we have reason to believe will work well, but which it is difficult to apply in old settled communities without preliminary experiment.

In international affairs this country should behave toward other nations exactly as an honorable private citizen behaves toward other private citizens. We should do no wrong to any nation, weak or strong, and we should submit to no wrong. Above all, we should never in any treaty make any promise which we do not intend in good faith to fulfill. I believe it essential that our small army should be kept at a high pitch of perfection, and in no way can it be so damaged as by permitting it to become the plaything of men in Congress who wish to gratify either spite or favoritism, or to secure to localities advantages to which those localities are not entitled. The navy should be steadily built up; and the process of up-building must not be stopped until—and not before—it proves possible to secure by international agreement a general reduction of armaments. The Panama Canal must be fortified. It would have been criminal to build it if we were not prepared to fortify it and to keep our navy at such a pitch of strength as to render it unsafe for any foreign power to attack us and get control of it. We have a perfect right to permit our coastwise traffic (with which there can be no competition by the merchant marine of any foreign nation—so that there is no discrimination against any foreign marine) to pass through that Canal on any terms we choose, and I personally think that no toll should be charged on such traffic. Moreover, in time of war, where all treaties between warring nations, save those connected with the management of the war, at once lapse, the Canal would of course be open to the use of our warships and closed to warships of the nation with which we were engaged in hostilities. But at all times the Canal should be opened on equal terms to the ships of all nations, including our own engaged in international commerce. That was the understanding of the treaty when it was adopted, and the United States must always, as a matter of honorable obligation and with scrupulous nicety, live up to every understanding which she has entered into with any foreign Power.

The question that has arisen over the right of this Nation to charge tolls on the Canal vividly illustrates the folly and iniquity of making treaties which cannot and ought not to be kept. As a people there is no lesson we need to learn more than the lesson not in an outburst of emotionalism to make a treaty that ought not to be, and could not be, kept; and the further lesson that, when we do make a treaty, we must soberly live up to it as long as changed conditions do not warrant the serious step of denouncing it. If we had been so unwise as to adopt the general arbitration treaties a few months ago, we would now be bound to arbitrate the question of our right to free our own coast-wise traffic from Canal tolls; and at any future time, we might have found ourselves obliged to arbitrate the question whether, in the event of war, we could keep the Canal open to our own war vessels and closed to those of our foes. There could be no better illustration of the extreme unwisdom of entering into international agreements without paying heed to the question of keeping them. On the other hand, we deliberately, and with our eyes open, and after ample consideration and discussion, agreed to treat all merchant ships on the same basis; it was partly because of this agreement that there was no question raised by foreign nations' as to our digging and fortifying the Canal; and, having given our word, we must keep it. When the American people make a promise, that promise must and will be kept.

Now, friends, this is my confession of faith. I have made it rather long because I wish you to know just what my deepest convictions are on the great questions of today, so that if you choose to make me your standard-bearer in the fight you shall make your choice understanding exactly how I feel—and if, after hearing me, you think you ought to choose someone else, I shall loyally abide by your choice. The convictions to which I have come have not been arrived at as the result of study in the closet or the library. but from the knowledge I have gained through hard experience during the many years in which, under many and varied conditions, I have striven and toiled with men. I believe in a larger use of the governmental power to help remedy industrial wrongs, because it has been borne in on me by actual experience that without the exercise of such power many of the wrongs will go unremedied. I believe in a larger opportunity for the people themselves directly to participate in government and to control their governmental agents, because long experience has taught me that without such control many of their agents will represent them badly. By actual experience in office, I have found that, as a rule, I could secure the triumph of the causes in which I most believed, not from the politicians and the men who claim an exceptional right to speak in business and government, but by going over their heads and appealing directly to the people themselves. I am not under the slightest delusion as to any power that during my political career I have at any time possessed. Whatever of power I at any time had, I obtained from the people. I could exercise it only so long as, and to the extent that, the people not merely believed in me, but heartily backed me up. Whatever I did as President I was able to do only because I had the backing of the people. When on any point I did not have that backing, when on any point I differed from the people, it mattered not whether I was right or whether I was wrong, my power vanished. I tried my best to lead the people, to advise them, to tell them what I thought was right; if necessary, I never hesitated to tell them what I thought they ought to hear, even though I thought it would be unpleasant for them to hear it; but I recognized that my task was to try to lead them and not to drive them, to take them into my confidence, to try to show them that I was right, and then loyally and in good faith to accept their decision. I will do anything for the people except what my conscience tells me is wrong, and that I can do for no man and no set of men; I hold that a man cannot serve the people well unless he serves his conscience; but I hold also that where his conscience bids him refuse to do what the people desire, he should not try to continue in office against their will. Our Government system should be so shaped that the public servant, when he cannot conscientiously carry out the wishes of the people, shall at their desire leave his office and not misrepresent them in office; and I hold that the public servant can by so doing, better than in any other way, serve both them and his conscience.

Surely there never was a fight better worth making than the one in which we are engaged. It little matters what befalls any one of us who for the time being stand in the forefront of the battle. I hope we shall win, and I believe that if we can wake the people to what the fight really means we shall win. But, win or lose, we shall not falter. Whatever fate may at the moment overtake any of us, the movement itself will not stop. Our cause is based on the eternal principles of righteousness; and even though we who now lead may for the time fail, in the end the cause itself shall triumph. Six weeks ago, here in Chicago, I spoke to the honest representatives of a Convention which was not dominated by honest men; a Convention wherein sat, alas! a majority of men who, with sneering indifference to every principle of right, so acted as to bring to a shameful end a party which had been founded over half a century ago by men in whose souls burned the fire of lofty endeavor. Now to you men, who, in your turn, have come together to spend and be spent in the endless crusade against wrong, to you who face the future resolute and confident, to you who strive in a spirit of brotherhood for the betterment of our Nation, to you who gird yourselves for this great new fight in the never-ending warfare for the good of humankind, I say in closing what in that speech I said in closing: We stand at Armageddon, and we battle for the Lord.

We come here to-day to commemorate one of the epoch-making events of the long struggle for the rights of man—the long struggle for the uplift of humanity. Our country—this great Republic—means nothing unless it means the triumph of a real democracy, the triumph of popular government, and, in the long run, of an economic system under which each man shall be guaranteed the opportunity to show the best that there is in him. That is why the history of America is now the central feature of the history of the world; for the world has set its face hopefully toward our democracy; and, O my fellow citizens, each one of you carries on your shoulders not only the burden of doing well for the sake of your own country, but the burden of doing well and of seeing that this nation does well for the sake of mankind.

There have been two great crises in our country's history: first, when it was formed, and then, again, when it was perpetuated; and, in the second of these great crises—in the time of stress and strain which culminated in the Civil War, on the outcome of which depended the justification of what had been done earlier, you men of the Grand Army, you men who fought through the Civil War, not only did you justify your generation, not only did you render life worth living for our generation, but you justified the wisdom of Washington and Washington's colleagues. If this Republic had been founded by them only to be split asunder into fragments when the strain came, then the judgment of the world would have been that Washington's work was not worth doing. It was you who crowned Washington's work, as you carried to achievement the high purpose of Abraham Lincoln.

Now, with this second period of our history the name of John Brown will be forever associated; and Kansas was the theater upon which the first act of the second of our great national life dramas was played. It was the result of the struggle in Kansas which determined that our country should be in deed as well as in name devoted to both union and freedom; that the great experiment of democratic government on a national scale should succeed and not fail. In name we had the Declaration of Independence in 1776; but we gave the lie by our acts to the words of the Declaration of Independence until 1865; and words count for nothing except in so far as they represent acts. This is true everywhere; but, O my friends, it should be truest of all in political life. A broken promise is bad enough in private life. It is worse in the field of politics. No man is worth his salt in public life who makes on the stump a pledge which he does not keep after election; and, if he makes such a pledge and does not keep it, hunt him out of public life. I care for the great deeds of the past chiefly as spurs to drive us onward in the present. I speak of the men of the past partly that they may be honored by our praise of them, but more that they may serve as examples for the future.

It was a heroic struggle; and, as is inevitable with all such struggles, it had also a dark and terrible side. Very much was done of good, and much also of evil; and, as was inevitable in such a period of revolution, often the same man did both good and evil. For our great good fortune as a nation, we, the people of the United States as a whole, can now afford to forget the evil, or, at least, to remember it without bitterness, and to fix our eyes with pride only on the good that was accomplished. Even in ordinary times there are very few of us who do not see the problems of life as through a glass, darkly; and when the glass is clouded by the murk of furious popular passion, the vision of the best and the bravest is dimmed. Looking back, we are all of us now able to do justice to the valor and the disinterestedness and the love of the right, as to each it was given to see the right, shown both by the men of the North and the men of the South in that contest which was finally decided by the attitude of the West. We can admire the heroic valor, the sincerity, the self-devotion shown alike by the men who wore the blue and the men who wore the gray; and our sadness that such men should have had to fight one another is tempered by the glad knowledge that ever hereafter their descendants shall be found fighting side by side, struggling in peace as well as in war for the uplift of their common country. all alike resolute to raise to the highest pitch of honor and usefulness the nation to which they all belong. As for the veterans of the Grand Army of the Republic, they deserve honor and recognition such as is paid to no other citizens of the Republic; for to them the republic owes its all; for to them it owes its very existence. It is because of what you and your comrades did in the dark years that we of to-day walk, each of us, head erect, and proud that we belong, not to one of a dozen little squabbling contemptible commonwealths, but to the mightiest nation upon which the sun shines.

I do not speak of this struggle of the past merely from the historic standpoint. Our interest is primarily in the application to-day of the lessons taught by the contest of half a century ago. It is of little use for us to pay lip-loyalty to the mighty men of the past unless we sincerely endeavor to apply to the problems of the present precisely the qualities which in other crises enable the men of that day to meet those crises. It is half melancholy and half amusing to see the way in which well-meaning people gather to do honor to the man who, in company with John Brown, and under the lead of Abraham Lincoln, faced and solved the great problems of the nineteenth century, while, at the same time, these same good people nervously shrink from, or frantically denounce, those who are trying to meet the problems of the twentieth century in the spirit which was accountable for the successful solution of the problems of Lincoln's time.

Of that generation of men to whom we owe so much, the man to whom we owe most is, of course, Lincoln. Part of our debt to him is because he forecast our present struggle and saw the way out.

He said:

'I hold that while man exists it is his duty to improve not only his own condition, but to assist in ameliorating mankind.'

And again:

'Labor is prior to, and independent of, capital. Capital is only the fruit of labor, and could never have existed if labor had not first existed. Labor is the superior of capital, and deserves much the higher consideration.'

If that remark was original with me, I should be even more strongly denounced as a Communist agitator than I shall be anyhow. It is Lincoln's. I am only quoting it; and that is one side; that is the side the capitalist should hear. Now, let the working man hear his side.

'Capital has its rights, which are as worthy of protection as any other rights.... Nor should this lead to a war upon the owners of property. Property is the fruit of labor; . . . property is desirable; is a positive good in the world.'

And then comes a thoroughly Lincoln-like sentence:

'Let not him who is house-less pull down the

house of another, but let him work diligently and build one for himself, thus by example assuring that his own shall be safe from violence when built.'

It seems to me that, in these words, Lincoln took substantially the attitude that we ought to take; he showed the proper sense of proportion in his relative estimates of capital and labor, of human rights and property rights. Above all, in this speech, as in many others, he taught a lesson in wise kindliness and charity; an indispensable lesson to us of today. But this wise kindliness and charity never weakened his arm or numbed his heart. We cannot afford weakly to blind ourselves to the actual conflict which faces us to-day. The issue is joined, and we must fight or fail.

In every wise struggle for human betterment one of the main objects, and often the only object, has been to achieve in large measure equality of opportunity. In the struggle for this great end, nations rise from barbarism to civilization, and through it people press forward from one stage of enlightenment to the next. One of the chief factors in progress is the destruction of special privilege. The essence of any struggle for healthy liberty has always been, and must always be, to take from some one man or class of men the right to enjoy power, or wealth, or position, or immunity, which has not been earned by service to his or their fellows. That is what you fought for in the Civil War, and that is what we strive for now. At many stages in the advance of humanity, this conflict between the men who possess more than they have earned and the men who have earned more than they possess is the central condition of progress. In our day it appears as the struggle of freemen to gain and hold the right of self-government as against the special interests, who twist the methods of free government into machinery for defeating the popular will. At every stage, and under all circumstances, the essence of the struggle is to equalize opportunity, destroy privilege, and give to the life and citizenship of every individual the highest possible value both to himself and to the commonwealth. That is nothing new. All I ask in civil life is what you fought for in the Civil War. I ask that civil life be carried on according to the spirit in which the army was carried on. You never get perfect justice, but the effort in handling the army was to bring to the front the men who could do the job. Nobody grudged promotion to Grant, or Sherman, or Thomas, or Sheridan, because they earned it. The only complaint was when a man got promotion which he did not earn.

Practical equality of opportunity for all citizens, when we achieve it, will have two great results. First, every man will have a fair chance to make of himself all that in him lies; to reach the highest point to which his capacities, unassisted by special privilege of his own and unhampered by the special privilege of others, can carry him, and to get for himself and his family substantially what he has earned. Second, equality of opportunity means that the commonwealth will get from every citizen the highest service of which he is capable. No man who carries the burden of the special privileges of another can give to the commonwealth that service to which it is fairly entitled.

I stand for the square deal. But when I say that I am for the square deal, I mean not merely that I stand for fair play under the present rules of the games, but that I stand for having those rules changed so as to work for a more substantial equality of opportunity and of reward for equally good service. One word of warning, which, I think, is hardly necessary in Kansas. When I say I want a square deal for the poor man, I do not mean that I want a square deal for the man who remains poor because he has not got the energy to work for himself. If a man who has had a chance will not make good, then he has got to quit. And you men of the Grand Army, you want justice for the brave man who fought, and punishment for the coward who shirked his work. Is not that so?

Now, this means that our government, national and State, must be freed from the sinister influence or control of special interests. Exactly as the special interests of cotton and slavery threatened our political integrity before the Civil War, so now the great special business interests too often control and corrupt the men and methods of government for their own profit. We must drive the special interests out of politics. That is one of our tasks to-day. Every special interest is entitled to justice—full, fair, and complete—and, now, mind you, if there were any attempt by mob-violence to plunder and work harm to the special interest, whatever it may be, and I most dislike and the wealthy man, whomsoever he may be, for whom I have the greatest contempt, I would fight for him, and you would if you were worth your salt. He should have justice. For every special interest is entitled to justice, but not one is entitled to a vote in Congress, to a voice on the bench, or to representation in any public office. The Constitution guarantees protections to property, and we must make that promise good But it does not give the right of suffrage to any corporation. The true friend of property, the true conservative, is he who insists that property shall be the servant and not the master of the commonwealth; who insists that the creature of man's making shall be the servant and not the master of the man who made it. The citizens of the United States must effectively control the mighty commercial forces which they have themselves called into being.

There can be no effective control of corporations while their political activity remains. To put an end to it will be neither a short nor an easy task, but it can be done.

We must have complete and effective publicity of corporate affairs, so that people may know beyond peradventure whether the corporations obey the law and whether their management entitles them to the confidence of the public. It is necessary that laws should be passed to prohibit the use of corporate funds directly or indirectly for political purposes; it is still more necessary that such laws should be thoroughly enforced. Corporate expenditures for political purposes, and especially such expenditures by public-service corporations, have supplied one of the principal sources of corruption in our political affairs.

It has become entirely clear that we must have government supervision of the capitalization, not only of public-service corporations, including, particularly, railways, but of all corporations doing an interstate business. I do not wish to see the nation forced into the ownership of the railways if it can possibly be avoided, and the only alternative is thoroughgoing and effective regulation, which shall be based on a full knowledge of all the facts, including a physical valuation of property. This physical valuation is not needed, or, at least, is very rarely needed, for fixing rates; but it is needed as the basis of honest capitalization.

We have come to recognize that franchises should never be granted except for a limited time, and never without proper provision for compensation to the public. It is my personal belief that the same kind and degree of control and supervision which should be exercised over public-service corporations should be extended also to combinations which control necessaries of life, such as meat, oil, and coal, or which deal in them on an important scale. I have not doubt that the ordinary man who has control of them is much like ourselves. I have no doubt he would like to do well, but I want to have enough supervision to help him realize that desire to do well.

I believe that the officers, and, especially, the directors, of corporations should be held personally responsible when any corporation breaks the law.

Combinations in industry are the result of an imperative economic law which cannot be repealed by political legislation. The effort at prohibiting all combination has substantially failed. The way out lies, not in attempting to prevent such combinations, but in completely controlling them in the interest of the public welfare. For that purpose the Federal Bureau of Corporations is an agency of first importance. Its powers, and, therefore, its efficiency, as well as that of the Interstate Commerce Commission, should be largely increased. We have a right to expect from the Bureau of Corporations and from the Interstate Commerce Commission a very high grade of public service. We should be as sure of the proper conduct of the interstate railways and the proper management of interstate business as we are now sure of the conduct and management of the national banks, and we should have as effective supervision in one case as in the other. The Hepburn Act, and the amendment to the act in the shape in which it finally passed Congress at the last session, represent a long step in advance, and we must go yet further.

There is a wide-spread belief among our people that under the methods of making tariffs, which have hitherto obtained, the special interests are too influential. Probably this is true of both the big special interests and the little special interests. These methods have put a premium on selfishness, and, naturally, the selfish big interests have gotten more than their smaller, though equally selfish brothers. The duty of Congress is to provide a method by which the interest of the whole people shall be all that receives consideration. To this end there must be an expert tariff commission, wholly removed from the possibility of political pressure or of improper business influence. Such a commission can find the real difference between cost of production, which is mainly the difference of labor cost here and abroad. As fast as its recommendations are made, I believe in revising one schedule at a time. A general revision of the tariff almost inevitably leads to logrolling and the subordination of the general public interest to local and special interests.

The absence of effective State, and, especially, national, restraint upon unfair money-getting has tended to create a small class of enormously wealthy and economically powerful men, whose chief object is to hold and increase their power. The prime need is to change the conditions which enable these men to accumulate power which is not for the general welfare that they should hold or exercise. We grudge no man a fortune which represents his own power and sagacity, when exercised with entire regard to the welfare of his fellows. Again, comrades over there, take the lesson from your own experience. Not only did you not grudge, but you gloried in the promotion of the great generals who gained their promotion by leading the army to victory. So it is with us. We grudge no man a fortune in civil life if it is honorably obtained and well used. It is not even enough that it should have gained without doing damage to the community. We should permit it to be gained only so long as the gaining represents benefit to the community. This, I know, implies a policy of a far more active governmental interference with social and economic conditions in this country than we have yet had, but I think we have got to face the fact that such an increase in governmental control is now necessary.

No man should receive a dollar unless that dollar has been fairly earned. Every dollar received should represent a dollar's worth of service rendered—not gambling in stocks, but service rendered. The really big fortune, the swollen fortune, by the mere fact of its size acquires qualities which differentiate it in kind as well as in degree from what is possessed by men of relatively small means. Therefore, I believe in a graduated income tax on big fortunes, and in another tax which is far more easily collected and far more effective—a graduated inheritance tax on big fortunes, properly safeguarded against evasion and increasing rapidly in amount with the size of the estate.

The people of the United States suffer from periodical financial panics to a degree substantially unknown among the other nations which approach us in financial strength. There is no reason why we should suffer what they escape. It is of profound importance that our financial system should be promptly investigated, and so thoroughly and effectively revised as to make it certain that hereafter our currency will no longer fail at critical times to meet our needs.

It is hardly necessary for me to repeat that I believe in an efficient army and a navy large enough to secure for us abroad that respect which is the surest guaranty of peace. A word of special warning to my fellow citizens who are as progressive as I hope I am. I want them to keep up their interest in our internal affairs; and I want them also continually to remember Uncle Sam's interest abroad. Justice and fair dealing among nations rest upon principles identical with those which control justice and fair dealing among the individuals of which nations are composed, with the vital exception that each nation must do its own part in international police work. If you get into trouble here, you can call for the police; but if Uncle Sam gets into trouble, he has got to be his own policeman, and I want to see him strong enough to encourage the peaceful aspirations of other peoples in connection with us. I believe in national friendships and heartiest good-will to all nations; but national friendships, like those between men, must be founded on respect as well as on liking, on forbearance as well as upon trust. I should be heartily ashamed of any American who did not try to make the American Government act as justly toward the other nations in international relations as he himself would act toward any individual in private relations. I should be heartily ashamed to see us wrong a weaker power, and I should hang my head forever if we tamely suffered wrong from a stronger power.

Of conservation I shall speak more at length elsewhere. Conservation means development as much as it does protection. I recognize the right and duty of this generation to develop and use the natural resources of our land; but I do not recognize the right to waste them, or to rob, by wasteful use, the generations that come after us. I ask nothing of the nation except that it so behave as each farmer here behaves with reference to his own children. That farmer is a poor creature who skins the land and leaves it worthless to his children. The farmer is a good farmer who, having enabled the land to support himself and to provide for the education of his children leaves it to them a little better than he found it himself. I believe the same thing of a nation.

Moreover, I believe that the natural resources must be used for the benefit of all our people, and not monopolized for the benefit of the few, and here again is another case in which I am accused of taking a revolutionary attitude. People forget now that one hundred years ago there were public men of good character who advocated the nation selling its public lands in great quantities, so that the nation could get the most money out of it, and giving it to the men who could cultivate it for their own uses. We took the proper democratic ground that the land should be granted in small sections to the men who were actually to till it and live on it. Now, with the water-power with the forests, with the mines, we are brought face to face with the fact that there are many people who will go with us in conserving the resources only if they are to be allowed to exploit them for their benefit. That is one of the fundamental reasons why the special interest should be driven out of politics. Of all the questions which can come before this nation, short of the actual preservation of its existence in a great war, there is none which compares in importance with the great central task of leaving this land even a better land for our descendants than it is for us, and training them into a better race to inhabit the land and pass it on. Conservation is a great moral issue for it involves the patriotic duty of insuring the safety and continuance of the nation. Let me add that the health and vitality of our people are at least as well worth conserving as their forests, waters, lands, and minerals, and in this great work the national government must bear a most important part.

I have spoken elsewhere also of the great task which lies before the farmers of the country to get for themselves and their wives and children not only the benefits of better farming, but also those of better business methods and better conditions of life on the farm. The burden of this great task will fall, as it should, mainly upon the great organizations of the farmers themselves. I am glad it will, for I believe they are all able to handle it. In particular, there are strong reasons why the Departments of Agriculture of the various States, and the United States Department of Agriculture, and the agricultural colleges and experiment stations should extend their work to cover all phases of farm life, instead of limiting themselves. as they have far too often limited themselves in the past, solely to the question of the production of crops. And now a special word to the farmer. I want to see him make the farm as fine a farm as it can be made; and let him remember to see that the improvement goes on indoors as well as out; let him remember that the farmer's wife should have her share of thought and attention just as much as the farmer himself. Nothing is truer than that excess of every kind is followed by reaction; a fact which should be pondered by reformer and reactionary alike. We are face to face with new conceptions of the relations of property to human welfare, chiefly because certain advocates of the rights of property as against the rights of men have been pushing their claims too far. The man who wrongly holds that every human right is secondary to his profit must now give way to the advocate of human welfare, who rightly maintains that every man holds his property subject to the general right of the community to regulate its use to whatever degree the public welfare may require it.

But I think we may go still further. The right to regulate the use of wealth in the public interest is universally admitted. Let us admit also the right to regulate the terms and conditions of labor, which is the chief element of wealth, directly in the interest of the common good. The fundamental thing to do for every man is to give him a chance to reach a place in which he will make the greatest possible contribution to the public welfare. Understand what I say there. Give him a chance, not push him up if he will not be pushed. Help any man who stumbles; if he lies down, it is a poor job to try to carry him; but if he is a worthy man, try your best to see that he gets a chance to show the worth that is in him. No man can be a good citizen unless he has a wage more than sufficient to cover the bare cost of living, and hours of labor short enough so that after his day's work is done he will have time and energy to bear his share in the management of the community, to help in carrying the general load. We keep countless men from being good citizens by the conditions of life with which we surround them. We need comprehensive work-men's compensation acts, both State and national laws to regulate child labor and work for women, and, especially, we need in our common schools not merely education in book learning, but also practical training for daily life and work. We need to enforce better sanitary conditions for our workers and to extend the use of safety appliances for our workers in industry and commerce, both within and between the States. Also, friends, in the interest of the working man himself we need to set our faces like Mint against mob-violence just as against corporate greed; against violence and injustice and lawlessness by wage-workers just as much as against lawless cunning and greed and selfish arrogance of employers. If I could ask but one thing of my fellow countrymen, my request would be that, whenever they go in for reform, they remember the two sides, and that they always exact justice from one side as much as from the other. I have small use for the public servant who can always see and denounce the corruption of the capitalist, but who cannot persuade himself, especially before elections, to say a word about lawless mob-violence. And I have equally small use for the man, be he a judge on the bench, or editor of a great paper, or wealthy and influential private citizen, who can see clearly enough and denounce the lawlessness of mob-violence, but whose eyes are closed so that he is blind when the question is one of corruption in business on a gigantic scale. Also remember what I said about excess in reformer and reactionary alike. If the reactionary man, who thinks of nothing but the rights of property, could have his way, he would bring about a revolution; and one of my chief fears in connection with progress comes because I do not want to see our people, for lack of proper leadership, compelled to follow men whose intentions are excellent, but whose eyes are a little too wild to make it really safe to trust them. Here in Kansas, there is one paper which habitually denounces me as the tool of Wall Street, and at the same time frantically repudiates the statement that I am a Socialist on the ground that is an unwarranted slander of the Socialists.

National efficiency has many factors. It is a necessary result of the principle of conservation widely applied. In the end it will determine our failure or success as a nation. National efficiency has to do, not only with natural resources and with men, but is equally concerned with institutions. The State must be made efficient for the work which concerns only the people of the

State; and the nation for that which concerns all the people. There must remain no neutral ground to serve as a refuge for lawbreakers, and especially for lawbreakers of great wealth, who can hire the vulpine legal cunning which will teach them how to avoid both jurisdictions. It is a misfortune when the national legislature fails to do its duty in providing a national remedy, so that the only national activity is the purely negative activity of the judiciary in forbidding the State to exercise power in the premises.

I do not ask for over centralization; but I do ask that we work in a spirit of broad and far-reaching nationalism when we work for what concerns our people as a whole. We are all Americans. Our common interests are as broad as the continent. I speak to you here in Kansas exactly as I would speak in New York or Georgia, for the most vital problems are those which affect us all alike. The national government belongs to the whole American people, and where the whole American people are interested, that interest can be guarded effectively only by the national government. The betterment which we seek must be accomplished, I believe, mainly through the national government.

The American people are right in demanding that New Nationalism, without which we cannot hope to deal with new problems. The New Nationalism puts the national need before sectional or personal advantage. It is impatient of the utter confusion that results from local legislatures attempting to treat national issues as local issues. It is still more impatient of the impotence which springs from over division of governmental powers, the impotence which makes it possible for local selfishness or for legal cunning, hired by wealthy special interests, to bring national activities to a deadlock. This New Nationalism regards the executive power as the steward of the public welfare. It demands of the judiciary that it shall be interested primarily in human welfare rather than in property, just as it demands that the representative body shall represent all the people rather than any one class or section of the people.

I believe in shaping the ends of government to protect property as well as human welfare. Normally, and in the long run, the ends are the same; but whenever the alternative must be faced, I am for men and not for property, as you were in the Civil War. I am far from underestimating the importance of dividends; but I rank dividends below human character. Again, I do not have any sympathy with the reformer who says he does not care for dividends. Of course, economic welfare is necessary, for a man must pull his own weight and be able to support his family. I know well that the reformers must not bring upon the people economic ruin, or the reforms themselves will go down in the ruin. But we must be ready to face temporary disaster, whether or not brought on by those who will war against us to the knife.

Those who oppose all reform will do well to remember that ruin in its worst form is inevitable if our national life brings us nothing better than swollen fortunes for the few and the triumph in both politics and business of a sordid and selfish materialism.

If our political institutions were perfect, they would absolutely prevent the political domination of money in any part of our affairs. We need to make our political representatives more quickly and sensitively responsive to the people whose servants they are. More direct action by the people in their own affairs under proper safeguards is vitally necessary. The direct primary is a step in this direction, if it is associated with a corrupt-practices act effective to prevent the advantage of the man willing recklessly and unscrupulously to spend money over his more honest competitor. It is particularly important that all moneys received or expended for campaign purposes should be publicly accounted for, not only after election, but before election as well. Political action must be made simpler, easier, and freer from confusion for every citizen. I believe that the prompt removal of unfaithful or incompetent public servants should be made easy and sure in whatever way experience shall show to be most expedient in any given class of cases.

One of the fundamental necessities in a representative government such as ours is to make certain that the men to whom the people delegate their power shall serve the people by whom they are elected, and not the special interests. I believe that every national officer, elected or appointed, should be forbidden to perform any service or receive any compensation, directly or indirectly, from interstate corporations; and a similar provision could not fail to be useful within the States.

The object of government is the welfare of the people. The material progress and prosperity of a nation are desirable chiefly so far as they lead to the moral and material welfare of all good citizens. Just in proportion as the average man and woman are honest, capable of sound judgment and high ideals, active in public affairs—but, first of all, sound in their home life, and the father and mother of healthy children whom they bring up well—just so far, and no farther, we may count our civilization a success. We must have—I believe we have already—a genuine and permanent moral awakening, without which no wisdom of legislation or administration really means anything; and, on the other hand, we must try to secure the social and economic legislation without which any improvement due to purely moral agitation is necessarily evanescent. Let me again illustrate by a reference to the Grand Army. You could not have won simply as a disorderly and disorganized mob. You needed generals; you needed careful administration of the most advanced type; and a good commissary—the cracker line. You well remember that success was necessary in many different lines in order to bring about general success.

You had to have the administration at Washington good, just as you had to have the administration in the field; and you had to have the work of the generals good. You could not have triumphed without that administration and leadership; but it would all have been worthless if the average soldier had not had the right stuff in him. He had to have the right stuff in him, or you could not get it out of him. In the last analysis, therefore, vitally necessary though it was to have the right kind of organization and the right kind of generalship, it was even more vitally necessary that the average soldier should have the fighting edge, the right character.

So it is in our civil life. No matter how honest and decent we are in our private lives, if we do not have the right kind of law and the right kind of administration of the law, we cannot go forward as a nation. That is imperative; but it must be an addition to, and not a substitution for, the qualities that make us good citizens. In the last analysis, the most important elements in any man's career must be the sum of those qualities which, in the aggregate, we speak of as character. If he has not got it, then no law that the wit of man can devise, no administration of the law by the boldest and strongest executive, will avail to help him. We must have the right kind of character—character that makes a man, first of all, a good man in the home, a good father, a good husband— that makes a man a good neighbor. You must have that, and, then, in addition, you must have the kind of law and the kind of administration of the law which will give to those qualities in the private citizen the best possible chance for development. The prime problem of our nation is to get the right type of good citizenship, and, to get it, we must have progress, and our public men must be genuinely progressive."

Conclusion

There is a side to Theodore Roosevelt that is forgotten in most of the literature about him and his success. Teddy, Teedy, or TR, whichever version of his name one prefers, was the personification of the term "mind over matter." Whatever physical impediment stood in his way, he not only used the psychical resources available to him to overcome them, but he also used a mental process to break it down. Among all the presidents who have come and gone, Teddy was singularly unique in his ability to move mountains with his mind.

His mind was not limited to intelligence and discipline. Sure, he was a Harvard College alum; that fact just gives credence to his ability to absorb academic information. He graduated magna cum laude, which just says that he was able to grapple with and absorb information better than his peers.

But his mind was something altogether different from most of the men we have seen occupy the office. It was about the ability to manifest things that were otherwise thought to be impossible. As a young child, his family was concerned that Teedy, as he was called by aunts and grandmothers, was in frail health.

His core medical issues were congenital. At birth, he already had an eye condition that resulted in severe myopia. Since children who are born myopic do not know how to explain that distant objects are a blur, he suffered from the consequences of headaches and tired eyes from a young age. That was the first of his problems.

His second issue at birth was his severe bronchial allergy. The slightest irregularity in the quality of air around him would result in a full allergic reaction. This resulted in low oxygen absorption that further fueled his headaches and rendered his eyesight poorer. Allergy sufferers today have many more options in sourcing relief compared with the mid-nineteenth century when Roosevelt was born and spent his childhood.

The bronchial allergy led to bronchial asthma attacks that were categorized as violent. Teedy was still an infant at that time. His bronchial tubes would inflame and swell while they released mucus that filled the lungs. It was almost like drowning in some ways. That swelling then spread to the upper respiratory tract, and soon his airways would constrict in size and flood with mucus.

These events, painful for the infant and heartbreaking for his parents, happened at frequent intervals—perhaps even three to four times a week. It was not just something in the air. It could even be triggered by food that he ingested. These episodes would turn his usually fair skin to a worrying tinge of blue as the rosy complexion drained to reveal the oxygen deprivation.

There was always someone stationed in young Teedy's nursery because there were attacks while he slept. The midnight attacks were commonplace, and the household and the hands who aided the Roosevelts of Oyster Bay had their act together whenever there was an episode. They would all jump to action and stand ready to offer aid.

The rest of the home was busy with the traffic of tutors coming and going, assigned with imparting knowledge on a wide array of subjects to the home-schooled, brilliant young boy. Along the way, days turned to months, and little Teedy continued to fight the good fight. He learned his ABCs and 123s and found delight in the pursuit of information and opinion. He was naturally good at math, and he was a quick reader. He could devour entire novels in as short as a day, while he stayed home for stretches during the pollen season.

The nighttime attacks left Teedy all the worse for wear. The sudden disturbance of his sleep and the energy that was extracted in the fight to live would render this young man incapacitated and at the brink of exhaustion by the time the allergies would start to ebb, and he would fall asleep in his father's arms—the only place that seemed to give him respite.

Thus was the life that Theodore Roosevelt Jr. experienced at the starting line of his amazing race. It was the cauldron in which the bond between father and son were forged and the circumstances under which an appreciation for life took root.

The doctors could not get a full handle on the allergy and myopia that spurred the deterioration of other elements of his health. It was a miserable time. Even though the Roosevelts, Theodore and Martha Bulloch, were wealthier than most in one of the busiest cities in the country, the long list of eminent doctors of New York City were just not able to properly diagnose and medicate young Teedy. The Roosevelt's first course of action was to then limit Teedy to their midtown Manhattan brownstone mansion with medical care at a moment's notice and a retinue of staff at the ready to provide aid.

His allergies were not just respiratory in nature. They also affected his intestinal tract. Food allergies would result in severe gastrointestinal pain followed by diarrhea. This would further add to the complications and cause general weakness due to the inability to retain nutrition or calories. The result was a young boy who was frequently deprived of adequate oxygen, hydration, and nutrition. His meek stature as he grew older was in total contrast to his father's large and imposing presence.

The element that always remained in the dark and beyond the conversation of historians is the element of fear that took up permanent residency in the heart of this young boy. He began to associate several factors to the near-death experiences that he would have. Everything from food to sleep and spring days would send a shiver up little Teedy's spine, as they were all associated with near-death experiences for him.

He was not the only one in the family with his battle to be fought. His younger sister came to have the same problem, and so the house had two little Roosevelts who would make emergencies daily routine.

The family was counseled that Teedy would either die young or the ailments would resolve themselves as he grew older. Neither happened. As he matured, they tried different strategies, from smoking cigars to drinking dark and strong coffee. The cigars were designed to dry his lungs, while the caffeine was designed to dilate his passages. The former nauseated him, while the latter brought some much-appreciated relief. It was also a good thing since it kept him up, and that allowed him to read even more.

Roosevelt Senior kept an eye on the medical advancements that were happening in a rapidly changing world. He was always in search of medical solutions for his two children. The family even tried traveling to different countries so that they could expose the siblings to cleaner air or air that was not as humid as that in New York City. They tried cooler climates, and they tried dryer ones as well as ones that were higher in elevation. The best combination was the mountain resorts that offered cooler and thinner air that was less polluted. New York in the 1850s was fairly polluted from all the factories and ships that were the engine of the economy.

Back in New York, Theodore Senior decided to take matters into his own hands by going in the opposite direction of conventional wisdom. The doctors ordered complete rest, while Senior determined that the opposite was best. Instead of telling him to rest more and be inactive, he was told to work out more and build up. The young Roosevelt who was scrawny had a set of instructors to guide him on the gym equipment that his father had installed in the rooftop balcony of the mansion.

He had come to this decision after an incident that occurred in upstate New York where some kids had bullied the frail TR. TR had an awakening of sorts and consulted with his father to shed his meager stature and build himself up to something that could keep up with his mind.

Here, Teedy would lift weights, do push-ups, run, do sit-ups, and build his muscles, his stamina, and his will. Each time he got to the end of his body's ability, his trainers would demand more. It is here that he learned that his mind could override his body's commands. He and his father had decided that it was time they beat back the congenital issues with cerebral solutions, and it worked. As he built up his strength and his mind, his asthma attacks, gastrointestinal issue, and bronchial allergies gradually reduced in frequency until they were all gone.

In Teedy's young mind, he associated activity with health, sportsmanship with activity, and mental will to eventual action. It was the founding characteristic of the man that would be president by the time he turned forty-three.

A few things happened in the wake of this manner of childhood. The first was that he grew exceptionally fond of his father and incredibly close. His father had become the strong protective figure under which young Teedy felt loved and safe. He was certainly close to his mother, but the bond between father and son spilled over into a relationship that is rarely found in many filial relationships.

The second was the connection in his mind that he made between several elements. He began to hate the indoors. He associated that with being sick. He loved the outdoors, especially places with bright sunshine and cool air. He hated the opposite—dark places where he was frequently kept when he was in distress or where he was when the distress emerged. He loved athletic activities. He saw them as the path to salvation. It was the workouts, the vigorous workouts that he had endured on the roof-top gym where the trainers would push him hard to carry more, crunch more, run more. It was always the practice of pushing through seeming difficulty that led to feeling better later, and the pushing became part of his character. It is one of the reasons why he was able to succeed at whatever he took on or was faced with. As long as he pushed hard, he would come out the other side.

By the time he was fifteen years of age, he had turned the corner. Much of the medical stresses he was under had all but evaporated, but the strategies that he picked up to counter them had been internalized. Those strategies became the core of his character, from the ability to act to the ability to not give up in the face of adversity. They were all learned in the time between the cradle and the gym.

The strategy he learned the most, however, was not just the ability to convert thought to action but the ability to make intentions and thoughts manifest as the outcome. He was the personification of mind over matter. It was a gift forged in the throes of death and the loving arms of a strong father.

Roosevelt was intense. His passion and gregarious nature differentiated him from those around him. A significant body of reasons for this characteristic lay in the fact that he grew up secluded from the rest of the world until he was in his early teens. His lack of social interaction with the outside world shaped his view of the world in general.

Except for some travel with his family and some time he spent away from home convalescing, he did not have a tainted or poor view of the outside world. Everyone was a possible friend. Everyone was potentially good. He arrived at Harvard in the fall of 1876 and immediately stood out from the crowd of 161 incoming freshmen. His cohorts were composed, calm, and reserved. Roosevelt thundered and gesticulated as a matter of practice. Since knowledge, conversation, and getting to the bottom of things came naturally, the Harvard debate team was an obvious attraction. He loved to argue because he enjoyed getting at the truth of everything, not because he was obnoxious. He could also be dramatic. He would pound his hands and gesticulate to drive a point during every debate. It was earth-shattering and effective. Outside the debate stage, he loved having friends. He loved the opportunity to go out and make new acquaintances. It was the main reason why he joined many societies, clubs, and organizations. The boxing club and debate society were just two of many.

Young Roosevelt was also fairly awkward in social settings. If he saw a friend he recently met across the yard, he would shatter the silence by thundering a greeting. Even with his prickly manners, he was able to make many friends who may have bristled at first but eventually adored him dearly.

Academically, he did well even with a mountain of extracurricular activities. He graduated twenty-first in his class and had good enough grades to be accepted to any law school he chose.

It was during this period of newly found freedom at Harvard that he met Alice Lee. The two courted and then decided to marry once school was over. Roosevelt was a fairly traditional and conservative young man. He was not in the frame of mind that prioritized fooling around or acting ungentlemanly. His conservative attitude dictated that marrying Alice also came with significant responsibility. That responsibility demanded that he was able to support her and the family they eventually built. To be successful, he needed to be the breadwinner of the family. For that to happen, he needed to complete school first. That was his primary motivation to stay in school until he was fully capable of looking after a family.

He had fallen in love with Alice. It was not a fleeting fancy. He had surrendered his heart. In return, she loved him deeply as well. In spite of her deep and often obvious adoration, however, all evidence points to Roosevelt being inherently jealous and romantically possessive. If any man had the gall to make a move on Alice, Roosevelt would get highly wound up and go so far as to challenge him to a duel. To this end, Roosevelt even purchased pistols to be able to duel with anyone who took up his challenge.

His college years moved along several parallel paths. His view on academic pursuits was not about a paper chase. Roosevelt was not interested in the diploma. He was interested in the experience. The experience in this sense went beyond the practical dimension of the knowledge he acquired from books. It was to explore the impression it made on the young men and women around him in classrooms and social points of contact.

Just by these two elements (there were many others) that surfaced into view during his college years, it is plain to see that he stood in stark contrast to the rest of the blue bloods that attended Harvard.

It has been mentioned that much of his personality can be traced to the developmental years. From as far back as he could remember, life had been a struggle. He defined life through those lenses. All that had changed by this point, and he felt alive in the truest meaning of the word. He felt like a spring that was first coiled and kept compressed since its making and then being released one day.

www.ingramcontent.com/pod-product-compliance
Lightning Source LLC
Chambersburg PA
CBHW030143100526
44592CB00009B/100